WOMEN'S ACTIVISM IN AFRICA

WOMEN'S ACTIVISM IN AFRICA

Struggles for Rights and Representation

Edited by Balghis Badri and Aili Mari Tripp

ZED
Zed Books
London

Women's Activism in Africa was first published in 2017 by Zed Books Ltd, The Foundry, 17 Oval Way, London SE11 5RR, UK.

www.zedbooks.net

Editorial copyright © Balghis Badri and Aili Mari Tripp 2017
Copyright in this collection © Zed Books 2017

The rights of Balghis Badri and Aili Mari Tripp to be identified as the editors of this work have been asserted by them in accordance with the Copyright, Designs and Patents Act 1988.

Typeset in Plantin and Kievit by Swales & Willis Ltd, Exeter, Devon
Cover design by Clare Turner
Cover photo © Nyani Quarmyne/Panos
Printed in the USA by Edwards Brothers Malloy

A catalogue record for this book is available from the British Library.

ISBN 978-1-78360-909-3 hb
ISBN 978-1-78360-908-6 pb
ISBN 978-1-78360-910-9 pdf
ISBN 978-1-78360-911-6 epub
ISBN 978-1-78360-912-3 mobi

CONTENTS

ACKNOWLEDGEMENTS

The Regional Institute of Gender, Diversity, Peace and Rights at Ahfad University for Women in Omdurman, Sudan would like to extend its gratitude to the Norwegian Agency for Development Cooperation, which supported the holding of the conference at Ahfad University on 'African Women Mobilising for Change', where most of the papers in this book were presented. We are also grateful to the Zed Books team, especially Ken Barlow, for their generous support of this book project.

1 | AFRICAN INFLUENCES ON GLOBAL WOMEN'S RIGHTS: AN OVERVIEW

Aili Mari Tripp and Balghis Badri

Introduction

Prior to, but especially since, independence, women activists in Africa have been engaged in a variety of movements and forms of collective action around issues ranging from rights to land and inheritance, to increasing female political representation, and ending domestic violence. While some of these women's rights agendas have been inspired by international feminisms and supported by external donor strategies, African women themselves have contributed significantly to global understandings and implementation of women's rights. This book – and this chapter in particular – seeks to highlight the various contributions of African women to these debates and to global understandings and framings of women's rights.

The chapter challenges assumptions that African women activists have simply absorbed external agendas and definitions of feminism and shows how instead they have creatively and actively forged their movements with reference to their own concerns as they have defined and conceptualised them. There has been considerable scholarly interest in how international norms are interpreted locally (Hodgson 2011; Merry 2006a, 2006b; Levitt and Merry 2009; Yuval-Davis 2009), and also in how there are differences between international/ universal and local norms (Abu-Lughod 2002; Hodgson 2011; Ilumoka 2009). This chapter – and the book – adopts a somewhat different perspective in showing how African movements themselves have shaped and are shaping global understandings of women's rights and feminism.

The key challenge for movements globally has been how to transform power structures that limit women. Up until the early 1990s, the focus of women's mobilisation in developing countries had been on women's poverty and economic empowerment (Snyder 2015). After the Human Rights Conference in Vienna (1993), and especially after the United Nations Conference on Women in Beijing (1995), the emphasis shifted to a frame that situated 'women's rights as human rights' and to subsequent efforts to address violence against women. While violence and other human rights violations have been key concerns of women's movements in Africa, it is interesting to note that the focus of women's movements has never simply been on women as victims, even though the international media often portrays African women primarily as victims of HIV/AIDS, Ebola, trafficking, famine, violence and war. Rarely do we read or hear in the international media about the women activists who have sought to challenge the structural constraints that underlie violence, cultural manifestations of women's marginalisation, and discrimination more generally. Nevertheless, the focus of women activists since the 1990s has been on: 1) the political representation of women; 2) transforming economic structures by providing women with greater financial resources and support for businesses, and by incorporating gender-related reviews of national budgets; 3) initiatives around peace-making and peacebuilding; 4) violence against women; and 5) legal and constitutional reform of women's rights, including challenges to traditional authorities and customary law.

From time to time, some of these movements have indeed gained international visibility, such as the environmental Green Belt Movement, led by the late Nobel laureate Wangari Maathai, when it became an important force for political change in Kenya in the 1990s. In 2003, one of the regional women's peace organisations active in Sierra Leone, Liberia and Guinea – the Mano River Women's Peace Network, better known as MAROWPNET – was awarded the United Nations Prize for Human Rights by the UN General Assembly to recognise its 'outstanding achievement in the promotion of human and women's rights'. The peace movement in Liberia, involving thousands of women, helped bring an end to civil war in that country in 2003. This movement gained international recognition when Leymah Gbowee and Ellen Johnson Sirleaf won Nobel Peace Prizes in 2011. Women in Morocco, Tunisia and Egypt were at the forefront of movements for political reform and equality in 2011. Most recently, Tunisia passed a constitution in 2014 that is one of the most progressive in terms of women's rights anywhere in the world. In spite of this international recognition, the full extent of women's mobilisation and its influence on global trends in Africa has not been adequately acknowledged. Even this chapter provides only a cursory account, while the case studies in the book provide further evidence of these trends.

Changes in women's mobilisation

The trajectory of post-1990s women's mobilisation in Africa has had its own sources arising out of Africa's democratising trends; the economic crisis and structural adjustment of the 1980s and 1990s; the decline of conflict, especially after the 1990s; the influence of Africa's regional and sub-regional institutions; UN influences; the influx of donor funds; and the expansion of new communications mechanisms. Contemporary movements in Africa have also drawn on their roots in indigenous women's strategies that pre-date Islamisation, Christianisation and colonisation. They have drawn on women's experiences in anticolonial resistance and national liberation movements, as well as women's experiences in party- or state-directed women's organisations in the era of single parties and military rule.

During the first three decades after independence, women's organisations were generally tied to the patronage politics of the single-party state. Their activities were monitored and directed to ensure that they would support various party or government initiatives. This meant that women's organisations tended to be focused on welfare and domestic concerns and espoused a discourse of 'developmentalism'. At the grassroots level, women's associations were mostly producing handicrafts, promoting literacy, farming, participating in income-generating projects, fighting AIDS, subscribing to faith-based organisations, engaging in cultural expression and other such activities.

This changed in the 1990s, with the diffusion of new women's rights norms and strategies throughout the world. The UN and international and regional women's organisations influenced women's rights norms throughout Africa, but African women's movements were themselves active in helping shape these global trends. Similarly, the African women's rights movement engaged the African Union, Southern African Development Community (SADC) and other sub-regional organisations, which, in turn, put pressure on member states to advance women's rights. The 1985 UN Conference on Women held in Nairobi and later the 1995 UN Conference on Women in Beijing were especially important in serving as catalysts for many organisations and activists. International donors, tired of state corruption and inefficiency, began to focus on non-governmental organisations (NGOs), including women's associations, providing them with new resources, independent of the state and party patronage.

Women activists had fought for greater democracy from the 1990s onwards, while the new democratising trends opened up political space for women's mobilisation along with activism by environmentalist, human rights, indigenous peoples and other new forces. In the 1990s, single-party regimes transformed themselves into multiparty systems; military dictatorships dissolved into civilian rule; while freedom of the press, association and assembly expanded, albeit unevenly, with much backtracking.

The decline of conflict in Africa, especially after 2000, also speeded up the push for women's rights in post-conflict countries. The end of a significant number of conflicts after the 1990s created important political opportunities for women's movements, especially where women's peace movements overlapped with women's movements.

All of these changes – the diffusion of international norms regarding gender equality, new donor strategies, political liberalisation, and the decline of conflict – created conditions that allowed new women's movements to emerge and have an impact on policy, practice and public opinion. The expansion of the use of new media also facilitated these trends. A wide variety of new women's organisations emerged in most African countries, especially in countries that liberalised politically. New organisations began promoting a women's rights agenda to push for constitutional and legislative changes regarding gender equality. They began to introduce new agendas ranging from issues of reproductive rights to violence against women, peace, the environment, women's education, the expansion of credit facilities for businesswomen and women farmers, access to land, women's inheritance rights, media representation of women, women's political representation, and many other concerns.

New feminist influences

Another, more recent, development after the mid-2000s was that women's rights activists in Africa increasingly began to refer to themselves as feminists, but most still do not self-identify in this way even though they may share the goals of feminists. This is because 'feminism' has often been conceived of disparagingly as a Western or foreign concept. Although there are still opponents of women's rights who make this claim, this is changing rapidly, as African feminists – especially the younger generations – are redefining feminism in African terms. After independence, some were wary that such a competing ideology would detract from the pressing project of national development. Even government leaders who supported gender equality often argued that they could not attend to women's rights concerns until development had been achieved. Feminism was sometimes seen as an individualistic ideology that pitted men against women. For others it was seen as a challenge to indigenous values and traditions and a form of cultural imperialism (Tripp et al. 2009).

However, today there is a younger generation of self-identifying feminists emerging throughout Africa who are redefining feminism from an African perspective. Organisers of the first African Feminist Forum, held in Ghana in 2006, issued an open challenge to women's organisations that were focusing on reforms to improve the conditions under which women live and work but were not challenging discriminatory and patriarchal structures and institutions that might bring about more major transformations in gender relations. They criticised the 'hypocritical' and 'sexist' defence of 'African culture and tradition' to justify discrimination against women; the practice of giving women token positions of power; sexist attitudes when it came to sexual and reproductive health and rights; the use of notions of motherhood in state policies to minimise women's contributions; and the feminisation of HIV/AIDS and poverty.

The forum came up with a 'Charter of Feminist Principles' that articulated this perspective. It represented a deliberate departure away from the ambivalence and defensiveness about using the term 'feminism' in Africa, while recognising that there is a plurality of views within both women's and feminist movements regarding strategy, ideology and priorities, and that these differences are markers of the vitality and breadth of these movements. However, as the Feminist Forum organisers pointed out, there was consensus on the need to address issues such as 'poverty, illiteracy, health and reproductive rights, political participation and peace'.[1]

---

1 http://www.africanfeministforum.com/feminist-charter-introduction/ (accessed 30 September 2016).

This first Feminist Forum meeting reflected a shift in thinking that by 2010 was evident as feminist discourse became commonplace on online websites, blogs and journals, on Twitter, Facebook and YouTube. Journals such as *Feminist Africa* provided new perspectives. New feminist novels, including *Dust* by Yvonne Adhiambo Owuor (Kenya), *Kintu* by Jennifer Nansubuga Makumbi (Uganda) and *Americanah* by Chimamanda Ngozi Adichie (Nigeria), offered new ways of imagining women. Adichie issued a clarion call to women in her video *We Should All be Feminist*, which received international acclaim and in which she explores what it means to be an African feminist today. In Kenya today there are vigorous new debates about gender-based violence, lesbian, gay, bisexual and transgender (LGBT) rights, the policing of women's dress, and women in pop culture, particularly music videos. Facebook and Twitter debates about African feminism abound: for example, #FeministWhileAfrican, #WhenWomenSpeak, #MyBodyMyHome, #MyDressMyChoice, and #BringBackOurGirls.[2]

The range of issues being debated and addressed by feminists today goes well beyond the concerns of the movements that emerged in the 1990s, as many taboos are being shattered. The rights of LGBT people, which were visible primarily in South Africa and Namibia in the mid-1990s, emerged after 2010 in countries such as Uganda and Kenya as a concern of some women's rights organisations. Abortion – which, like LGBT rights, is still largely taboo – has also gained increasing prominence in countries where large numbers of women die from unsafe self-abortions. Marital rape, the working conditions of domestic servants, the plight of single mothers in North Africa, and other such concerns are gaining recognition as self-identifying feminists become more influential.[3]

African influences on women's rights globally

Margaret Snyder has characterised the UN as the 'unlikely godmother' of the global feminist movement. Women the world over have relied on the UN to help define and coalesce women's concerns, to put forward programmes for legislative change, to provide forums for meeting across borders, and to participate in discussions on

2 http://thewidemargin.org.
3 http://www.africanfeministforum.com/ (accessed 30 September 2016).

issues of concern to women's lives (Snyder 2006). The UN, starting with the 1975 First World Conference on Women in Mexico City (1975) and the subsequent conferences in Copenhagen (1980), Nairobi (1985) and Beijing (1995), coupled with the declaration of the United Nations Decade for Women (1976–85), offered opportunities for African women to bring their unique experiences to the rest of the UN community. African women attended the conferences in various capacities as NGO representatives, serving on official national delegations, as members of UN agencies, and as professionals and organisers. They served as a stimulus for many programmes for women's advancement on the continent, but they also provided forums for African women to share their experiences and influence the global women's movement.

African women activists were visible in planning and running key UN conferences on women. Aida Gindy from Egypt held the first meeting on 'Women in Economic Development' in 1972. From the outset, at the time of preparations for the first UN conference on women, Kenyan women sought to hold the conference in Kenya. Phoebe Asiyo, who had been a delegate to the UN Committee on the Status of Women, had unsuccessfully lobbied the Kenyan government to have Kenya host the first World Conference on Women, but Kenya ended up hosting the 1985 conference ten years later (Snyder 2015). Tanzania's Gertrude Mongella was general secretary of the UN Beijing Conference, while Sierra Leonean Filomina Steady was one of the key convenors of the Earth Summit (1992). The Kenya Women's Group helped in the planning and running the Nairobi UN Conference in 1985. The Egyptian National Preparatory Committee for NGOs, led by Aziza Hussein, helped organise the International Conference on Population and Development that was held in Cairo in 1994. The Cairo Conference was important because it shifted the debate over population control away from the traditional family planning focus on quotas and targets to one that emphasised women's rights and women's health.

In the preparations for the 1995 Beijing Conference, many African-based and/or African-oriented organisations formed part of the NGO Forum Planning Committee; these included the African Women's Development and Communication Network (FEMNET), which was also charged with the overall coordination of the African regional input.[4] In addition, African women were members of international bodies on this planning committee, such as Women's World Banking, Young Women's Christian Association, Girl Guides Association, International Federation of University Women, among many others.

From the very outset, women from African countries were visible in these international venues. Jeanne Martin Cissé became the first woman to be president of the UN Security Council when she served as Guinea's permanent representative to the UN from 1972 to 1976. She had been general secretary of the Conference on African Women and had been active in the Guinean women's movement, serving as Guinea's representative to the UN Committee on the Status of Women. She had also been a parliamentarian and minister. Liberia's Angie Brooks was the only African female president of the UN General Assembly in 1969 and only the second woman from any country to hold this position. Women's rights activist Anna Tibaijuka from Tanzania served as an under-secretary-general of the UN and executive director of the UN Human Settlements Programme (UN-HABITAT) from 2006 to 2010. She was the second-highest-ranking African woman in the UN system after Dr Asha-Rose Migiro, another Tanzanian, who served as the deputy UN secretary-general.

African women's movements have influenced global trends since at least the 1970s. The Association of African Women for Research and Development (AAWORD), formed in 1976, was one of the first regionally based organisations of women in Africa. In part, its creation was a result of some of the experiences African women encountered first at the UN Conference on Women held in Mexico in 1975 and then at the 1976 Wellesley College conference, where many of the African participants felt that Western women were attempting to set the agenda in ways that did not accord with their priorities. They promoted research networking among African women scholars to offset the domination of research on women in Africa by Western scholars and to tackle the dearth of research on women in Africa

---

4 Other participating organisations included Akina Mama Wa Afrika London Women's Centre, Association of African Women for Research and Development (AAWORD), Association of Uganda Women Medical Doctors/Advocacy for Women's Health, CADEF – Women's Rights in Mali, Country Women of Nigeria, and Women in Africa/the African Diaspora.

and the lack of availability of work by African scholars on women at the time. In forming AAWORD, African scholars also rejected the perceived condescending and patronising attitudes of Western scholars (AAWORD 1982: 107).

The All African Women's Conference was one of the six organisations that drafted the 1979 Convention on the Elimination of Discrimination Against Women (CEDAW) and was the only regional organisation involved (Zwingel 2004: 12). African women have continued to be part of the Monitoring International Group for CEDAW.

As early as the 1970s, African women's organisations pressed the UN Economic Commission for Africa to establish a training centre for women. The then African Training and Research Centre for Women (ATRCW), which was formed in Addis Ababa, became the first regional centre in the world and soon became a model for the UN system as other such centres were established. This centre has played a major role in articulating the role of women and ensuring the formulation of relevant policies, conventions and charters from the women's perspective. The centre was heavily involved in planning and facilitating women's participation at the various conferences, including the Beijing+ Conference and related activities. When they came to the 1980 UN Conference on Women in Copenhagen, African women representatives had prepared draft policy proposals regarding women and development, having worked on them in advance at a Lusaka regional conference that drew on research carried out by the ATRCW. The proposals formed the basis of the Women and Development section of the Organisation of African Unity's 1982 Lagos Plan of Action. It laid out a strategy for women's economic empowerment, involving education, claims to administrative and political power, the need for research, the exchange of information regarding economic changes as they affected women, and ways to build strategic collaborations between governments, international agencies and women's NGOs. As Devaki Jain explained, 'African women were several steps ahead of the rest of the world's women during the 1960s and 1970s' because they were already carrying out research and making policy recommendations directed at government officials and regional institutions. Women such as Jacqueline Ki-Zerbo had already developed the idea of 'gender mainstreaming' in 1960 at a meeting of the UN Economic Commission for Africa, where she spoke of the importance of maintaining 'a double stream, to have specific support for women while at the same time trying to involve them in the mainstream of decisions and actions' (Snyder and Tadesse 1995: 38; Jain 2005: 100–1).

At the 1985 Nairobi Conference, African women were able to influence official discussions of the UN conference to focus on issues of national liberation and apartheid that were not receiving the attention they deserved. A decade later, at the UN Conference on Women held in Beijing in 1995, African women once again played a key role in promoting, among other things, their concerns regarding the girl-child, which became one of the twelve areas of critical concern in the core of the Beijing Platform for Action. This had been part of a proposal coming out of the NGO forum for the region (Fifth Conference on African Women, Dakar, Senegal 1994), and was accepted by the official African Conference.

Obviously, not all African attempts to influence global debates have been successful, nor do all African women's rights activists agree on priorities and strategies between and within countries. Moreover, priorities have changed over time to reflect new realities and changes in perception. For example, some African women health advocates at the 1994 population conference in Cairo did not regard reproductive rights as an issue that could be separated from other women's concerns of gaining a livelihood or accessing clean water, shelter and health services. Others did not want to prioritise contraception and abortion over other concerns or even to consider them 'rights' (Ilumoka 2009). In the end, 179 UN member states adopted a Platform of Action that called for universal education, universal access to reproductive health care, and lower infant, child and maternal mortality rates – all key demands of African women. This represented what was termed the 'Cairo consensus' between women's rights activists and population experts.

The next sections explore some key issue areas in which women activists in Africa have been global leaders, namely in the political representation of women, in finance and entrepreneurship, in peace-making and peacebuilding, and in challenging customary law and traditional authorities.

Leaders in the political representation of women

African women have been world leaders in the arena of female political representation, changing global expectations in this area. In fact, across the continent, the rates of women in parliament tripled between 1990 and 2010. Women's movements were key advocates of these changes in political representation. Rwanda's women parliamentarians were the first in the world to exceed 50 per cent of the legislative seats; today they claim 64 per cent of the legislative seats, the highest share in the world. There are female speakers of the house in one fifth of African parliaments. This is higher than the world average of 14 per cent. Women began to claim positions in key ministries (for example, defence, finance, foreign affairs) across the continent, and increasing numbers of women began to run for executive positions after 2010.

Women's representation in Africa, in particular, challenged existing global theories of legislative change, many of which had focused on the importance of electoral systems. While proportional representation systems fared better than plurality systems in advancing women's parliamentary presence, the major changes in women's representation between 1990 and 2010 could be attributed primarily to the adoption of gender quotas. The largest number of countries in Africa that adopted legislative quotas did so after the UN Conference on Women in Beijing in 1995, where a Platform of Action prodded member states to take steps to increase female leadership in all areas. An analysis of the role of quotas points to the importance of women's movements in increasing rates of representation. In countries with quotas, women claimed 25 per cent of parliamentary seats, while in countries without quotas women claimed an average of 14 per cent of the seats in 2015.

Existing theories also suggested that oil-producing countries had lower rates of female representation because the existence of oil rents reduces the number of women in the workforce and hence their capacity to press for change in electoral laws (Ross 2008). However, these theories do not adequately account for women's movements and coalitions that have pressed for quotas and have increased the representation of women even in oil-producing countries. In Africa, oil-producing countries are increasing rates of female representation without significant changes in female labour force participation. The top oil producers[5] in Africa have roughly the same rate of female

---

5 These are Algeria, Angola, Cameroon, Chad, Republic of Congo, Equatorial Guinea, Gabon, Libya, Nigeria and Sudan.

representation in parliament on average (20.70 per cent) as the non-oil producers (20.61 per cent). Today, women in oil-producing states such as Angola hold 37 per cent of the legislative seats, while the proportions are 32 per cent in Algeria and 31 per cent in Sudan, primarily as a result of the adoption of quotas.

Other theories of representation suggest that culture – and, in particular, the preponderance of a population adhering to Islam – serves as a constraint on female representation (Inglehart and Norris 2003). In Africa, however, many countries with the highest rates of female representation have significant Muslim populations, such as Senegal, Algeria, Tanzania, Tunisia, Morocco, Mauritania and Sudan. They have adopted quotas and increased rates of representation of women. In fact, predominantly Muslim Senegal has one of the highest rates of female representation in the world as a result of a vigorous campaign led by the Conseil Senegalais des Femmes (COSEF), which started in 2005 and ended in the adoption of quotas in 2012. Once again, these changes are obscured by the lack of attentiveness to women's movements and coalitions that pressed for them.

In general, post-conflict countries have double the rates of representation for women in parliament compared with non-post-conflict countries. War disrupted gender relations in ways that allowed for women to rise to power. It unintentionally created conditions that opened up possibilities for women at many levels, from the executive to local government. For example, Ellen Johnson Sirleaf of Liberia was elected the first female president in Africa in 2005 after years of civil war. Catherine Samba-Panza was elected interim president of the Central African Republic amidst a bloody civil war. Both Johnson Sirleaf and Samba-Panza are strong advocates of women's rights. Earlier, Ruth Perry was appointed head of the National State Council of Liberia as the interim head of state in 1996 amidst conflict, and had been a founding member of the Liberian Women's Initiative. Women gained greater visibility during and after war because institutional changes opened up opportunities for them to demand women's rights and representation in the context of peace talks, constitutional changes, legislative changes, truth and reconciliation processes and electoral reforms, which included the introduction of quotas (Tripp 2015).

One sees similar changes in the judiciary, with the advancement of women magistrates up to the top levels. African women judges are even entering the international arena: Fatou Bensouda from Gambia is the chief prosecutor in the International Criminal Court. Curiously, all but one of the current five African judges at the International Criminal Court are women.

Pressures to increase women's representation in Africa extend to the local level: women hold almost 60 per cent of local government positions in Lesotho and Seychelles; they comprise 43 per cent of the members of local councils or municipal assemblies in Namibia; and they hold over one-third of local government seats in Mauritania, Mozambique, Tanzania and Uganda.

At the regional level, women make up 50 per cent of the African Union (AU) parliament; this is in contrast to the European Union Parliament, where only one-third of the seats are held by women. In July 2012, South Africa's Nkosazana Dhlamini-Zuma took over the leadership of the AU Commission. From 2004 to 2009, Gertrude Mongella of Tanzania chaired the AU's Pan-African Parliament as the first president of the body. Fatoumatta Ceesay from Gambia heads up the parliament of the Economic Community of West African States (ECOWAS), which is made up of fifteen member states, and Margaret Nantongo Zziwa serves as speaker of the East African Legislative Assembly.

African women activists have thus played an important role in advancing the debate regarding women's political leadership and, in particular, the use of quotas. Drude Dahlerup and Lenita Freidenvall (2003) have argued that the incremental model of increasing women's representation in parliament that led to high rates of female representation in the Nordic countries in the 1970s has been replaced by the fast-track model one finds in Africa, where dramatic jumps in parliamentary representation are brought about by the introduction of electoral quotas. These jumps in representation occurred in Africa under specific contexts that allowed women's rights activists to have influence: often they were adopted after conflict and after political opening, which allowed women's rights activists the space to organise coalitions that pressed for change. They occurred in the context of support from those in power, and from international actors such as the UN and donors.

Leaders in finance and entrepreneurship

Women activists' efforts to improve women's economic status have focused on improving their access to credit and microcredit, struggles for legal change around land and inheritance, and gender budgeting. Women's economic involvement in Africa, for example, helped inspire the formation of Women's World Banking, the first such international lending organisation. A pre-conference seminar of eleven women from five continents prior to the 1975 Mexico City UN Conference on Women discussed how women might be able to access financial services to improve their economic situation. There, the successful Ghanaian agribusiness entrepreneur, industrialist and philanthropist Esther Ocloo pioneered the idea of formalising local women's credit associations. She asked: 'Why are we talking about women as victims or as passive beneficiaries of social services. Poor women are the world's farmers, traders, informal sector industrialists. Women need access to financial services – not charity, not subsidies' (Nancy Barry tribute to Ocloo, 4 March 2002). Ocloo worked with Ela Bhatt, founder of the Self-Employed Women's Association in India, and Michaela Walsh, a New York investment banker, and together they founded Women's World Banking in 1979. Ocloo became the first chair of its board of trustees, serving in that capacity from 1980 to 1985. As of 2005, Women's World Banking was providing financial services to over 12 million women and operating in forty-five countries around the world. It was the precursor of the Grameen Bank, formed in 1980, BRAC, Accion, and other such popular micro-lending initiatives.

Although much of the focus on credit has been at the level of microfinance, women's businesses are scaling up in Africa and larger amounts of credit are required. Today, in a country such as Uganda, women own 40 per cent of businesses and yet only 7 per cent of all credit is allocated to them. As a result, new models of banking led by women are emerging. The Uganda Women's Finance Trust, which was formed in 1984 by a group of women professionals to provide microcredit to women, serves as an example of the type of transition that is taking place in the financial world. In 2014, the Trust was transformed into the Uganda Finance Trust Bank, the first commercial bank wholly established by enterprising women to provide financial services to low- and medium-income people, especially women. It has a staff of 400 and a network of thirty-three branches, with 70 per cent of its branches in rural areas. It is owned by the Uganda Women's Finance Trust, Uganda Women Entrepreneurs and Ugandan Sun Mutual Cooperative Saving, as well as by the Dutch Oikocredit and the French Investment & Partner (Sanya 2014). This bank is a good example of the ways in which financial institutions are scaling up from microcredit to meet the needs of a new group of female entrepreneurs, particularly at the middle range, while continuing to support small-scale entrepreneurs (Tripp 2015).

Women's role in finance is evident in other areas as well. A Ugandan woman, Edigold Monday, became the first woman to direct a top Africa-wide bank in 2008. Under her leadership, the Bank of Africa strengthened its financial position, growing its assets by 91 per cent, deposits by 85 per cent and loans and advances by 74 per cent (Ladu 2014). The African Development Bank was the first multilateral bank to appoint a Special Envoy on Gender in 2013, Geraldine J. Fraser-Moleketi (Tripp 2015).

Women's changing needs in finance reflect their growing clout as businesswomen. In fact, Africa is a world leader when it comes to women starting businesses, with almost equal numbers of male and female entrepreneurs. In countries such as Ghana, Nigeria and Zambia, the number of women entrepreneurs exceeds that of men, according to the Global Entrepreneurship Monitor's *2013 Global Report*. Overall, there are proportionately more entrepreneurs in Africa than elsewhere in the world.[6]

Today in Uganda, for example, there are women who have built up major businesses, have significant real estate holdings and large-scale investments, and are engaged in international trade. Many women are now demanding business management training, rather than simply cooking and handicraft skills. One indication of women's changing role in business was the election of Olive Zaitun Kigongo as the first woman president of Uganda National Chamber of Commerce and Industry as early as 2002. The women's movement organisations have supported these changes and have pressed for greater reforms. For example, women have formed their own business associations such as Ugandan Women Entrepreneurs Association (UWEAL), which has promoted the purchase of locally made products, created awareness

6 http://edition.cnn.com/2014/05/13/business/numbers-showing-africa-entrepreneurial-spirit/.

of business and entrepreneurship among young women, established a mentoring programme, helped women transition from the micro-enterprise to small- and medium-sized enterprise level by improving the performance of their business (Tripp 2015).

Today, women in Africa are global leaders in the boardroom. An African Development Bank (2015) study looked at data for 307 companies in twelve African countries and compared it with data for other parts of the world; it found that, even though the number of women is still limited in boardrooms, women in Africa are only slightly behind European (18 per cent) and US (17 per cent) women, with a rate of 14.4 per cent. This puts them ahead of the Asia Pacific region (9.8 per cent), Latin America (5.6 per cent) and the Middle East (1 per cent). They are best represented in the boardrooms of financial services, basic materials and construction, and automotive industries. The countries with the highest rates of female boardroom representation of the countries surveyed included Kenya (19.8 per cent), South Africa (17.4 per cent), Botswana (16.9 per cent), Zambia (16.9 per cent) and Ghana (17.7 per cent).

A new breed of businesswoman is emerging. At one end of the spectrum one finds women such as Mosunmola 'Mo' Abudu, whom *Forbes* described as 'Africa's Most Successful Woman'. She is the first woman in Africa to own a pan-African TV channel. She herself is a talk show host, TV producer, media personality, entrepreneur and philanthropist. Folorunsho Alakija is the wealthiest woman in Nigeria and is managing director of the Rose of Sharon Group, which is involved in the fashion, oil and printing industries.

More typical middle-range entrepreneurs might include Alice Karugaba, who runs a successful and well-known furniture outlet, Nina Interiors, in Uganda. Another Ugandan, Benedicta Nanyonga, makes bags, belts and shoes from used drinking straws and sells them in international markets. Regina Mukiibi is the first female funeral director in Uganda. Scot Carol Cooke noted, when making a film about Ugandan businesswomen, that the country's 'growing band of female entrepreneurs ... are defying the statistics, cultural stereotypes and credit restrictions and are taking the business world by storm. They are putting so-called hard working Western business women like me to shame on a daily basis.'[7]

---

7 http://barefootinbusiness.com.

While most women in Africa are still working in agricultural or informal sectors, we highlight these developments in the business sector as an outcome of women's rights advocacy and as an area in which women in Africa are fast becoming world leaders.

Another area that first generated considerable momentum in Africa and then spread beyond the continent has been the adoption of 'gender budgets', or attempts to make the gender implications of spending priorities in the national budget more explicit and improve the status of women by bringing attention to the gender gaps. After the 1995 Beijing Fourth UN Conference on Women, many African countries, starting with Tanzania and Uganda, adopted women's budgets designed along the lines of South Africa's 1994 budget exercise, which itself was inspired by the 1984 budgets of federal and state governments in Australia. Approximately forty gender-sensitive budget initiatives were underway globally by 2002, the largest number of which were in Africa, in countries such as Uganda, Botswana, Zimbabwe, Malawi, Mozambique, Namibia and Tanzania. Gender budgeting subsequently spread more widely in the West; the European Union has endorsed this as an approach, as have the parliaments of some of its member states, such as Germany. African experiences with this form of gender mainstreaming have become an important factor in increasing their popularity (Elson and Sharp 2010; Stotsky et al. 2016; Tripp et al. 2009).

Contributions to peace-making and peacebuilding

African women's contributions to policy were also visible in the area of peace-making and peacebuilding, given that so many of the wars between 1990 and 2000 were located on the continent. Many of these conflicts were long in duration. After 2000, the number of conflicts starting decreased while the number of conflicts ending increased, resulting in a marked drop in conflicts in Africa. African women activists were heavily involved in bringing about an end to these conflicts, primarily at the local level, by demonstrating against war, negotiating with militias and militia leaders, holding ceremonies to turn in arms, negotiating the release of kidnapped people, and seeking to ensure that peaceful elections were held. They were proactive in promoting issues of peace, not only at the local level but also in international forums.

Women's marginalisation from politics meant that they brought a different set of interests to bear on peace processes. African women, in particular, made peace a central issue at the UN Beijing Conference on Women in 1995. Their efforts contributed greatly to the passing of UN Security Council Resolution 1325 on 31 October 2000, which covered the inclusion of women in peace negotiations and gave them roles in peacekeeping missions around the world. The resolution requires the protection of women and girls against sexual assault in civil conflicts and heightened efforts to place women in decision-making positions in international institutions. In 2000 in Namibia, they provided leadership in developing the Windhoek Declaration and Namibia Plan of Action on mainstreaming a gender perspective in multidimensional peace support operations. The declaration advocated for women's participation in peace operations and peace negotiations, 50 per cent women in leadership positions, women as gender specialists within missions, and gender considerations in all aspects of peace-making and peacebuilding (Windhoek Declaration 2000). This paved the way for Namibia to bring forward to the UN Security Council Resolution 1325, which called for gender balance and equality in prevention, protection and participation in conflict situations.

Many of the changes in thinking about gender-based violence globally came out of African experiences within conflict, as these sharpened awareness of the nature and gravity of the problem. The International Criminal Tribunal for Rwanda (ICTR) judgment against former Rwandese mayor Jean-Paul Akayesu in 1988 for his role in the Rwandan genocide of 1984 helped to fundamentally transform existing norms regarding gender violence, not only within Africa but globally. For the first time, rape and sexual violence were explicitly recognised as 'an act of genocide and a crime against humanity' (Copelon 2000: 227). Two of the three judges in this case were from Africa: Judge Laïty Kama from Senegal and Navanethem Pillay from South Africa. Pillay is known, among other things, as having founded the international women's rights organisation Equality Now, which works to protect and promote the human rights of women and girls around the world.

Cultural rights and women's rights

Finally, although it is true that there are areas in which universal women's rights regimes clash with the cultural understandings of local actors, as has been argued by Dorothy Hodgson, Pamela Scully and others, it is also the case that African women activists are shaping and defining for themselves new cultural norms that promote equality, non-discrimination and healthy satisfying lives for both men and women. African women's rights advocates were also among the first to openly discuss the tensions between women's rights and cultural rights that are so contentious today. One example of this is the leadership African women have exerted on the Inter-African Committee on Traditional Practices Affecting the Health of Women and Children, which was formed in 1984 and works with governments, international organisations and donors to develop and evaluate policies, laws and programmes to protect and promote the bodily integrity of women and young girls.

Today, many of these debates over cultural rights are occurring in the context of constitutional and legal reform. Virtually all African countries have rewritten their constitutions since 1990, many precipitated by the shift to multipartyism and others in the post-conflict context. Since 1995, forty-four constitutions have been rewritten in sub-Saharan Africa (or are in the process of being rewritten).

Many of these contemporary struggles in Africa regarding women's rights have focused on customary law and the role of traditional and religious authorities. In Africa, women's rights activists have increasingly pressed for constitutions to adopt clauses regarding customary law, mostly in post-conflict countries. These struggles have their origins in the legal systems established during colonial times, which were reinforced after independence. Contemporary African legal systems are the result of a mix of legal traditions that were built on colonial common law traditions (for example in former British colonies) and civil law traditions (in former French, Portuguese, Belgian, German, Italian and Spanish colonies). Both legal traditions have coexisted at different levels of comfort with customary law (Tripp et al. 2009).

Since the 1990s, women's rights organisations in Africa have sought to introduce clauses that allow the constitutional guarantees of equality to prevail should there be a clash between women's rights and customary laws and practices that violate women's rights, discriminate against women, or infringe on bill of rights provisions regarding gender equality. These are extremely profound challenges.

They are, in effect, attempts to legitimise new legal-based sources of authority for rights governing relations between men and women, family ties, and relationships between women and traditional, clan and religious leaders. In the past, even when laws existed to regulate marriage, inheritance, custody and other such practices, customary laws and practices coexisted and generally took precedence when it came to family and clan matters. Even though, in practice, these customary norms still prevail today, even with the constitutional reforms, women's movements now have the means to challenge these practices through constitutional and legislative means. But challenges to customary law have been particularly difficult because there can be strong feelings of support for customary practices, even among women themselves (Logan 2009). Therefore, it has been much harder to pass legislation affecting these institutions, such as laws ensuring women's rights to property and land through inheritance. Much of the active and organised resistance to improving women's legal status, particularly in the area of family law, has come from religious leaders, chiefs, elders, clan leaders and individuals who are wedded to older norms and cultural practices. Many of these people also stand to benefit politically – and even economically – from older practices and beliefs (Tripp 2015).

Generally, issues that pertain to the family and the clan, particularly with respect to family law and customary law, have met with more resistance compared with legislative changes affecting gender equality in markets or in state institutions. Thus, education for girls, legislative quotas for women, maternity leave, discrimination in employment practices and other such concerns have been much less controversial than reforms to family law. There has been considerable resistance in many countries to such issues as the reform of land and property inheritance by women, female genital cutting, child marriage, forced marriage, bride wealth, polygyny and marital rape. Legal change often precedes actual changes in such practices.

While most African constitutions protect traditional authorities and customary law, 42 per cent of countries have introduced provisions that allow the constitution or statutory law to override customary law. Some, such as the Ethiopian constitution, even go so far as to charge the state with eliminating such practices.

Women's rights activists pressed hard for these changes in Uganda through the Constitutional Commission and later the Constituent

Assembly. As a result, Article 33 of the 1995 Ugandan constitution states that: 'Laws, cultures, customs and traditions which are against the dignity, welfare or interest of women or any other marginalised group … or which undermine their status, are prohibited by this Constitution.'

However, even countries that have tried to harmonise the contradictory impulses of supporting women's rights while at the same time protecting customary law adjudicated by traditional authorities have run into problems in practice. The limits to these contradictory constitutional provisions in Uganda emerged with the debate over the amendments to the 1998 Land Act. When the women's movement started to demand a co-ownership (common property) clause so that women could inherit land or keep their share of land if they were divorced or thrown out by their husbands, there was immediate pushback in defence of the clan and customary practices.

Some of the main opponents of gender-related reforms have continued to be clan leaders, traditional authorities, and some religious institutions. Nevertheless, in some instances they have become advocates for changes in women's status. In 2006, for instance, a group of distinguished Islamic scholars assembled at Al-Azhar University in Cairo to issue a set of recommendations recognising that female genital mutilation 'is a deplorable, inherited custom, which is practiced in some societies and is copied by some Muslims in several countries'.[8] They concluded that 'there are no written grounds for this custom in the Qur'an with regard to an authentic tradition of the Prophet' and acknowledged that 'female genital circumcision practiced today harms women psychologically and physically' and should be 'seen as a punishable aggression against humankind'. They demanded that 'the practice must be stopped in support of one of the highest values of Islam, namely to do no harm to another' and called for its criminalisation.

In northern Uganda, the prime minister of the Acholi Ker Kwaro, Hon. Kenneth Oketta, described to Aili Tripp how one of the main functions of his office involved conflict mediation. Land inheritance and domestic violence were two of the main issues that came to his

---

8 http://www.target-human-rights.com/HP-00_aktuelles/alAzharKonferenz/index.php?p=beschluss&lang=en.

attention for mediation. The local women lawyers' chapter of FIDA confirmed that they worked closely with his office on women's rights concerns and had run training sessions with the local court system on how to handle land matters. The Acholi leader saw his role as an interpreter of culture and as such was concerned that women were treated justly in such cases (Tripp 2015).

In countries such as Liberia and Namibia, where women have gained positions of power in formal structures, there appears to be some spillover into traditional institutions. For example, Heike Becker (2006) and Janine Ubink (2011) found that Ovambo traditional authorities were putting more women into positions of power as head women and in community courts in Namibia. While these may be indications of some change, generally these traditional and religious institutions are among the more conservative elements within society and have been most resistant to change.

Outline of this book

The narratives in this book are analysed by African authors who themselves are part of the activist groups and have witnessed or participated in the mobilisation process to end discrimination and gender-based violence. They are feminist scholars who have unique personal theoretical standpoints as well as a commitment to a feminist research methodology which is participatory and reflective. Most studies look at women's mobilisation in either North Africa or sub-Saharan Africa. This book looks at eight country case studies in the continent as a whole.

The chapters in this volume challenge the stereotype that African women are passive, underprivileged and simply under the domination of patriarchy. The authors' adopt a variety of disciplinary paradigms and methods to highlight various aspects of African women's mobilisation and struggles for change. They consider the constraints they faced, and the contexts that led to achievements and their strategies. They document changes in women's roles, status and well-being as well as their traditional positions of leadership. The chapters examine mobilisation for resistance since precolonial times up to the present as well as the national and regional context that has impacted women's mobilisation strategies and outcomes.

The chapters explore diverse types of women's mobilisation, from grassroots organisations to urban informal-sector groups, from civil society groups to religious organisations, those that were an outgrowth of political parties as well as independent organisations. Some look at state-led organisations and government bureaucracies, while others focus on individual-led mobilisation, for example the chapter on Kenya by Regina Mwatha. Yet others focus on individual women leaders, as does Lilia Labidi, writing on Tunisia.

The authors offer diverse conceptualisations of feminism, women's movements and women's mobilisation based on how these are conceived in the context of their own countries. For example, Sheila Meintjes from South Africa shows how the transition from authoritarianism to democracy in South Africa 'meant a shift from "movement activism" to more issue-specific interventions and pragmatic strategies' for women's rights activists. Regina Mwatha found that in Kenya 'the women's movement is viewed as one that emphasises common objectives, continuity and coordination'. The Tanzanian case shows how women's rights activists can mobilise across religious, ethnic, and even class differences. They can build effective networks in which different organisations complement the work of others and draw on each other's various strengths.

The strategies, approaches and techniques used also show the wealth of lessons to be shared for replication and those to be avoided. They range on a continuum from state-supported strategies to those of mobilisation against state laws and policies. Fatima Sadiqi from Morocco highlights changes in feminist consciousness since colonial times, culminating in present-day mobilisation around the identity politics of all disadvantaged groups, including Amazigh (Berber) demands. Feminists and Amazigh movements have formed coalitions, and she argues that 'feminist consciousness is increasingly congruent with Berber consciousness, since the two share secularism as a guiding tenet. This has translated into reciprocal networking on the ground.'

Current strategies include those of younger generations who focus on social media, which was widely used during the 'Jasmine Spring' in Tunisia. Lilia Labidi states: 'Whereas for the women writers of the 1980s, the book and the international solidarity networks were essential, for those of the 2000s mastery of communications technology provides one of the foundations for an expansion of freedom.' She shows how increasingly a new generation of women authors are producing creative works that reveal their engagement in a culture that is global and universal, as they 'contribute to the construction of a humanist feminism and a transnational modernity'.

Nana Pratt argues for the importance of regional networking and international solidarity as a useful strategy in the case of Sierra Leone, where an African Women's Peace Mission was sent under the auspices of Female African Solidarity (FAS) and the Women's International League for Peace. That mission acknowledged the important role women played in the negotiations and consultations that led to the elections in 1996 and commended the Sierra Leonean Women's Forum for leading the mobilisation of the peace efforts, even as they were supported by donors and the UN agencies.

The chapters take a close look at the inner workings of the movements to show that, in spite of their common struggles for gender equality, there also exist philosophical, ideological, religious and class-based or rural–urban-based differences between organisations. For example, the secular and Islamist divide is highlighted by authors in the context of predominantly Muslim countries such as Morocco (Fatima Sadiqi) and Sudan (Samia Al Nagar and Liv Tønnessen). It is also interesting to note that in many polarising contexts, even those of civil war, many of these divides were bridged by women peace activists in forging a common women's rights agenda, as Nana Pratt shows in the case of Sierra Leone. In Liberia, too, women famously built a strong peace movement that included women of all walks of life and ethnicities as well as both Muslims and Christians. In Somalia, women activists formed a coalition of all contending clans. In Burundi, during the peace talks, women came together across party and ethnic lines to establish a common agenda. A similar bridging of difference in the context of the women's movement is evident in the cases of Kenya (Regina Mwatha) and South Africa (Sheila Meintjes).

More specifically, the African writers of this volume have shown the importance of coalitions and the ways in which their successes in engaging with the state were tied to the coordination between women's organisations, other members of civil society, women in political parties and women parliamentarians. The professionalisation of the main women actors, the focus on particular issues to recruit supporters, and taking advantage of changes in circumstances were crucial for success. Networking using social media and modern communication techniques helped activists work within and across national boundaries and to work at regional and international levels.

The authors reflect on the gains of women's mobilisation that led to improved political representation and the promotion of social development indicators in education, employment and socioeconomic conditions. Gender-sensitive constitutional rights and legal reforms represent additional gains of the past decades and have been particularly important in Muslim countries. Women's movements have succeeded in bringing issues including violence against women to the fore as public concerns, as well as the need to change stereotypical images of women in the media. However, most of the authors refer to the need to fundamentally challenge patriarchy. A strong patriarchal culture remains the main obstacle preventing women's organisations from fundamentally transforming gender power relations. Patriarchy bestows privilege and prestige on men at the expense of women and operates at all levels of society, from the household to the state house. Patriarchal values sustain oppression, whether through the use of religious dogma, traditional values, or secular value systems to legitimise male domination and gender injustice. Both men and women are culpable in maintaining patriarchy, but, by the same token, they can be partners in fighting it, as many of the chapters show. In some cases, men not only support women's demands but also initiate the call for women's rights and gender equality. Their participation is essential to the process of dismantling patriarchy. These men may be heads of state, religious scholars, political party leaders, members of the family or work colleagues, and they are discussed in the chapters by Sadiqi for Morocco, Labidi for Tunisia, Al Nagar and Tønnessen for Sudan, Mwatha for Kenya, Meintjes for South Africa and Tripp for Tanzania.

Most of the chapters in this book highlight women's activism that aims to redress the injustice, discrimination and subordination women face. Aili Tripp examines the historical roots of the movement in Tanzania, beginning with women's mobilisation during the independence period. She looks at the role of the country's first president, Julius Nyerere, in shaping norms around gender equality based on his socialist orientation; the influence of the Women's Union during the one-party era; and the impact of international women's movement pressures. She also considers the various ways in which the women's movement in Tanzania asserted leadership both on the continent and internationally as it pioneered women's political leadership and gender budgeting (the analysis of national budgets for their gendered impacts).

In contrast, Regina Mwatha from Kenya provides a different narrative and analysis, elaborating on the evolution and types of women organising in the country from before colonisation to the current period. She shows, for example, how in traditional communities women assisted each other in different economic, socio-cultural and political matters, and later used the same networks to fight against colonial domination. She explains how the women's movement is made up of rural grassroots organisations, formal women's organisations and individual women. She explores their changing relationship to the state over time. She also brings out their emphasis on common objectives and coordination across a diverse movement. She highlights Kenyan women's global leadership in environmental issues through the activities led by Wangari Maathai.

Akua Britwum and Angela Akorsu focus on a case study based on fieldwork with a traditional union of women traders in Cape Coast, Ghana, a country known for its matrilineal descent system. The majority of people in the country work within the informal economy, and women form the bulk of this sector, working as traders in urban and rural markets. Women traders organised traditional unions around different types of trades, each of which was headed by a queen. The market became a space for political mobilisation during electoral campaigns and was a potential site for women to address their needs and demands. It was not only a market place, but also a place where women came into direct daily contact with different state bodies. The state has an ambivalent posture towards the traders, and while it pays lip service to job creation and skills acquisition, many of its policies undermine the livelihoods of traders. Women in this informal economy do not enjoy any social benefits and must rely on their own self-help associations to sustain themselves and regulate trade activity.

In another West African country – Sierra Leone – Nana Pratt highlights the important roles women played in a nationwide peace movement during the country's eleven-year civil war (1991–2002). Pratt was not only an eyewitness to the war, she was actively engaged in the movement during the period of conflict and post-conflict.

She details the evolution and achievements of the women's peace movement, which draws on traditions that go back to the early 1900s. She shows how women were involved in the broader peace movement but also had their own independent activities. They were involved in peace restoration and the call for non-violent elections during the democratisation process.

Sheila Meintjes analyses the South African women's movement, looking at how women took advantage of the end of apartheid to advance their demands. They formed a broad coalition of women's organisations, which led to the endorsement of a women-friendly constitution, enhanced representation and legal justice. The women movement's encompassed a wide spectrum of organisations, from small grassroots groups to large church-based organisations, political party wings and other coalitions. The movement shifted from one that had worked in a conflict setting against the state to one that engaged the state in the process of drafting the constitution. These changes have highlighted the diversity of women's activism in South Africa and the particular challenges it faces going forward.

The chapters on North Africa, which is predominantly Muslim, highlight the divide between secularist and Islamist groups. This is particularly evident in the chapters by Samia Al Nagar and Liv Tønnessen on Sudan and Fatima Sadiqi on Morocco. Al Nagar and Tønnessen focus their chapter on the shift that has occurred within women's mobilisation in Sudan, from a focus on the role of women in the public sphere of politics and economic activity to the private sphere, with an emphasis on family law, divorce, female genital mutilation and child marriage. Since independence, the women's movement has fragmented into different groups, displaying divisions along generational, ideological and urban–rural lines. The most significant division is between the secularists, who argue for a human rights orientation, and the Islamists, who adopt a religious view of women's rights. The authors examine the implications of these divisions.

Fatima Sadiqi provides an overview of the past seventy years of mobilisation in Morocco. She classifies the diverse types of women's mobilisation into three groupings: secular feminists, state-led feminists and Islamic feminists. Secular feminists evolved under colonialism and largely represent the upper-class, educated women. The 1980s and 1990s saw the emergence of organisations demanding changes in family law along with the expansion of the movement to include a wider range of economic classes. By the 2000s, the movement had expanded through social media and was openly allying itself with the Amazigh (Berber) nationalist movement, although it had a strong urban base. The origins of the Islamic women's movement lie in a response to the secularist women's movement. Sadiqi notes the great achievements made by women, especially in the area of legal reform of Islamic family law, achievements that challenged both patriarchal values and conservative interpretations of Islamic principles guiding gender and family relations.

Lilia Labidi of Tunisia offers a different way of discussing African women's mobilisations by focusing on key women's life stories and their activism from the time of colonisation. She draws on personal expressions of resistance through literary writing, fiction and journalistic writings as well as the use of social media and cartoons during the Tunisian uprisings of 2011. Hence, her focus is on literature, the arts and social media as strategies for mobilisation to advance goals of equality, justice and recognition. The chapter also highlights the role of men who are religious Muslim scholars, political leaders and family members in both the initiation of and support for women's rights campaigns. She is interested in the contexts in which memoirs and journals that used to be produced primarily by men in lofty positions of politics, medicine and other professions now seem to be written by women as well. She examines closely the biographies of a few Tunisian women writers who have engaged in a literature of denunciation against political violence and looks at their lives both before and after the 2011 uprisings.

Thus, these chapters, when taken as a whole, offer narratives of what has been achieved in terms women's rights through women's mobilisation. They offer glimpses into who led the achievements, what challenges they faced, what opportunities were missed, and the broader contexts that supported their agency. A larger debate continues over the extent to which these achievements are substantial or whether they are simply window dressing. Yet, the compilation of all these experiences is crucial for the exchange of lessons to be learned and for future generations to reflect on how to move these struggles forward.

Conclusions

As African women's movements have taken advantage of changing international gender norms and transnational feminist movements to advance their own agendas domestically, they in turn have influenced global understandings and implementation of women's rights. These influences are particularly evident in UN agencies, policies and conferences. African women have been leaders and have been influential, particularly in areas such as the political representation of women, in advancing women as economic actors, in adopting strategies to promote peace, and in tackling cultural constraints on women.

African women's movements pressed for changes in these areas in the context of democratisation, a decline in overall conflict on the continent, changing international and regional norms regarding women's rights, and new donor support. They also utilised new social media to advance their goals. African women's movements became especially visible after the 1990s, when women's organisations were increasingly characterised by their associational autonomy from government and from the dominant political party. In contrast to the first three decades after independence, they acquired their own resources, selected their own leaders, and forged their own women's rights agendas in ways that were no longer dictated by the ruling party or government, as had been the case in the early post-independence years prior to political liberalisation in the 1960s, 1970s and 1980s. Although the older welfare-oriented and developmental agendas persisted after the 1990s, a new emphasis on political participation and advocacy emerged. New women's organisations formed to improve leadership skills, encourage women's political involvement, promote women's political leadership, press for legislative and constitutional changes, and conduct civic education.

As women's movements in Africa responded to the challenges of poverty, conflict, domestic violence and political marginalisation in their own societies, they engaged regional and global actors in order to advance their own goals at home. They were connected with international women's movements to influence UN and other multilateral agencies as well as foreign donors. They relied on international treaties and conventions to press their own agenda at home. And they engaged regional organisations such as SADC, ECOWAS and the Economic Community of Central African States

(ECCAS) to do the same. In doing so, they also influenced global discussions on women's rights, particularly in areas where they were world leaders.

These developments speak to broader changes in global feminisms. Non-Western countries today, in fact, have claimed much of the momentum of feminist and women's rights advocacy globally (Tripp 2006). They have helped influence the combination of the rights-based and development-based approaches to women's advancement, which has energised activists in the global South. Global feminism is a more South-centred movement than ever before, and African women leaders have helped significantly in bringing about this transformation.

References

AAWORD (1982) 'The Experience of the Association of African Women for Research and Development'. *Development Dialogue*, 1–2, 101–13.

Abu-Lughod, L. (2002) 'Do Muslim Women Really Need Saving? Anthropological Reflections on Cultural Relativism and its Other'. *American Anthropologist*, 104, 783–90.

African Development Bank (2015) *Where are the Women: Inclusive Boardrooms in Africa's Top Listed Companies?* Abidjan, Côte d'Ivoire: African Development Bank.

Becker, H. (2006) '"New Things After Independence": Gender and Traditional Authorities in Postcolonial Namibia'. *Journal of Southern African Studies*, 32, 29–48.

Dahlerup, D. and Freidenvall, L. (2005) 'Quotas as a "Fast Track" to Equal Representation for Women'. *International Feminist Journal of Politics*, 7, 26–48.

Elson, D. and Sharp, R. (2010) 'Gender-responsive Budgeting and Women's Poverty' in Chant, S. (ed.) *The International Handbook of Gender and Poverty: Concepts, Research and Policy*. Cheltenham: Edward Elgar, pp. 522–7.

Hodgson, D. (2011) '"These are not our Priorities": Maasai Women, Human Rights and the Problem of Culture' in Hodgson, D. L. and Scully, P. (eds) *Gender and Culture at the Limit of Rights*. Philadelphia: University of Pennsylvania Press.

Ilumoka, A. (2009) 'Advocacy for Women's Reproductive and Sexual Health and Rights in Africa Between the Devil and the Deep Blue Sea' in Adomako Ampofo, A. and Arnfred, S. (eds) *African Feminist Politics of Knowledge: Tensions, Challenges, Possibilities*. Uppsala: Nordiska Afrikainstitutet.

Inglehart, R. and Norris, P. (2003) *Rising Tide: Gender Equality and Cultural Change around the World*. Cambridge and New York: Cambridge University Press.

Jain, D. (2005) *Women, Development, and the UN: A Sixty-year Quest for Equality and Justice*. Bloomington: Indiana University Press.

Ladu, I. M. (2014) 'Uganda's First Female Bank MD Bows Out'. *Daily Monitor*, 14 April.

Levitt, P. and Merry, S. (2009) 'Vernacularization on the Ground: Local Uses of Global Women's Rights in Peru, China, India and the United States'. *Global Networks*, 9, 441–61.

Logan, C. (2009) 'Selected Chiefs, Elected Councillors and Hybrid Democrats: Popular Perspectives on the Co-existence of Democracy and Traditional Authority'. *Journal of Modern African Studies*, 47(1), 101–28.

Merry, S. E. (2006a) *Human Rights and Gender Violence: Translating International Law into Local Justice*. Chicago: University of Chicago Press.

Merry, S. E. (2006b) 'Transnational Human Rights and Local Activism: Mapping the Middle'. *American Anthropologist*, 108, 38–51.

Ross, M. (2008) 'Oil, Islam, and Women'. *American Political Science Review*, 102, 107–23.

Sanya, S. (2014) 'First Women's Commercial Bank Launched in Uganda'. *New Vision*, 17 January.

Snyder, M. (2006) 'Unlikely Godmother: The UN and the Global Women's Movement' in Ferree, M. M. and Tripp, A. M. (eds) *Global Feminism: Transnational Women's Activism, Organizing, and Human Rights*. New York: New York University Press, pp. 24–50.

Snyder, M. C. (2015) 'Four Decisive Decades: The Birth and Growth of a Global Women's Movement'. Keynote address at the Women's Caucus, African Studies Association Annual Meeting, San Diego.

Snyder, M. C. and Tadesse, M., with African Training and Research Centre for Women (1995) *African Women and Development: A History*. Johannesburg, London and Atlantic Highlands NJ: Witwatersrand University Press and Zed Books.

Stotsky, J. G., Kolovich, L. and Kebhaj, S. (2016) *Sub-Saharan Africa: A Survey of Gender Budgeting Efforts*. IMF Working Paper WP/16/152. Washington DC: International Monetary Fund (IMF).

Tripp, A. M. (2006) 'The Evolution of Transnational Feminisms: Consensus, Conflict and New Dynamics' in Marx Ferree, M. and Tripp, A. (eds) *Global Feminism: Transnational Women's Activism, Organizing, and Human Rights*. New York: New York University Press.

Tripp, A. M. (2015) *Women and Power in Post-conflict Africa*. New York: Cambridge University Press.

Tripp, A. M., Casimiro, I., Kwesiga, J. and Mungwa, A. (2009) *African Women's Movements: Transforming Political Landscapes*. Cambridge and New York: Cambridge University Press.

Ubink, J. (2011) 'Gender Equality on the Horizon? The Case of Uukwambi Traditional Authority, Northern Namibia'. Enhancing Legal Empowerment Working Paper Series. Rome: International Development Law Organization.

Windhoek Declaration (2000) 'Windhoek Declaration and Namibia Plan of Action on "Mainstreaming a Gender Perspective in Multidimensional Peace Support Operations" On the 10th Anniversary of the United Nations Transitional Assistance Group'. Windhoek, Namibia, 31 May. Available at http://www.un.org/womenwatch/osagi/wps/windhoek_declaration.pdf.

Yuval-Davis, N. (2006) 'Human/Women's Rights and Feminist Transversal Politics' in Ferree, M. M. and Tripp, A. M. (eds) *Global Feminism: Transnational Women's Activism, Organizing, and Human Rights*. New York: New York University Press.

Zwingel, S. (2004) 'From International Regime to Transnational Implementation Network: Effects of the Convention on the Elimination of all Forms of Discrimination Against Women (CEDAW) on Women's Lives'. Paper presented at the 45th Annual Convention of the International Studies Association, 'Hegemony and Its Discontents: Power, Ideology and Knowledge in the Study and Practice of International Relations', Montreal, Canada.

2 | THE EVOLUTION OF THE WOMEN'S MOVEMENT IN SIERRA LEONE

Nana Claris Efua Pratt

This chapter looks at the evolution of the women's movement in Sierra Leone, its achievements and milestones, with a focus on the postcolonial era. It looks at the status of the women's movement since independence in 1961 and considers significant developments that have occurred since then. It highlights the major factors that have influenced the growth of the movement, such as education and the eleven-year civil war (1991–2002). The motivating and visionary leadership of diverse women's groups in the nationwide movement has recognised the empowering influence of education and skill acquisition. This was so even as early as 1915, when the oldest women's civil society organisation – the Young Women's Christian Association (YWCA) – was established. Women realised the need for more women and girls throughout the nation to access education. Some of the reasons and motivations behind this realisation are discussed in this chapter. The women's movement in Sierra Leone champions and rallies around the issues of women's and girls' education, women's rights and gender inequality (including in politics) and, particularly nowadays, issues of sexual and gender-based violence. Achievements over the years include sustained contributions to and the promotion of women's and girls' education by organisations within the movement. This has been achieved through different methods, including the establishment of learning centres, vocational schools and institutes, scholarship programmes for girls, and the provision of school supplies. The women's movement continues to work with relevant institutions and organisations (such as government ministries, departments, non-governmental organisations (NGOs) and United Nations (UN) agencies) on these issues. The outcomes of some of these interventions have included the establishment of policies and legal measures to mitigate or remove some of the barriers to the advancement of women and girls. The women's movement in Sierra Leone has always actively initiated its own programmes as well as supporting others' actions for peace restoration during violent conflicts and for non-violent elections during the democratisation process. This chapter highlights women's activism during and after the 1991–2002 civil war and its interventions and collective achievements in peace restoration, peacebuilding and continuing democratisation processes from 2002 to date.

The elements of solidarity among the diverse groups within the Women's Forum include a decentralised system of operation with a rotating chair and members who are ready and willing to meet and take almost unanimous collective positions on issues dealing with gender equality, both at national and local levels and in socio-economic and political fields. Challenges that need to be grappled with include divisiveness arising from the intergenerational gap, declining volunteerism in the face of limited resources, limited involvement of women in critical areas of expertise (such as the fields of land rights, science and technology) and weak information management skills. The chapter also looks ahead at ways in which these issues might be confronted in order to maintain the momentum of the movement.

Background

Sierra Leone is situated in West Africa and became independent from British colonial rule on 27 April 1961. The country has a long history of women uniting for a common cause or shared goals and organising nationwide for socioeconomic and political change. The evolution of a women's movement in Sierra Leone has in large measure involved the volunteering spirit and inspiring and tireless efforts of women's faith-based and social reform organisations. One common goal that has encouraged shared action on the part of women has been a shared understanding, even in the face of patriarchal subjugation, of the issue of low literacy and educational levels of women and girls. This issue has inspired concern, particularly among women, who recognise the significant role education plays in livelihood opportunity, general enlightenment, and improvement of social status. The focus on women's and girls' access to education has continued since the colonial years, as the aspiration for many more women and girls to receive an education, especially at secondary and tertiary levels, remains a key concern. The women's movement's efforts around issues of education and skills training have deepened, but today they are framed in terms of the need for human and women's rights. Women's interventions seek not just to grant women access to 'available opportunities' but also to pursue gender equality, equity of access to opportunity, and control of the resulting benefits. The women's movement in Sierra Leone has engaged not only in lobbying and advocacy for the provision of opportunities for women's and girls' education, but also in the issues of women and gender, peace and security. Women have always recognised that peaceful and stable environments are critical in the promotion and realisation of educational or any other empowering aspirations.

The women's movement's activism against the 1991–2002 civil war in Sierra Leone and its contribution to the restoration of peace won admiration and recognition as actions worthy of emulation both in and outside the country. A diverse set of groups and individuals within the movement fostered solidarity, especially during the war years. This was possible because the leadership continuously organised strategy sessions in order to encourage information sharing on the effects of the war as well as on key messages that would promote the cessation of violence.

The women's movement prior to the war

The aims of the women's movement after independence and before the terrible civil conflict (1961–91) involved strategic organisation and mobilisation for change and empowerment in the realm of education and vocational skills training. Visible components of the women's movement in the 1960s included women's faith-based associations and social transformation groups such as the YWCA, which was established in 1915 by the wives of members of the Young Men's Christian Association (YMCA), who realised that for societal transformation their own women's organisation was needed. At its founding, women came together in prayer for world peace with the outbreak of the First World War in 1914. The Sierra Leone chapter of the YWCA became affiliated with the world YWCA in 1925. By 1995, the YWCA had branches all over the western area and the provinces, bringing in large numbers of women from the rural areas.

One of the landmark achievements of the women's movement was the creation of the YWCA Vocational Institute Freetown, the first such residential facility for women and girls in Sierra Leone, which was established in September 1961. Also, the YWCA established and maintained pre-primary schools in Freetown and in rural areas to promote access to education for children, especially girls, following independence. Over the years, various other organisations within the movement have sustained regular education scholarship programmes, which have enabled girls and women to enrol in and complete schooling at primary, secondary and tertiary levels.

At the time of Sierra Leone's independence from British colonial rule in 1961, the YWCA had been able to mobilise women and girls of different traditions nationwide to form a local women's advocacy movement based on the worldwide global YWCA. It aimed to empower women through education and skills training and to promote the realisation of their human rights while also enhancing the abilities of participating women so that they could take leadership roles and positively lead change at all levels. As part of this, it established learning centres, continuing education programmes, and primary and nursery schools in nearly all areas of the country.

The focus on women's and girls' access to available educational opportunities expanded over time so that by 1976 some educators among the leadership of the YWCA had motivated women in other professions nationwide. Together they created the Sierra Leone Association of University Women (SLAUW), which is affiliated with the International Federation of University Women (IFUW). The renowned educationalist Elizabeth Hyde was among the women who spearheaded the formation of SLAUW. SLAUW rallied support for the aspiration for many more women and girls to receive an education, particularly at secondary and tertiary levels. There was a need to sensitise people and deepen their knowledge and understanding, especially in rural areas, on the ways in which women who had gained higher education were able to contribute to self-development as well as national development. SLAUW initiated programmes to bring out the latent potential in women and girls and to enhance the promotion of access to education at all levels through regular awards of scholarships and career guidance workshops.

From the 1970s to the 1990s, the women's movement lobbied and advocated for women's socioeconomic empowerment with campaigns that gained momentum. In addition, women realised the need to ensure that the mushrooming of groups did not intensify emerging movement fragmentation, which would lead to a weakening of women's voices. Women's activism was increasing and women's issues and concerns had begun to receive some attention within poverty alleviation programmes, not only from government quarters but also from other developmental agencies. These interventions were based on the Women In Development (WID) approach.

In 1990, many diverse women's associations, including community-based organisations from all the regions, came together in a National Women's Conference chaired by a notable and widely acclaimed female paramount chief from the Southern Region, Madam Ella Koblo Gulama. She was supported by other dynamic women of influence, including other female paramount chiefs from the Southern Region, such as Madam Honoria Bailor-Caulker of Kagboro Chiefdom, Moyamba District, and members of the YWCA (including Lettie Stuart), SLAUW, the Girl Guides (Jeanne John) and the Police Wives Association, to name but a few, as well as a couple of women parliamentarians. The major outcome of the conference was the formation of a coalition of women's organisations called the National Organisation of Women, known as NOW (SL).

The coordinating thrust of the movement focused on both access to education, especially adult literacy, and facilitating women's economic empowerment, dealing, in particular, with access to available opportunities in the agriculture and trade sectors. The aim was to support women's right to land and their active inclusion and full participation in the various poverty reduction programmes in a way that reflected the lived realities of women, particularly in the rural areas. Women's struggle for their unfettered right to land in rural areas, where customary law and patriarchal social norms prevail, is still continuing.

One of the most important contributions of the women's movement during this period was its involvement in the constitution-making process. In 1990, the women's movement, led by SLAUW, made recommendations to the Constitutional Review Committee concerning the 1978 constitution. The revised constitution and its articles were more sensitive to issues of women's development than the 1978 constitution had been. These recommendations were adopted by the committee and resulted in the current constitution; this includes Article 6(2) of 1991, which provides for the state to 'promote national integration and unity and discourage discrimination on the grounds of place of origin, circumstance of birth, sex, religion, status, ethnic or linguistic association or ties'. Also, under Chapter II, Article 9(1), the Sierra Leone 1991 constitution enjoins the government to direct educational policy objectives 'towards ensuring that there are equal rights and adequate opportunities for all citizens at all levels' and 'safeguarding the rights of vulnerable groups, such as children, women and the disabled in securing educational facilities'.

The snag, however, is that these principles of policy are in general de jure gender equality and cannot be realised. The 1991 constitution is currently under review by a Constitutional Review Committee, and the women's movement and wider civil society are campaigning and advocating for relevant gender equality provisions in various spheres of life and for de facto equality objectives that are enforceable.

The women's movement during the war

When the Sierra Leonean civil war broke out in March 1991, sections of the women's movement leadership were particularly vociferous and spoke out against the insurgency. They advocated for peace and a return to democratic civilian rule. To this end, women lobbied the international community for help. Because of this action by women for peace and electoral democracy, NOW (SL) was proscribed by the military government of the National Provisional Ruling Council (NPRC). Some NOW (SL) members became lukewarm in their attitude and were not disposed to openly identify with the NOW (SL) leadership; others actively participated in a new collective, called the Sierra Leone Women in Development Movement (SILWODMO), which was fostered by the wives of the military rulers. Perhaps the behaviour of the NOW (SL) members who joined SILWODMO was justified in a way, because NOW (SL) had been banned. No one could blame them for seeking to continue some action in support of women, working with elements that had plunged the country into an undemocratic mode. Nevertheless, fearless and passionate NOW (SL) members continued their participation in ongoing WID programmes with which they had previously been engaged as members of their respective organisations. The country experienced a brutal eleven-year internecine conflict that started in the Eastern Region bordering Liberia in March 1991. The war eventually engulfed the entire country and reached the capital city, Freetown, by May 1997. The role of women in peace-making, peacebuilding and democratisation in Sierra Leone increased significantly with the outbreak of war in 1991 and the establishment of the NPRC military rule in 1992. From December 1994, the women of Sierra Leone began actively organising themselves around the issue of the continuing civil war. The fighting caused massive displacement and a collapse of the economy, with increased physical violence against women and children.[1]

When the war intensified in 1995 and the NPRC government failed to bring the war to an end as they had promised after they seized power in 1992, women began to speak out, calling for peace and an end to the fighting. They lobbied, advocated and raised consciousness about violence. They questioned the will of the government to bring the war to an end. The women called for elections leading to a democratically elected president and parliament.

In 1994, the Women's Forum was created as a new umbrella organisation made up of all the women's associations and groups in Sierra Leone, inspired by SLAUW. Two office holders in SLAUW, Haja Alari Cole and myself, attended a training workshop on the theme 'Women Organising for Change' in Geneva, Switzerland, organised by the IFUW in 1993. We returned home and fulfilled the commitment made at the workshop to replicate it. SLAUW, with two staff members acting as resource people, trained about thirty women invited from women's civil society organisations with varied mandates and interests, who, as an outcome of the workshop, unanimously decided to establish a strong network to be called the Women's Forum, Sierra Leone.

This was created in response to the need for women to persist in their efforts in the face of difficulties and to take a collective stand on issues relating to women, war and peace, and the nation as a whole. The Women's Forum was the platform that provided a unifying force for women's advocacy on all issues relating to women's concerns, needs and interests. These ranged from equality of opportunity in all spheres of national development and growth, to the prevention of violence against women and their families, and to the restoration

1 FAS (1997) 'Background to women's participation in the peace process' in *Women's Participation in the Peace Process in Sierra Leone: Peace and Solidarity Mission Organised by Femmes Africa Solidarité (FAS), 20–25 February 1997, Freetown, Sierra Leone*. Geneva: Femmes Africa Solidarité.

of peace and democracy in Sierra Leone. The founding members of the Women's Forum included SLAUW, YWCA, Partners Women's Commission (PWC), NOW (SL), Federation of Muslim Women's Associations (FOMWASAL), Network of the Methodist Women's Association, Women's International League for Peace – Sierra Leone (WILPF-SL), and the Women's Wing of the Sierra Leone Labour Congress, to name but a few. The YWCA has always played a key role in coordinating the institutionalisation and operationalisation of the Women's Forum since its inception and its first meeting in 1994 on the premises of the first girls secondary school in Sierra Leone. The school is known as the Annie Walsh Memorial School, and was established in 1849 by the Church Missionary Society. SLAUW then had its office at the school; the school's principal at the time was Europa Wilson Agwu, who was also the treasurer of SLAUW. The YWCA freely offered a more readily accessible meeting space for the monthly forum meetings, the chairing of which is rotated among the constituent member organisations. Currently, the Women's Forum consists of about 300 member organisations from all three provincial regions and the western area. Coincidentally – or perhaps because of a willingness to volunteer, which has been the sustaining characteristic of SLAUW – both the immediate past National President, Rosaline McCarthy, and the current President of the Women's Forum, Maude Peacock, are energetic members of SLAUW.

In 1996, under the aegis of the Women's Forum, passionate and proactive groups formed, including the Women Organised for a Morally Enlightened Nation (WOMEN). In 1995, the YWCA, FOMWASAL and NOW (SL) insisted on better and equitable representation of women at the Bintumani II National Consultative Conference on peace, which led to elections being held. In the end, the strategic arguments and skilfully worded one-line messages of the women's movement's delegates inspired other delegations. The women succeeded in motivating a landslide vote that secured 'elections before peace' for Sierra Leone as opposed to the NPRC's stalling argument for 'peace before elections'. In addition to the Bintumani II National Consultative Conference, the women's movement successfully mobilised and coordinated interventions for other advocacy and lobbying activities leading to democratic elections and the transfer of power from the military regime to the democratically elected government in 1997. After the elections, the important role that women played during that period was widely recognised and acclaimed by various stakeholders. Among outstanding women champions of the interventions were the then National President of the YWCA, Amy Smythe (who was appointed after the elections as the minister of the first ever Ministry of Gender Affairs in Sierra Leone), Zainab Hawa Bangura (currently the UN Secretary-General's Special Representative on Sexual Violence in Conflict) and Cecilia Greenwood (then Assistant Coordinator, NOW (SL)).

In 1997 (20–21 February), an African Women's Peace Mission was fielded to Sierra Leone under the auspices of Femmes Africa Solidarité (FAS) at the invitation of WOMEN and WILPF-SL. That mission acknowledged the important role played by women in the negotiations and consultations that led to elections in March 1996 and commended the Women's Forum for mobilising women for campaigning, advocacy and lobbying. During the war years, several programmes and projects that centred on relief and humanitarian assistance were initiated by various women's civil society organisations. Projects were aimed at promoting and providing educational access, especially for school-aged children and young women in refugee or internally displaced camps. These projects were sometimes implemented collectively or singly and supported by donor agencies and the UN family, especially the UN Children's Emergency Fund (UNICEF) and UN Development Fund for Women (UNIFEM) (which later became UN Women).

The Forum for African Women Educationalists (FAWE), founded in 1995, was among those organisations within the women's movement that were highly visible and most recognised for providing access to education for children during the war years. The FAWE Sierra Leone chapter was established by the current female head of the National Electoral Commission (NEC), Dr Christian Thorpe, who at the time was the Minister of Education. FAWE ensured that young women and girl war survivors as well as other girls and boys on the street continued to access some form of education or training. To that end, the organisation set up the FAWE schools located in Grafton outside Freetown as well as in the city.

In April 2000, the Mano River Women's Peace Network (MARWOPNET), a sub-regional women's movement composed of women's civil society organisations from Guinea, Sierra Leone,

Liberia and subsequently Côte d'Ivoire, was established in Abuja, Nigeria, through the immense support and promotion of FAS under the auspices of the Economic Community of West African States (ECOWAS), with aim of engendering the peace process in the Mano River Basin. Many of the women's organisations within the women's movement in Sierra Leone are founding members of MARWOPNET.

The post-war women's movement

The Women's Forum – along with other, primarily male-dominated groups within the wider, vibrant Sierra Leonean civil society – actively pushed for effective democratisation as a key step in peace consolidation, peacebuilding and enduring stability after the official declaration of the end of the war in 2002. Women had always emphasised the need for their involvement in all areas of the recovery, consolidation, democratisation and development processes. Despite the acknowledged contribution of women to peace-making and peace-restoration in Sierra Leone, little opportunity was afforded them for full participation and representation, particularly in decision-making positions in the various governance institutions established in the peace-recovery and peacebuilding processes.

In 2002, the nucleus of the group called 50/50 was developing within the Women's Forum. It was led by the transformative leadership of indefatigable women such as Dr Nemata Majeks-Walker. With funding support from the British Council, more women from all over the country – and from all the registered political parties – were mobilised for training on increasing women's political participation in democratic politics. The training was conducted by Lesley Abdela (the founder of the 300 Group, which had worked for gender parity in the British House of Commons and in public life), at the invitation of the British Council and in collaboration with the incipient 50/50. 50/50 was established after the training to advocate and campaign for women's increased political participation and equal representation in decision-making processes at all levels in Sierra Leone.

Achievements after the war

Between 2000 and 2007, the 50/50 group and NOW (SL) actively collaborated and together spearheaded the relevant activities that culminated in the development and publication of the Sierra Leone

Women's Manifesto for the 2002 and 2007 general elections. During the respective election periods, the manifesto brought together the various demands made by women over the years as part of their struggle to attain gender equality, including empowerment towards claiming women's rights at all levels and in every field of endeavour. The training of women aspirants by members within the movement and the sensitisation of the wider populace intensified advocacy and lobbying of political parties, particularly by the 50/50 group. They mounted advocacy campaigns even at local community levels – where especially pervasive gender inequality weighs heavily on women's lives – and provided much needed leverage for women aspirants to seek their respective parties' nomination to contest elections at both national and local government levels in 2002, 2007 and 2012. Many more women than in previous years were elected to the national parliament and to local governments.

The women's movement advocated and worked with the Ministry of Social Welfare, Gender and Children's Affairs for the provision of measures, policies and legal instruments to address women's concerns and needs and to improve institutional frameworks in order to moderate or eliminate discriminatory practices against women and promote gender equality. The positive outcomes of women's contributions include the following: the National Policy on the Advancement of Women (2001), the National Policy on Gender Mainstreaming (2001), the Sierra Leone National Action Plan for the implementation of UN Security Council Resolutions 1325 and 1820 (2010), the passage of gender-related laws such as the Registration of Customary Marriage and Divorce Act (2007), Devolution of Estate Act (2007) and Domestic Violence Act (2007), the Sexual Offences Act (2012), the National Strategy for the Reduction of Teenage Pregnancy (2013) and Pillar 8, the stand-alone Gender Equality Pillar of the Agenda for Prosperity (PRSP III) (2013–18).

Challenges to the women's movement

Over the years, the women's movement in Sierra Leone has recorded many notable achievements. These successful outcomes have been assisted by the volunteering and self-sacrificing spirit and resilience of actors within the movement. The movement continues its interventions to empower and advance the status and position of women, prevent gender-based discrimination, and actively participate in national and community peacebuilding efforts in the patriarchal Sierra Leonean society. However, many challenges remain.

These challenges include, for example, the lack of an adequate funding base that would ensure sustainable interventions throughout the length and breadth of the country. Donors have often dictated an organisation's activities; funding is usually tied to project activities aligned to donors' priorities and ceases with a shift in those priorities. Organisations face challenges in implementing activities that relate to their core issues. Additionally, many donors are reluctant to provide institutional support to organisations, which hinders the effective functioning of their offices. Most of the time, organisations do not have adequate funds to hire full-time, appropriately qualified personnel and have to rely on volunteers who may not be fully committed or even possess the technical and managerial skills necessary to run their offices.

There remains a lack of understanding of issues relating to gender and development among a critical mass of women. This inhibits the concerted action and full participation of many women. For example, when laws and policies are introduced, they are not adequately disseminated. This in turn contributes to the lack of ownership of processes, which leads to weak enforcement. Many women, particularly rural women, may not understand the principles behind the laws and policies. This means that they continue to be subjected to traditions and customs instead of consistently teaming up with other women to take advantage of the legal rights afforded them.

The continuing patriarchy and male dominance in Sierra Leone take the wind out of the sails of the women's movement. Men often use rural women's illiteracy and ignorance to undercut support for women leaders who understand the issues and are poised to mobilise women from all regions. Men often tell rural women that the actions to be taken will benefit only educated women.

Sometimes it can be difficult to convince women of the need to hold the government accountable on certain issues. This is because women from various political parties may not reach a consensus on the actions that need to be taken to benefit the greatest number of women, as they are more loyal to their political parties than to the women's concerns and interests being championed by the movement.

The lack of proper mechanisms for information sharing poses challenges to the promotion of the women's movement. Some women prefer to work on their own and pursue their own agenda. Thus, they are reluctant to share information about the activities of their individual organisations. They provide little support to the national network because they feel that planned actions may not benefit them personally. Also, some women are not good communicators; even when they represent organisations, they fail to relay what transpired at the meetings back to their membership. They are not good at presenting written reports. As a result, follow-up action on the meeting is not possible. The dearth of regular documentation, weak data and poor information keeping and retrieval limit the timeliness and efficiency of operational activities and the conducting of research by the women's movement. Moreover, the overall lack of professionalism hinders the maintenance of organisational standards. For example, keeping discussions and activities focused and maintaining the standard of minutes and reports pose problems for some women, as does ensuring that assignments, tasks and duties are completed.

Many women, especially among the younger generation of the movement's leadership, seem less committed to volunteering and harnessing their expertise as needed to maintain the momentum of the women's movement. As a result, they are not willing to make sacrifices for the promotion of the movement's goals. Many from the older generation see them as always being on the receiving end, especially when it comes to financial gains. At the same time, the younger generation also has its complaints. Could it be that the older generation, still on the front line of the women's movement, is perceived as being not adequately empowering and not affording opportunities more fairly and widely? Thus intergenerational tensions may stand in the way of collaboration.

Poverty abounds in Sierra Leone and it is being felt within the women's movement. This tends to cloud the vision of women and makes them unable to contribute adequately and in a timely manner to the welfare of the organisation. The paucity of women in Sierra Leone involved in today's strategic fields – land rights, science, engineering and technology, for instance – is a big challenge, particularly in provincial areas. The result is that the few women who undertake roles in these fields usually become overburdened. Hence, there is an urgent need to address the need, particularly in rural areas, for more young women to train and engage in these fields.

The way forward

There is a need to continue to build up the momentum that is picking up again as a result of the women's movement championing advocacy activities relating to non-violent electoral processes during the November 2012 parliamentary and local government elections. These activities were based on the strategy of the Women's Situation Room, a strategy that was first implemented by the women of Liberia and was replicated in Senegal in collaboration with the Angie Brooks Centre and FAS.

A weakening of the cohesion between member organisations tended to creep in at various moments, resulting in some ebb and flow in the momentum of the women's movement's activities in Sierra Leone. When one considers how women rallied around the issues of the 1990s, culminating in the 1996 elections and beyond, it becomes imperative to consider proactive ways to confront the issues facing the women's movement. This is necessary so that the momentum for action that is picking up can be increased and maintained.

Thus, the women's movement needs to initiate and conduct capacity-building training for organisations within the movement, and this needs to include leadership skills, team building, partnership and networking. It should organise and conduct training sessions, especially targeting young women, to equip them with the knowledge, understanding, tools and effective skills for interpersonal communication, conflict prevention, management and resolution. This would contribute to strengthening capacity to maintain cohesiveness, solidarity and effective participation within the women's movement in order to engender transformation in society. It should mobilise resources (human, financial and technological) and train office holders and staff members on information management. There needs to be more effort to build the advocacy skills of member organisations to equip them with the tools needed for social, economic and political activism, including for the collective needs and interests of women and peace. Collaboration and partnership with the Ministry of Social Welfare, Gender and Children's Affairs should be strengthened to enhance the women's movement's ability to influence desirable policy change. For example, the Ministry should be supported in its effort to get the 30 per cent Gender Quota Bill passed in parliament. And, finally, donors need to provide more sustained and dedicated resources (financial, technical and human) to the women's movement to assist its efforts to transform society through women's active engagement at all levels.

3 | MARKET WOMEN'S ASSOCIATIONS IN GHANA

Akua Opokua Britwum and Angela Dziedzom Akorsu

Introduction

Market women in Ghana operate within the informal economy that until Keith Hart's (1973) 'discovery' in the 1970s was largely invisible to academics and had no place in national policy formulation. Its subsequent recognition as a livelihood option has since attracted numerous studies. There remain, however, contentions about suitable definitions that capture succinctly its true form and nature (Aksikas 2007; Beneria 2001; Davies 2004; Hormeku 1998; Ninsin 1991; Hansen and Ninsin 1989; Overton 2000). Beginning with descriptive definitions (Matsebula et al. 1996) that listed its supposed characteristics, the concern now is how to conceptualise it without taking formality as a reference point (Peattie 1987; Reddy 2007; William 2008).

How one thinks of the starting point for analysis is important because, in a country such as Ghana, 86 per cent of the working population is located in the informal economy (Ghana Statistical Service 2013), yet government attitudes towards it remain largely ambivalent. Public statements and interventions to tackle youth employment give recognition to its contribution, employment skills acquisition, and job creation. Urban planning policies, however, show outright hostility to informal workers and their livelihoods (Britwum 2013; Lindell 2010). They are accused of creating disorder in the cities and causing unsanitary conditions that bedevil Ghanaian urban centres (Brown and Lyons 2010).

The informal economy saw rapid expansion in Ghana at the height of the country's economic decline in the 1980s. The ensuing reforms from the mid-1980s to the 1990s to restructure the Ghanaian economy resulted in a drastic loss of formal sector jobs (Britwum 2011). Most households turned to domestic-based activities as income-earning alternatives. The loss of male formal sector jobs intensified reliance on female income-earning activities, which were mainly extensions of women's gendered tasks such as cooking and trading (Britwum 2009). Today, women form the bulk of the Ghanaian informal economy workforce. The proportion of the economically active female population in the informal economy is 91 per cent while the corresponding figure for men is 81 per cent (Ghana Statistical Service 2013). Trading tends to be the second main source of employment for informal economy workers after agriculture. Women in the informal economy in Ghana are more likely to be traders and food processors. The female working population in trading and retail is about 25 per cent while that for men is 12 per cent (Ghana Statistical Service 2013).

In the face of their exclusion from formal economic and social protection systems, women have resorted to trade associations that embody support and regulatory systems to guide their economic activities in urban markets while serving a vast array of customers (Britwum 2013). The economic and political import of market-based trade associations has been captured in several studies. Women's groups in Ghana have been studied for a number of reasons; one area of interest has been their political and economic roles (Awo 2010; Assimeng 1990; Tsikata 1989).

The special interest in market traders' associations derives from their economic and mutual assistance activities as well as their political influence (Awo 2010; Prag 2010). Numerous studies note the ingenuity and entrepreneurial skills of market traders (Clark 2010; Clark and Manuh 1991), while others focus on the effect of female trading cartels on farmer incomes and national economies (Britwum 2013; Clark and Manuh 1991). It is, however, an interest in their socio-political role for women's gendered positioning that leads us to examine the activities of market traders in the Cape Coast Metropolis in Ghana.

Study context

This study is specific to Cape Coast, the capital of the Central Region of Ghana and the seat of local government administration. At the last census, the population of the Cape Coast Metropolitan Assembly (CCMA) was 169,894, with a larger female presence of 87,084 as against 82,810 males (Ghana Statistical Service 2013). The rate of population growth and the rapid expansion in urban infrastructure have drawn satellite communities such as Pedu, Abura, Nkanfoa, Esuekyir, Ebubonko and Ankaful into the ambit of the CCMA. About 63 per cent of the working population are engaged in private informal activities. Markets happen to be the focal point for urban-based informal economy activities. In fact, markets in Ghana, like those in other West African countries, are an aggregation point for women traders selling wares ranging from imported and processed goods to farm produce (Britwum 2013; Clark 1994, 2010; Prag 2010).

Trading is a centuries old venture in West Africa. Written records provide evidence of not just local but international trade dating back to the tenth century (Hymer 1970). According to Clark (2010), market trading was male dominated until the cocoa boom in 1910. However, the shift to more lucrative cash crop production meant a relocation of male interests, leading to a gradual takeover by women traders in the markets of Ghana. The study covered the four markets in the CCMA: the Anaafo, Abura, Kotokuraba and Thursday markets. These constitute the oldest, youngest, largest and smallest markets in the CCMA respectively. The study involved key individual and group interviews with leaders and members of the traders' groups in these markets. In addition, there was the opportunity to observe women as they traded their wares in the markets and to interact in some of their group meetings. The interviews were conducted in September and October 2011 and follow-up was undertaken in June 2012.

Informal economy workers as political actors

A major problem for informal economy workers is their place in national policy formulation and their right to dedicated policy attention to promote their economic activities. Forced to develop their own routes to claim visibility in the policy arena, informal economy workers face limits on voicing their concerns and influencing national policies to their advantage, limits that are recognised by Brown and Lyons (2010). This situation has not daunted their efforts and their alternative organisational forms continue to engage policy at several levels, be it national or local government. Lindell (2010) laments the paucity of information on the political action of informal economy workers. In her introduction to a collection of works focusing on forms of collective action by urban informal economy actors, she highlights their attempts to influence dominating powers through collective action. Their collective actions, however, provide opportunities to overcome the limitations of their visibility and clout, provided they are strong and can identify which institutions to access. Traders' associations, Brown and Lyons (2010) contend, have this potential, given the scale of their collective membership and the interests that shape the spaces in which they undertake their economic activities, as well as the myriad form of power they have to engage.

Current attention, however, has turned to the potential contribution of such organisational forms to the struggle for representational equality (Boampong 2010; Lindell 2010; Meagher 2010). Although there is a diversity of women's groups in Ghana, both formal and informal market women's associations stand out as the most enduring, with the longest history of collective action (Tsikata 1989). While writers examine the immediate impact of organisational forms in mediating short-term interests, the potential of such actors to transform the social systems that form the basis of their disadvantage is hardly questioned. An examination of the possible contributions of such associations towards the struggle for representational democracy in Ghana has important implications for the promotion of women's employment rights and livelihood security.

Lindell (2010) asserts that informal economy organisations are 'scaling up' as political actors, using a variety of actions and formal structures to claim their rights to livelihood. Several dynamics are located within such organisational forms for collective action. They include internal constraints on their organising strategies as well as what Lindell describes as their complex and 'multiple subjectivities' arising out of their 'heterogeneous composition' as groups of people with markedly different employment statuses engaging 'multiple fields of power that intersect and interact to shape configurations of advantage and disadvantage in specific contexts' (Lindell 2010: 10, 14). Group heterogeneity arises out of a membership that includes all actors located in the commodity distribution chain, such as wholesalers of Ghanaian farm and factory produce, suppliers of imported products for the West African sub-region and beyond. The group members can also include retailers and other ancillary service providers such as head porters and drivers. Clark (2010) is upbeat about this state of affairs, and hails this internal heterogeneity as ensuring stronger in-group solidarity.

The markets in Ghana, like those of other West African countries, are an aggregation point for women traders selling wares that include imported items and farm produce (Britwum 2013; Clark 2010). Market trading, according to Clark (2010), was male dominated prior to the cocoa boom in 1910. Tracing the development of trading over time, from the tenth-century trans-Saharan trade routes to precolonial trade with European merchants and the infamous slave trade and continuing with economic activity under colonial and post-independence civilian and military governments, Clark (2010) shows the resilience of women's market groups.

Clark (2010) attributes the emergence of traders' associations to efforts by Fante fish traders in Kumasi to access space for marketing their smoked fish in the early part of 1915. It was not until the 1930s and 1940s that the present system was formalised through efforts on the part of market women to negotiate fee schedules and access to marketing sites with colonial officers. Their economic contribution to local government revenue was noticed very early, forcing colonial authorities to bend local government rules in their favour (Clark 2010). Traders' relationships with governments have not always been smooth (Assimeng 1990; Tsikata 1989). Their convoluted relations with successive governments, according to authors such as Clark (2010) and Assimeng (1990), stem, on the one hand, from government control over prices, which affect workers' incomes, and, on the other, from the traders' demands for better working conditions.

Time and again, traders have shown their ability to succeed under dire economic conditions, even where formal institutions fail. However, since colonial rule, market women have served as scapegoats for the economic woes of the nation. In the era of price controls, under both colonial and post-independence governments, market traders have been blamed for shortages largely attributed to their desire to force up prices through hoarding. Civilian as well as military governments have on occasion clashed with market women or have actively courted their cooperation. The most controversial periods in Ghana's history for market women were the price control regimes under colonial rule and their open flogging under military rule (Assimeng 1990; Clark 2010; Clark and Manuh 1991). Some studies recognise that informal economy workers' groups face organisational challenges including limited time and other resources such as finances, leadership skills, and the conflicting interests of members as well as hostile political entities (Brown and Lyons 2010; Webster and Von Holdt 2005).

Beyond the strength of trade unions as a workers' representational form, Brown and Lyons (2010) recognise market traders' associations as a form of employment representation used by informal economy actors to secure their work-related needs. Traders' groups such as unions prioritise the interests of their members over those of others and as a result tend to be exclusionary. In the particular case of market women's associations, their boundaries of inclusion are marked by the commodities they trade in and sometimes the markets where they carry out their trade. Traders organise around a shared commodity, according to Clark (2010), which facilitates fast and seamless adaptation of market women to shifts in official policy and market demands. They are also identified as providing social networks for their members as well as economic support in accessing credit and other market information. There are issues about members' ability to exercise their rights as citizens through systematised relations with urban authorities who control their market operations. Their organisational challenges limit their ability to engage the authorities in a structured and consistent manner. This affects how they secure their claim to policy space in order to promote sustainable livelihoods in an economy that, over centuries, has failed to secure decent jobs for women. In order to interrogate more deeply their organisational challenges, we follow Lindell's advice about the need for a conceptual framework that takes into account the various relations and interactions traders' groups are undertaking. She insists that such relations are 'implicated in the construction and reconstruction of the collective identities of informal actors' (Lindell 2010: 26). Thus, we are interested in such collective identities that provide the basis for identification as members of the various associations.

Existing associations and their characteristics

Studies on market women's associations have highlighted their structure and focus, observing that traders' associations in the market tend to be commodity-based, tied to items sold or to the main crafts. In addition, Clark notes the variety of organisational models present in market traders' associations, with ethnic traditions shaping leadership skills. Other factors that have an impact on group structure and practice include religion, trade unions and cooperative movements (Clark 2010). Depending on the nature of the trade, the associations also tend to be single sex, and mainly focus on livelihood survival and membership welfare (Brown and Lyons 2010; Clark 2010; Prag 2010).

Their internal structures tend to relate closely to traditional systems of governance (Britwum 2013; Brown and Lyons 2010; Clark 2010). The associations covered in the four markets in Cape Coast have similar structures and form. They are organised according to the items or commodities traded at the markets, with the leaders of such associations called item or commodity queens – '*Obaahemba*' (e.g., tomato queen or pepper queen).

The study identified a total of thirty-four traders' associations in the four markets. There were about twenty-five item and trade associations at the Kotokuraba market, and seven at the Abura market. There are associations at the Anaafo and Thursday markets that, due to their small sizes, were trade-based associations covering all the market traders.

A number of the groups had been in existence for over twenty years. The youngest group is six months old and the oldest forty years. Group leaders reported a revitalisation of some dormant groups over the past ten years. Some, however, were functioning poorly if at all; their members had ceased paying dues and no meetings had been held for the past twelve months. The functional market associations that held regular meetings and had an active membership paying dues were commodity food groups such as the Tomato Traders, Plantain Sellers, Egg Sellers, Fresh Fish Sellers and Fish Processors, Salt Sellers and Provisions Sellers Associations. The non-food item groups included the Cloth Sellers and Cosmetics Sellers Associations. The craft-based groups included the Tailors and Dressmakers Association. The functional groups were mainly located in Kotokuraba, the largest market.

It appears that traders' groups in the markets become more differentiated as markets get larger and trader numbers increase. Item group differentiation was more pronounced in Kotokuraba market than in Abura. Kotokuraba had more item groups and the groups tended to be organised around single items. At Abura, the second largest market, traders' groups comprised a combination of item groups. Thus, textiles and cosmetics sellers formed a group, while fruit and vegetable sellers formed another. So did utensils and clothing sellers. The smaller markets – Anaafo and Thursday – had an umbrella traders' group at the market level with no item groups. The group activity level was also determined by market size. Item groups that were active and functioning were more likely to be located in Kotokuraba, the largest market, than in Abura.

The traders' groups covered in the study had hybrid structures, with a blend of the traditional and formal committee system. All traders' groups had leaders who were supported by committee-style executives such as an organiser, secretary, financial controller, treasurer and porter. However, the heads, or 'queens', were quite advanced in age; they held the position for life, with a new head installed upon the demise of the incumbent. Leadership was hereditary and passed down from one family member to another on the death of the serving market queen. Market queens' assistants were also likely to be family members.

The item associations of Kotokuraba and Abura belonged, in turn, to the market associations of their markets. The market associations were also part of an umbrella Federation of Market Associations in Cape Coast, which belonged to the Ghana Market Women's Association and the Ghana Union of Traders Association. Each woman trader belonged to multiple levels of trade associations by default. Some belonged to item-based associations in addition to being affiliated to the Federation of Market Associations of Cape Coast. Some were also part of national item or trade-based associations: for example, there were both national associations and local chapters of Tomato Traders, Tailors and Dressmakers, and Cloth Sellers. Thus, we found a multiplicity of levels and types of organisation representing markets and local government as well as national trade and item groups.

Membership of market associations is normally compulsory and is a requirement for trading in the markets. Continuous eligibility, however, depends on regular payment of dues, and acceptance of the associations' disciplinary actions and rulings in case of disputes. Some traders' associations impose additional requirements: for example, the Cosmetics Sellers Association demands that prospective members pass an admission interview. In principle, the associations were open to all women irrespective of religion, ethnicity or age. Even though there were no reports of discrimination on the basis of religion, ethnicity or age, some practices suggested subtle ethnic and religious biases. It was not possible to verify the ethnic origin of group members during the data collection, but information gathered revealed that group leaders were mainly Fantes, with evidence of very little variation in ethnic origin. Only one group had a leader who was non-Fante. The Cosmetic Sellers Association required all members, irrespective of their religious persuasion, to attend a monthly all-night prayer session organised by an all-women Christian charismatic sect, the Women's Aglow. The Queen of the Cosmetics Group said with satisfaction – and oblivious to the inherent discrimination in this provision – that 'even Muslims have to attend or risk their membership'.[1]

Functions of the market associations

The main functions of the traders' groups revolved around economic benefits, welfare, discipline and representation. The market associations allow women traders to establish direct contact with mainstream structures such as local government authorities (CCMA), banks and microfinance institutions, as well as revenue-collecting authorities. Group leaders were the official representatives of traders at public and traditional functions such as festivals and meetings with statutory bodies. Most groups were formed to provide a unified front for dealing in particular with the CCMA. They therefore had a structured relationship with the CCMA to the extent that the queens were invited to meetings to deliberate on major decisions such as the location or relocation of markets. The leaders constituted a conduit for channelling trader members' grievances to the CCMA, and for receiving and disseminating information from the public institutions among traders. They offered a platform for mobilising traders at short notice.

Generally, all the associations were established for welfare reasons. The welfare-oriented agenda of the associations, as reported during interview sessions, meant that they were a source of support in times of need as well as promoting members' well-being. All the groups provided support to members in times of crisis such as the death of a loved one, loss of income and ill health. Sharing life achievements such as weddings and childbirth were additional supports offered by the groups. Some groups reported providing scholarships for

1 Interview, June 2012.

members' children. Discipline was another function that engaged traders' groups; resolving inevitable conflicts in the markets was a prime function and market queens and executives all reported settling disputes among members as well as between members and customers. The associations worked to regulate the activities of the markets by determining market-trading practices, such as market entry, space allocation and commodity flows. Among the Tailors and Dressmakers Associations, knowledge sharing was a predominant function.

The traders' groups also had economic functions that revolved around debt recovery, either of those owed by members to suppliers or to members by customers and suppliers. The credit management function, for example, is remarkable in that the associations force members to be credit worthy, which in turn gives members credibility and should as a result facilitate access to credit. Some groups, such as the Cosmetics and Cloth Sellers at the Kotokuraba market, had in place revolving loan schemes, the '*susu*' system. Members contribute a daily fee into a fund and take turns to receive the accrued fund each week. This practice gives access to easy credit without collateral or interest. Item groups had decided to organise themselves in order to get easy access to loans, but this had had disappointing results for traders and it was a sore point. An interesting economic function was accessing insurance. The Tomato Sellers Association has negotiated this facility as security against travel risks. Some groups were also in discussions with representatives of the state pension scheme, the Social Security and National Insurance Trust, to work out ways to benefit from their informal economy pension schemes.

Organisational challenges of the associations

The challenges facing traders' groups emanated from the viability of the associations and their ability to influence state institutions in order to obtain the rights due to them as economic actors. A number of groups were not functioning because of membership apathy, which in turn affected the groups' clout as political actors, worthy of the attention of the CCMA. The market queens mentioned the limits of their abilities to improve the standard of living of their members. This, they said, tended to affect the payment of dues since most of the members are low-income earners and therefore want proof of the benefits from paying dues. The associations were unable to influence the business activities of the members and a number had failed to secure access to credit facilities to support their members. They also expressed frustration that several of their grievances presented to the local government authority, the CCMA, had not been addressed. Their grievances revolve around the absence of amenities such as sanitation, toilet facilities and running water in the markets. This was in spite of the fact that the CCMA never fails to collect the numerous tolls, levies and licensing fees.

A sore point for market traders was the group leaders' inability to assist their members to benefit from the state Microfinance and Small Loans Centre (MASLOC). There had been an initial invitation asking women to pay some processing fees, but group leaders had no information about when the loans would be disbursed to members. As a result, some group members in the Abura market, in particular, believed that the general market queen and her group of executives were short-changing them. Although challenges vary from one association to another, almost all the associations mentioned the lack of financial capital to expand their businesses as a major issue. Seeing that access to credit is one of the motivations cited for forming or joining an association, the groups' inability to access loans serves as a demotivator for group activity.

Conclusion

This study largely confirmed the existing literature on the potential of the market traders' associations to serve as political actors and social change agents. This was evident from their continued existence and activities, as well as their large presence in the markets. They were not among the invisible and hidden categories of the informal economy. The traders' associations were indeed important social networks for market women in the CCMA. They served as useful channels for championing members' welfare and were effective conflict resolution mechanisms, maintaining discipline in the trading activities of the markets. Trade groups in the CCMA engaged a variety of powerful actors through a variety of organisational structures at the local, regional and national level.

The general indications were that the associations were very weak in terms of advocacy and providing a voice for their members. However, the weak organisational capacity of these CCMA market associations has meant that they represent, for the most part, largely undeveloped political capital. This situation poses political mobilisation challenges for women and gender activists seeking to trigger an orientation towards a more political agenda among such women's associations. The strength of their operation lay in the existing structures of their associations, which ensured that all market groups had interconnectedness within and beyond the markets in which they operated. The organisational structures offered additional connections with state institutions and gave market women's groups the necessary legitimacy as official representatives of women traders in Ghana. Their weakness lay where it mattered most – in membership acceptance and ownership as well as in the utility of the groups to serve their interests. It is in this area that the social change potential stands a better chance of addressing women traders' needs.

References

Aksikas, J. (2007) 'Prisoners of Globalisation: Marginality, Community and the New Informal Economy in Morocco'. *Mediterranean Politics*, 12, 249–62.

Assimeng, M. (1990) 'Women in Ghana: Their Integration in Socio-Economic Development'. *Research Review*, 6, 57–68.

Awo, M. A. (2010) *Marketing and Market Queens: A Case of Tomato Farmers in the Upper East Region of Ghana*. Bonn: Friedrich-Wilhelms-Universität zu Bonn, Fakultät der Rheinischen.

Beneria, L. (2001) 'Shifting the Risk: New Employment Patterns, Informalization and Women's Work'. *International Journal of Politics, Culture and Society*, 15, 27–53.

Boampong, O. (2010) 'The Possibilities for Collective Organisation of Informal Port Workers in Tema, Ghana' in Lindell, I. (ed.) *Africa's Informal Workers: Collective Agency, Alliances and Transitional Organizing in Urban Africa*. London: Zed Books.

Britwum, A. O. (2009) 'The Gendered Dynamics of Production Relations in Ghanaian Coastal Fishing'. *Feminist Africa*, 12, 69–84.

Britwum, A. O. (2011) 'Trade Unions and the Informal Economy in Ghana' in Phelan, C. (ed.) *Trade Unions in West Africa, Historical and Contemporary Perspectives*. Oxford: Peter Lang.

Britwum, A. O. (2013) 'Market Queens and the Blame Game in Ghanaian Tomato Marketing' in Scherrer, C. and Saha, D. (eds) *The Food Crisis. Implications for Labor. Labor and Globalization*. Mering, Germany: Rainer Hampp Verlag.

Brown, A. and Lyons, M. (2010) 'Seen but not Heard: Urban Voice and Citizenship for Street Traders' in Lindell, I. (ed.) *Africa's Informal Workers: Collective Agency, Alliances and Trans-National Organizing in Urban Africa*. London: Zed Books.

Clark, G. (1994) *Onions Are My Husband: Survival and Accumulation by West African Market Women*. Chicago: University of Chicago Press.

Clark, G. (2010) 'Gender Fictions and Gender Tensions Involving "Traditional" Asante Market Women'. *African Studies Quarterly*, 11, 43–66.

Clark, G. and Manuh, T. (1991) 'Women Traders in Ghana and the Structural

Adjustment Program' in Gladwin, C. H. (ed.) *Structural Adjustment and African Women Farmers*. Gainesville: Center for African Studies, University of Florida Press.

Davies, M. (2004) 'Planet of Slums: Urban Involution and the Informal Proletariat'. *New Left Review*, 26, 5.

Ghana Statistical Service (2013) *2010 Population and Housing Census: National Analytical Report*. Accra: Ghana Statistical Service.

Hansen, E. and Ninsin, K. A. (1989) *The State, Development, and Politics in Ghana*. London: CODESRIA Book Series.

Hart, K. (1973) 'Informal Income Opportunities and Urban Employment in Ghana'. *Journal of Modern African Studies*, 11, 61–89.

Hormeku, T. (1998) 'The Transformation and Development of the Informal Sector and the Role of Trade Unions'. Paper presented at a Seminar on Trade Unions and the Informal Sector. Cairo: OATUU/ILO/ETUF.

Hymer, S. (1970) 'Economic Forms in Pre-Colonial Ghana'. *Journal of Economic History*, 30, 33–50.

Lindell, I. (2010) 'Introduction: The Changing Politics of Informality-Collective Organizing, Alliances and Scales of Engagement' in Lindell, I. (ed.) *Africa's Informal Workers: Collective Agency, Alliances and Transitional Organizing in Urban Africa*. London: Zed Books.

Matsebula, M. S., SAPES Trust and Southern Africa Regional Institute for Policy Studies (1996) *The Urban Informal Sector: A Historical and Structural Analysis with Special Reference to Swaziland*. Harare: SAPES Books.

Meagher, K. (2010) 'The Politics of Vulnerability: Exit, Voice and Capture in Three Nigerian Informal Manufacturing Clusters' in Lindell, I. (ed.) *Africa's Informal Workers: Collective Agency, Alliances and Transitional Organizing in Urban Africa*. London: Zed Books.

Ninsin, K. A. (1991) *The Informal Sector in Ghana's Political Economy*. Accra: Freedom Publications.

Overton, J. (2000) 'Academic Populists, the Informal Economy and Those Benevolent Merchants: Politics and Income Security and Reform in Newfoundland'. *Journal of Peasant Studies*, 28, 1–54.

Peattie, L. (1987) 'An Idea in Good Currency and How it Grew: The Informal Sector'. *World Development*, 15, 851–60.

Prag, E. (2010) 'Women Leaders and the Sense of Power: Clientelism and Citizenship at the Dantokpa Market in Cotonou, Benin' in Lindell, I. (ed.) *Africa's Informal Workers: Collective Agency, Alliances and Transitional Organizing in Urban Africa*. London: Zed Books.

Reddy, M. (2007) 'Modelling Poverty Dimensions of Urban Informal Sector Operators in a Developing Economy'. *European Journal of Development Research*, 19, 459–79.

Tsikata, E. (1989) 'Women's Political Organisations 1951–1987' in Hansen, E. and Ninsin, K. A. (eds) *The State, Development, and Politics in Ghana*. London: CODESRIA Book Series.

Webster, E. and Von Holdt, K. (2005) *Beyond the Apartheid Workplace: Studies in Transition*. Scottsville, South Africa: University of KwaZulu-Natal Press.

William, C. C. (2008) 'A Critical Evaluation of Competing Representations of the Relationship Between Formal and Informal Work'. *Community, Work and Family*, 11, 105–24.

4 | TUNISIAN WOMEN'S LITERATURE OF DENUNCIATION

Lilia Labidi[1]

Although some studies have been devoted to literature by women in the Arab world (Arebi 1994; Badran and Cooke 1990; Berrada 2008; Milani 1992; Shaaban 2009; Yazbek and Weiss 2012), they remain marginal in discussions of world literature, an imbalance that new communications technology can help to correct. I propose to treat here literature of a particular sort – the literature produced by feminists who denounce the conditions imposed on women and who call for both moral and legal remedies. Basing my discussion on life histories I collected from women of different generations and on my observations of and participation in women's movements in Tunisia, I will focus on the emergence of literary institutions where women, first as objects and then as subjects, played an important role; I will look closely at the biographies of a few Tunisian women writers who have practised a literature of denunciation against political violence; and I will explore the socio-political contexts within which these works were produced.

One of the characteristics of the Tunisian literary scene is its bilingual nature – Arabic and French – as is the case in Morocco, which excluded many countries of the region from censorship and from limitations related to publishing and distribution. La Ligue des Ecrivains Libres estimates that forty books were censored in Tunisia between 1995 and 2005.

My approach is anthropological and historical and aims to show how women's experiences influenced their writings both before and following the Arab Spring. I analyse the contexts in which memoirs

1 An earlier version of this chapter was presented to the Singapore Writers Festival, November 2012, organised by Arts House and the Middle East Institute (NUS), in a session devoted to an 'Introduction to the Literature of the Middle East'. I would like to thank Kevin Dwyer for translating this paper from French.

and journals, usually produced by men occupying important positions in politics, medicine and other fields, now seem to be produced and highly valued by women as well. Starting in the 1990s, a number of 1950s feminists who had experience in formal politics and in public space published memoirs and autobiographies. We also find some memoirs written by women testifying to their struggles against disease. Alia Mabrouk, author of several historical novels, published *Sombre histoire de cellules folles* (2001), a short text on her own trajectory in which, after having cared for her mother dying of cancer, she herself is struck by the same illness and struggles against death. Similarly, Raoudha Zarrouk recounts her experience as a mother struggling for the welfare of her son, a victim of a congenital disability, in *L'amour maternel triumphant* (2005).

Radhia Haddad, Alia Babou, Nazli Hafsia and Jelila Hafsia of the 1950s generation, and Azza Ghanmi, Neila Jrad and Sihem Ben Sedrine of the 1980s generation – to cite only a few – have employed such forms to bear witness to social and political events, both in the past and in the present. I have had discussions and interviews with members of both generations and have collected some of their life histories. As we move towards the present, I propose to discuss here the environment in which the following appeared: Sihem Ben Sedrine's *Lettre à une amie irakienne disparue (Letter to a Disappeared Iraqi Woman Friend)*, Lina Ben Mhenni's *Tunisian Girl, blogueuse pour un Arab spring*, and the rap songs of Shayma, a young Tunisian woman rap singer who also emerged with the Arab Spring.

All the creative figures I am dealing with here show a mastery of the linguistic codes and criticise various forms of oppression – patriarchy, colonialism/imperialism and dictatorship. This will help us see how the literature of denunciation subverts notions such as *sitr* (concealing) and *madh* (self-praise) and how, whenever Tunisian women have used writing to bear witness, their literature has contributed to expanding socio-cultural boundaries while also, from time to time, leading to negative reactions such as misogyny and violence.

The societal context for my discussion has, as its first landmark, the mid-nineteenth century and the expanding debate about new educational forms and education for girls and women, the arrival of women from abroad, and the role played by writers and political reformers regarding the condition of Tunisian women. The second landmark has two aspects. The first was the epistemological rupture that came with the promulgation of the Personal Status Code in 1956, giving to women a number of important rights – these were challenged by parts of the Zitounian religious elite. Mohamed Salah Ennaifer and his wife Souad Bakhta Kattèche Ennaifer, who headed the women's section of the Jeunes musulmans (Muslim Youth), chose exile in Algeria, while others chose Morocco or Egypt. The second landmark also involved the use of books in a mass educational system that would help construct a new Tunisian identity and work towards a new ethical and political conscience. Finally, the third landmark is the Arab Spring, which saw the appearance of new artistic forms and new women writers and artists comfortable in a variety of languages (Arabic, French and English), for whom the internet is the principal means of communication. As each stage ends not only do we see new gains in women's rights, but also we can find a feature film made by a woman that suggests a story emerging from the trauma of this struggle.

Early steps towards rights for Tunisian women

By the middle of the nineteenth century, reformers, writers and poets were trying to understand the situation of women and were looking for new models, following closely, for example, the suffragette movement in the US and Europe. This period constitutes a rupture in the domain of literature: at a time when the families of the bourgeoisie adopted the education of girls and their access to public space as an inevitable development, the role of women storytellers and oral poets, who were known for the vivacity and strength of their opinions, receded and then, with the spread of mass education, was further marginalised. Later efforts to recover this heritage were rare, although among feminists since the 1980s there has been a growing interest in the life histories of Tunisian women political figures who were active during the 1930s and whose testimony preserved the poetry of the spoken language (Labidi and Zghal 1985). Following the Arab Spring, a new online literature became accessible to a broad public and there was renewed interest in *zajal* – a poetic form that uses colloquial Arabic to express a poetic vision of the self and the world. Several women poets participated in public recitations of this sort in Sbeitla, Hammamet, Ain Draham and Tunis, among other places, during 2011 and later.

In this first section I will examine the role of reformists, women from abroad and the new intellectuals, and I will look at how the 'woman question' shifted to women's demands for their rights.

The reformers Ibn Abi Dhiaf (1804–74) was a historian and author of a long chronicle, published in 1856, *Risalah fi al-mar'a* (*The Woman's Epistle*); this was an answer to a list of twenty-three questions posed by Léon Roches, France's general consul in Tunis, discussing the social role of women in Tunisia, their rights and legal duties with regard to their families, their conjugal relations, and their presence in public space. The thirty-page document became widely known due to the historian Béchir Tlili's study (Tlili 1974). Ibn Abi Dhiaf's answers aimed to present the then current practices as normative. But, about ten years later, in 1868, Kheireddine Pacha (1822/23–90), a Tunisian of Circassian origin and a major reformer of this period, wrote an essay entitled *Aqwam al-masalik li ma'rifat ahwal al-mamalik* (*The Surest Path to Knowledge Regarding the Condition of Countries*), where he criticised Tunisian family attitudes that restricted girls' and women's education and argued that reforms undertaken in other sectors should also address broader questions regarding the condition of women in Tunisia.

This discussion, which corresponds to the introduction of new ideas to a part of the elite, faced delays and blockages, with the French occupation that lasted from 1881 to 1957. A number of authors continued on the path started by Kheireddine Pacha. In 1897, Mohamed Snoussi (1851–1900), a teacher at the Zeitouna University, published *L'Épanouissement de la fleur ou étude sur la femme en islam* (*The Flower's Blossoming, or a Study on Women in Islam*), in which he encouraged girls' education. Abdelaziz Thâalbi (1876–1944), a political figure, published *L'Esprit libéral du Coran* in 1905, along with two collaborators, as a work that favoured girls' education and the suppression of the hijab (Benattar et al. 1905). In 1906, Sadok Zmerli (1893–1983), an important intellectual figure of the period, stated during a lecture he gave abroad that he expected Tunisia would have to bring women teachers from the Middle East to compensate for the lack in Tunisia itself (Zmerli 1906).

French, Egyptian, Russian and Lebanese women alongside Tunisian women

In the context of this intellectual effervescence, several foreign women living in Tunisia played a crucial role in intellectual life and the history of ideas. Louise-Renée Millet, widow of a French military figure, gained the financial support of Bashir Sfar, President of Habous Administration, enabling her to open the first girls' school for Tunisians in 1900 (Bakalti 1990; Smith 2000). Subsequently, a number of other schools of this sort were founded in other cities. The Egyptian Princess Nazli Fadhel (1853–1913), of Turkish origin, started literary salons in Egypt. After becoming a widow, she married the Tunisian Khelil Bouhageb and lived in Tunisia from 1898 to 1913. She then opened a literary salon in La Marsa, near Tunis, in 1907, which was frequented by members of an intellectual youth movement called The Young Tunisians, among whom we find Ali Bach Hamba, editor-in-chief of *The Tunisian Weekly* (*l'Hebdomadaire Tunisien*) and other reformers (Nazli 2010). Nejia Thameur (1926–88), after studying in Lebanon, married an Algerian and the couple set up home in Tunisia, where she found the environment very favourable to her own literary creativity. She published *La femme et la vie* (a series of articles, 1956); *La justice du ciel* (a theatrical play, 1956); *Nous avons voulu la vie* (stories, 1956); *Veillées et maximes* (stories, 1972); *Asma, fille de Assad Ibn Al-Frourat* (stories, 1977); and *Les rides* (stories, 1978). She joined the radio, produced several programmes, and wrote articles that were published in several Tunisian and Arabic newspapers.

Among the first women to pursue higher education abroad was Tawhida Ben Cheikh, who obtained her secondary school baccalaureate in 1928. I collected her life story in the early 1980s. She went to Paris with Dr Burnet (then deputy director of the Institut Pasteur in Tunis) and his wife. Ben Cheikh had a French fellowship to study medicine and, earning her degree in Paris in 1936, she returned immediately to Tunis where she set up a private medical practice. Also, Badra Ben Moustapha Ouertani and her cousin Frida Agrebi, who were midwives, earned their diplomas in 1936 from the Algiers Medical School. None of these three women were able to practise in public hospitals, since such positions in state institutions were forbidden to Tunisians, as was the case for Tunisian engineers. Thus, Tawhida Ben Cheikh worked in the private sector until independence; Frida Agrebi worked with her doctor husband; and Badra Ben Moustapha Ouertani worked in the social services sector of the municipality of Tunis. Such careers had an important influence on families, which, during the 1940s and therefore well before independence, began sending their daughters to school and later to foreign universities (Labidi 1987).

How did female students react to education under occupation? The life histories of Zohra Chenik Mestiri, Radhia Haddad and Nebiha Ben Abdallah Ben Miled, which I collected among those of many other women who lived through this period, show how young girls were affected by this context and how they became involved in political struggle.

For example, the story of Zohra Chenik (born 1923) tells us much about the experience of young girls whose families were in favour of education and opposed to colonialism, yet who sent their daughters to colonial Catholic religious schools. I collected this life story in 2009. Zohra Chenik was the oldest of seven children. Unlike Tawhida Ben Cheikh, who, during her time in Paris, had been introduced by Dr Burnet and his wife to various groups of Parisian intellectuals but who had no contact with other Tunisian or Maghrebi students, Zohra Chenik had a close relationship with her Tunisian cohort. As an adolescent, she described herself as often depressed (as Habib Bourguiba had been at the same age), and the only means she possessed to counter this was at an individual level. She refused to retake her exams for the first part of the baccalaureate despite the insistence of her mostly European teachers. This was her way of expressing her rejection of an education she had assimilated but that to her represented the silence of the space, the coldness of the rooms, and other such impressions she had of the Western religious schools she had attended since her very early years. She also opposed traditional marriage engagement ceremonies that she knew were not the choice of her father, who was a pragmatic man, but rather the choice of the socio-cultural environment of the day. Her marriage to Said Mestiri, a surgeon, took place in 1950, the same year her father was again chosen as prime minister by the ruler Lamine Bey. Alongside her husband she embarked on socio-political activities and worked for the creation of 'Secours National' with Lamine Bey's daughter Zakia and her husband Dr Mohamed Ben Salem, to provide assistance for political prisoners. As the organisation's secretary-general, she became its lynchpin, setting up events to collect contributions, sending packages to prisoners, visiting the wounded, and so on.

These activities lasted only several months into 1952, ending when French forces attacked Tazarka and the area of Cap Bon, where they arrested many people and committed rapes and other acts of violence. It was in this context that her father and his ministers Mzali, Materi and Ben Salem were deported.

Nebiha Ben Abdallah Ben Miled (1919–2009), the daughter of Othman Ben Abdallah and Beya Mahjoub, learned embroidery from her mother and aunts and how to play a musical instrument from a woman musician. Later she took piano lessons and attended school. One day in school, encountering a French girl who was insulting Tunisians, Nebiha threw her into a rubbish bin. Her father would have political discussions during family dinners, and, because of Nebiha's active participation in these discussions, her father began to call her Mme Thorez, an allusion to the wife of Maurice Thorez, head of the French Communist Party.

She was asked to marry Dr Ahmed Ben Miled, who was fourteen years older than her, and she left school and married at the age of sixteen. The two books she received upon her engagement, Tahar Haddad's *Imra'atuna fi al-Shari'a wa al-Mujtama'* (*Our Women in Law and Society*) and Hassen Hosni Abdelwahab's *Chahirat tunsiyyat* (*Famous Tunisian Women*), broadened her intellectual horizons. Although married at sixteen and then having several pregnancies, she still prepared for degrees in nursing and social work and took Arabic courses given by Lamine Chabbi, who, after Tunisian independence, was Minister of Culture from 1956 to 1958. In addition, after her marriage she became active in several political organisations.

Also instructive is the case of Radhia Haddad (1922–2003), the daughter of Salah Ben Ammar, who worked at the government printing company, and of Kmar Zarrouk, the granddaughter of al-Arbi Zarrouk, who had opposed the Bardo treaty that installed the French protectorate in Tunisia in 1881. While attending a neighbourhood school in Franceville (today al-Omrane), she challenged a French woman teacher giving a history lesson on 'Our ancestors the Gauls' by arguing that the Arabs had a great cultural history, and she refused to listen to *La Marseillaise*. In addition, an Arabic language professor came to give her lessons at home. Radhia Haddad, like her mother, was hostile to the ways in which the colonial system humiliated Tunisians.

While her father was not opposed to her attending secondary school, he changed his mind just before the school year started, following a discussion he had with friends. Shocked by his decision, Radhia Haddad went on a hunger strike, only stopping this when her brother came down with typhoid. She continued her education at home, following the homework of her brother Hassib, who was two years her junior. Together they talked about the political activities of other youths, and she continued to be politically active. At independence she became president of L'Union nationale de la femme tunisienne (UNFT), a post she held from 1958 to 1972, and entered parliament in 1959, after the first Tunisian elections.

These last cases show how these girls and women, belonging to a well-off social class, like the first group that attended university, were hostile to the colonial educational system. They criticised its methods, pointed to the coldness of colonial architecture, disparaged the marginalisation of Arabic, and challenged the content of history lessons that promoted assimilation and did not give value to Arab history and civilisation. They were all strongly opposed to the racism shown by the teachers as well as by the children of the colonising power. In addition to all these problems, many families, fearing that their daughters might be converted to Christianity, chose to withdraw their daughters from school.

The demands of intellectuals and feminists

The discussion about the condition of women and about the veil expanded in the 1920s after Manoubia Ouertani, an unmarried sewing teacher at the nuns' school Les Vicaires, took off her veil in public in 1924 during a speech she was giving on the condition of women. Then, in 1929, Habiba Menchari, a secretary of Algerian origin, did the same. Articles were published in the press in both Arabic and French, some favourable, others opposed. Among the strong reactions we find an article by the lawyer and journalist Habib Bourguiba, entitled 'The veil' ('Le voile'), which sharply criticised the French socialist organisers of these events, for he saw the veil as an organic part of Tunisian identity.

Intellectuals and members of the group Taht Essour were active in the period between the two World Wars and included poets, writers and journalists such as Aboul Kacem Chebbi, Tahar Haddad, Béchir Khraief, Hédi Labidi, Zine el-Abidine Snoussi, Jalaleddine Naccache, Mahmoud Bourguiba, Bayram Tounsi and Ali Douagi. They were at the start of a renewal in literature and poetry, and they also published essays on the social conditions of women and workers, which increasingly filled the columns of the Arabic and French-language press. In addition, the theatre, songs and humour covered by the press won the public's interest and played a crucial role in social criticism (Di Falco 2007: 90). Tahar Bekri saw this movement as being composed of 'singers, journalists, anticonformists, the penniless, pessimists and those despairing of their situation, who took revenge on adversity through irony and black humor'.

Starting in 1928, Hédi Labidi opened up the columns of the newspaper *As-Sawab* to articles by Tahar Haddad on the liberation of women; Labidi was also the first to call upon women to form associations. In 1930, publication of Tahar Haddad's book *Our Women in Law and Society*, on the condition of women, launched a polemic between 'modernist' and 'traditionalist' Zeitounian *ulema*. This work drew a link between the struggle for women's emancipation and the emergence of the new intellectuals, and was challenged by the religious bourgeoisie of Tunis. Among those who strongly criticised Tahar Haddad was Sheikh Mohamed Salah Ben Mrad, a Zeitounian figure who, in response to Haddad's work, which had become a symbol for the emancipation of women and for the emergence of intellectuals coming from the cities of the interior, far from central authority, published a pamphlet denouncing it without, it seems, ever having read it. In addition, he opened up the columns of *Chams al-Islam (The Sun of Islam)* to his daughter Bchira Ben M'Rad, the founder of the Muslim Union of Women of Tunisia (Union musulmane des femmes de Tunisie), who, while promoting women's education and an improvement in their condition, also claimed that Tahar Haddad, a young Zeitounian intellectual, did not have the standing to express such views (Labidi 2009a). Ostracised and marginalised, living largely in solitude, Tahar Haddad died several years later.

The year 1930 saw not only the publication of Haddad's book but also the Carthage Eucharistic Congress and celebrations marking the one hundredth anniversary of the French colonisation of Algeria. This raised fears among Tunisian families that the girls' schools run by religious nuns on the European model and the removal of veils during discussions organised by the French socialist elite were all part of an effort to evangelise and assimilate Tunisian girls and women, especially since Tunisia was in the vulnerable situation of being under French colonial domination.

Other intellectuals continued this debate. Hassan Hosni Abdelwaheb (1884–1968), a teacher, founded Khaldounia in 1896; this was the first school in Tunisia to adopt a programme that included mathematics, law, science, geography and health. It was named after the famous fourteenth-century sociologist and historian Ibn Khaldoun, who was the first to publish a history of Tunisian literature in 1917 and founded several museums. In 1934, Abdelwaheb published *Chahirat tunsiyat (Famous Tunisian Women)*. And Tawhida Ben Cheikh's return to Tunisia in 1936 provided the occasion for the Muslim Union of Women of Tunisia to celebrate the country's first woman doctor; she had graduated from medical school in Paris and had been named director of the feminist magazine *Leila*, which had just started publication and lasted from 1936 to 1942. A rumour circulated that without enough women to write articles, some were being written by feminist men and signed with women's names, or were being written by women using pseudonyms. A further dispute arose when members of the church signed articles appearing in the magazine.

In this context, several other women's movements, or women's sections of political parties, were formed. In the late 1940s, Nebiha Ben Miled, after having worked with Bchira Ben M'Rad, joined the Union of Women of Tunisia (Union des femmes de Tunisie), a group with a communist orientation that focused on providing assistance to poor families and giving women information regarding health and contraception. This was an organisation she saw as more dynamic, corresponding to her personality, and it put her side by side with women including Zohra Ben Slimane, Chérifa Saadaoui, Gladys Adda, Neila Haddad and Gilda Khiari, among others. In the 1950s, Nebiha Ben Miled became the first Tunisian president of this association.

Chédlia Bouzgarou, Habib Bourguiba's niece, also emerged as a political figure starting in the mid-1930s. She distinguished herself first when, during the Bey's passage through the streets of the Medina, she decided to address him regarding the situation of deported political prisoners; to do this, she employed the ruse of calling out to him from a number of different balconies, creating the illusion of a broad demonstration. Her calls upset the normal routine and attracted the Bey's attention, as well as that of the dignitaries and journalists, to the situation of activists arrested by the colonial power. In April 1938 she organised a number of demonstrations that have since become legendary. On one occasion she led a protest with a group of only five women and, when France's Resident-General Eric Labonne arrived in Tunisia, they cried out: 'Down with privilege ...' This led to her arrest. On another occasion she organised a demonstration with a small group of women on the arrival of Resident-General Daladier. Once again, she was arrested and sentenced to a prison term. She pursued the struggle up until independence, and, even when in prison, she called upon common-law prisoners to mobilise against colonisation.

The Association of Young Muslims (Association des jeunes musulmans), led by Mohamed Salah Ennaifer (1902–93) and his wife Souad Bakhta Kattèche Ennaifer, head of its women's section, opened the School for the Muslim Girl (Ecole pour la fille musulmane) in 1947, with two branches at Bab Ennara and Bab El Khadra in Tunis and several branches in Tunisia's interior regions. They also trained teachers for these schools. Tunisian women such as Manana Righi financed the construction of schools for girls in Sousse. Noureddine Sraieb notes that there was a school system run by the Tunisian state before the French colonial period, and he cites Jules Ferry writing that 'the creation of an institution of upper primary schooling, with a teaching that is specialized and professional, is aimed to *Frenchify* the middle commercial and industrial class' (Sraieb 1993: 240, italics in the original).

In 1952, Zeitouna University set up a women's section, and, when the feminist newspaper *Ilhâm* appeared in 1954, a newspaper close to the Zeitounian religious elite, several women signed their names to their articles and studies. At that moment – when Tunisia was on the verge of recovering its political independence – more than 95 per cent of women did not know how to read or write.

During this first phase, which began around the mid-nineteenth century, an interest in the situation of women developed along with a rich literature on this subject, the hosting of a literary salon by a woman, and the creation of girls' schools in various Tunisian cities.

These all testified to a desire for progressive change. Starting in the 1920s, feminist women took off the veil and demanded other rights, while new intellectuals in different cities in the country's interior joined together in the Taht Essour (Under the Wall) group, to produce a new kind of literature. This period is also distinctive for the appearance of two feminist publications, *Leila* in French and *Ilham* in Arabic, and in the number of women writers who emerged.

The Personal Status Code

With independence, the promulgation in 1956 of the Personal Status Code (PSC) – abolishing polygamy, raising the minimum age for marriage, making divorce subject to judicial procedures, giving women the right to vote and be elected to political office, mandating that women receive the same salary as men for the same work, generalising education and guaranteeing women's access to public space – became central to the construction of a new Tunisian identity. Also central to this process was the development and spread of books. Between 1956 and 1987, more than 70 per cent of all books published were published by the state publishing institutions. With liberalisation of the sector, 1,249 non-school books were published in 2002 of which 885 were in Arabic; in 2007, 1,700 books were published of which almost one-third were children's books.

Literature and commitment

Together with the journal *El-Fikr*, founded in 1955, other publications appeared such as *Qisas* (a publication of The Story Club or Club de la nouvelle, founded in 1966), *al-Mar'a* (published by the UNFT, Union nationale des femmes tunisiennes), and the magazine *Faiza*, founded by Dorra Bouzid, Safia Farhat and Néfissa Ben Said. Starting in the 1960s, Néfissa Ben Said carried out interviews with literary and political figures, women and men, both Tunisian and foreign, such as Indira Gandhi, Léopold Sédar Senghor, Simone Weil and Rachid Driss. The role of women journalists was very important at this time in both the press and on the radio, as well as later on television. Also during this period the bilingual option – Arabic and French – was defended by many as a way to ensure access to the sciences and technology and to continue on the road forward. (To cite one example, the teaching of medicine and psychology, among other subjects, was and continues to be given in French, and French is the language of most publications in these fields.) The Tunisian Writers Union, founded in 1971, gave to writers an organisational structure. Selma Khadra Jayyusi founded a project for the translation of Arab literature into English (PROTA) in 1980 and set up East–West Nexus in the United States to make Arab literature better known.

Book publishing and sales flourished in Tunisia, with the SNED (Société Nationale d'Edition et de Diffusion) – later splitting into the STD (Société Tunisienne de Diffusion) and the MTE (Maison Tunisienne d'Edition) – contributing to the distribution of school books and to the publication of literary and scientific works. However, in the 1980s we see public institutions withdrawing from publishing, leading many Tunisian authors – as in other countries of the region – to publish at their own expense. Other media, such as the radio, television and print media, also contributed to the promotion and distribution of local production, providing the conditions for the emergence of a new elite and giving birth to a number of new women writers.

With the 1970s, Tunisia experienced the results of the failures of development theory, leading to crises on many levels. In 1975, three events sparked the imagination of the population. First, Selma Baccar's film *Fatma 75* – the first Tunisian film directed by a woman – which provided images of historic feminist figures from 1930 to 1975 and was contracted by the Ministry of Culture to celebrate the international decade for women's rights, was censored. Second, Hind Chelbi, professor at the Theological University of Tunis, who had been invited to give a speech on the occasion of *Laylat al-Qadr* (the Night of Power) during the month of Ramadan, refused to extend her hand to greet President Habib Bourguiba, testifying to her view that a good Muslim woman should not shake a man's hand and creating great surprise among the spectators. From this date the hijab, sometimes worn by girls against their parents' wishes, spread more widely, becoming visible in urban public space and increasingly becoming a sign of political protest. Legal decree no. 108, in effect since 1981 under Habib Bourguiba, and article 6 of decree no. 717 of 13 April 1993 under Zine el-Abidine Ben Ali (defining the norms for the national identity card) forbid wearing the hijab in public institutions and showing women wearing the hijab on television and on movie screens.

The Minister of the Interior in the first transitional government following the revolution of 14 January 2011 revised the laws relating to the identity card, allowing women to be photographed with the hijab for their identity card. However, eighteen months after the elections of October 2011, which led to a government led by the Islamically oriented Nahdha party, decree no. 108 remains in effect. Controversy over the hijab introduced a cleavage in discussion over women's rights that continued through the Arab Spring in 2011 and also continues today with respect to the niqab, with many feminists disagreeing with one another on whether these forms of dress should be seen as signs of submission or as possible forms of resistance. The sociologist Pierre Bourdieu (1993) said that the role of intellectuals should, in the context of a sociology of denunciation, aim to divert the strategies of domination to serve those who are dominated and thus legitimise a discourse of resistance.

During his inaugural speech, Moncef Marzouki, Tunisia's provisional president following the elections of October 2011, made a distinction between women wearing the niqab, the hijab, and the *safirat* – the latter meaning women who are not modest and do not follow religious principles – provoking much anger among women and feminists who wear neither hijab nor niqab and who see themselves as sincere Muslims. Third, with the end of the 1970s, Hélé Béji published *Le désenchantement national* (Béji 1982). This work, written from within the corridors of power (she is the niece of Wassila Ben Ammar, then Habib Bourguiba's wife), deals with the failures of decolonisation, the monopolisation of power, and the absence of freedom of expression – questions that she pursues in her subsequent writings.

In addition, from the end of the 1970s, the state was the target of growing criticism from the opposition and Islamists, and also from feminists who criticised it for, among other things, not appointing women to decision-making positions and not doing much to improve the situation of rural girls and women. In this context, where the demands of a variety of groups were being expressed, there was finally the appointment of Fethia Mokhtar Mzali (born 1927), professor of Arabic, as head of the UNFT in 1971 (she was a graduate of the Sorbonne and had published articles in *El-Fikr*; also, she had won the first elections for the UNFT presidency in the late 1950s, but President Bourguiba rejected this outcome and named Radhia

Haddad instead), and then as Minister for Women and the Family from 1983 to 1986. She was the first woman to be a government minister, in a government headed by her husband, Prime Minister Mohamed Mzali (1980–86). During the 2000s, she talked of the difficulties she encountered during this period as a woman minister in a masculine environment. Later, Souad Yaccoubi el-Ouahchi (born 1938) was appointed the first woman Minister of Public Health from 1984 to 1988, a half-century after Tawhida Ben Cheikh earned her doctorate in medicine. Both of these appointments were, in part, a response to pressure from the feminist movement. Since then, there have been a number of women ministers. Also in this context, the feminist magazine *Nissa* was founded by women journalists, researchers and academics who met at the Tahar Haddad Cultural Club, but this ceased publication after several numbers. During the same period, several opposition newspapers appeared and Islamic groups and leaders began to be increasingly noticed in public space (Labidi 1998).

Several women in prison were victims of violence for having challenged the dictatorships of the Habib Bourguiba and Zine el-Abidine Ben Ali regimes, or for having supported a spouse, a brother, a father or a friend who made such a challenge. Several organisations produced reports on violence against political prisoners committed during these periods, for example the International Association for the Support of Political Prisoners (Association Internationale de Soutien aux Prisonniers Politique or AISPP), the organisation Freedom and Equity (Liberté et Equité) and the Tunisian Human Rights League (La Ligue Tunisienne des Droits de l'Homme), but among the hundreds of cases they received, very few were submitted by women.

Why is the number of women so low? Ibtihel Abdelatif, president of the IVD's Women's Committee, points out that *al-Hay'at al-Haqiqat wa al-Karama* (IVD or Instance Vérité et Dignité/Authority for Truth and Dignity), which formed as a result of demands for transparency and accountability in the framework of the transitional justice of the Arab Spring in Tunisia, received only 1,626 cases presented by women, and only two of the total referred to rape, among the first 13,278 cases submitted to it.

According to Ibtihel Abdelatif, the reasons are many, such as the women's distance from Tunis, the cost of transportation, the need to have the husband's authorisation, and especially the fact that women victims of violence do not see themselves as victims even when they have been subjected to degrading insults, sexual touching, and forced nudity up to and including rape (sometimes accomplished with objects) (Bresillon 2015).

In this environment, starting in the 1980s, my own writings began to appear, focusing on two main themes. One theme deals with constructing the history of Tunisian women political figures, by drawing attention to historical figures in Tunisian feminism. An example of this is *Joudhour al-harakat al-nisa'iyya: riwayaat li-shakhsiyyaat tarikhiyya* (*Origins of Feminist Movements in Tunisia: Personal History Narratives*), now in its third edition (Labidi 2009a). The other theme concerns the deconstruction of discourse to show the different meanings relating to women of texts, hadith, essays, children's songs and press articles, an example of which is *Çabra Hachma: sexualité et tradition*, which received the 1989 Book Festival Prize in Tunis. This book, which sold out after six months, was brought to court by the public prosecutor for violating public morality, but the case was not pursued (Labidi 1989).

After President-for-Life Habib Bourguiba was deposed in 1987 by his Prime Minister Zine el-Abidine Ben Ali, a National Pact was signed in 1988 by the new government and a broad group of political movements, including the Islamic Tendency Movement in which Rachid Ghannouchi was a major figure. The National Pact guaranteed that the PSC would be kept as the philosophical foundation of the constitution. Between 1989 and 2000s, the authorities satisfied a variety of feminist demands, among them awarding Tunisian nationality to the child of a Tunisian mother and a foreign father, giving legal authorisation for feminist associations such as the ATFD (Association tunisienne des femmes démocrates) and AFTURD (Association de la femme tunisienne pour la recherche sur le développement), creating CREDIF (Centre de Recherche, d'Etudes, de Documentation, et d'Information sur la Femme/Centre for Research, Study and Documentation on Women) and creating a master's degree in women's studies.

At a time when the Ben Ali regime attempted to enlist the support of women and intellectuals for its security policies, it also suppressed public debate. Conferences that might have been the scene of critical discussion were systematically cancelled by the authorities. It is in this context that Moufida Tlatli's widely praised film *Samt el qusur* (*The Silence of the Palaces*) appeared, exploring the exploitation of women servants by the upper classes during the last decades of the French protectorate in Tunisia. The film focuses on a young woman singer who looks back on her past and that of her mother – a cook by day and a dancer obliged to provide sexual favours for the prince by night – and discovers that little has changed after independence. As Tlatli's film appeared, in the 1990s, independent feminist associations were being increasingly marginalised and repressed, with university colloquia closely monitored.

Literary institutions   Up until the 1970s, women's presence in intellectual and political spheres was limited. With no women university students in Tunisia in 1955, the UGET (Union générale des étudiants tunnisiens) invited some secondary school girl students known for their activism against colonialism to participate in the organisation's first congress and to represent women. Among this group was Layla Kabadou, along with Souad and Radhia Belkhodja, Radhia and Wided Jaouiada, and Fatma Kamel. The construction of literary institutions took several decades. In the 1960s there were twenty-one libraries for children and they were all headed by women (Said 1970). In 1976, Layla Kabadou was the first woman to open a bookstore – al-Kitab in the centre of Tunis – and, in 1978, she expressed her anger at the state monopoly on book publishing and became a member of the bookstore owners' union, a life story that I collected in 2005. Following this, a number of women have come to own and run bookstores. Other women founded publishing houses, among them the political activist Sihem Ben Sedrine, who headed Noir et Blanc in 1988 and founded Arcs in 1998 and Aloès in 1999.

Together with these developments, the government appointed some women to head cultural centres, among them Jalila Hafsia, a journalist and novelist, and Khédija Lasram Kammoun, a secondary school Arabic teacher, who followed one another as heads of the Tahar Haddad Cultural Centre. From the end of the 1970s, this was the special gathering place in the Medina of Tunis for the Tunisian feminist elite, which was to have such a significant impact on the history of ideas in Tunisia. Later, both of them hosted their own private literary salons. Now, with women having made their presence felt in education – women made up 55 per cent of primary school teachers in 2009, 42 per cent of university lecturers, and more than 60 per cent of university students – women were also strongly engaged in fields such as journalism, poetry, and the writing of novels and stories. Several names became very well known in literary criticism, in the theatre and in cinema.

In the area of literary criticism, figures such as Taoufik Baccar promoted women's writing starting in the 1970s; among recent women literary critics we can mention Abir Krifa (2008), Douja Mariem Mamelouk (2010) and Sonia S'hiri. Sonia S'hiri points to three novels written by women that dominated Tunisian literary life during the 1990s: Fadhila Chebbi's *Al-Ism wa al-Hadid* (*The Name and Decadence*), published in 1992 and characterised by its poetic language; Amal Mokhtar's *Nakhabu al-Hayat* (*A Toast of Life*), published in 1993, in which the protagonist is in search of herself and experiences 'a number of atavistic existential adventures' in Germany – a novel that resonates with some aspects of the Senegalese woman writer Ken Bugul's widely discussed *Le baobab fou* (Labidi 2003); and, in 1995, Aroussia Nalouti's *Tamass* (*Mutual Contact*), which explores the relationships between a mother and her children and between a wife and her husband (S'kiri 1997). We should also mention the inventories of Tunisian women's writing since independence compiled by Jean Dejeux, Jean Fontaine, Hédia Khadar and others.

Feminist associations, such as AFTURD, although constituting a small section of the population, became very active in setting up writing workshops for women (Binous et al. 1992, with a preface by Fatima Mernissi), publishing research studies (sometimes on controversial themes, such as Alia Chammari's study of divorce, or even on taboo subjects such as the collective work on inequality in inheritance led by the jurist Sanaa Ben Achour (AFTURD 2006)), holding public discussions where new works are presented, and so on. Finally, encyclopaedias have been devoted to women who were politically active (Labidi 2009b) and to women writers, and a website on this literature appeared in the West.[2]

This dynamism has been accompanied by new initiatives including the establishment of literary prizes, giving to Tunisian women's writing a new identity over recent decades. The Ministry of

2 http://www.limag.refer.org/.

Culture, the Municipality of Tunis, research centres, banks, holding companies and associations are the main promoters of literary prizes in Tunisia. As one of these initiatives, in the 1980s a group of independent women established the B'Chira Ben M'Rad Prize, awarded to women struggling to promote women's rights. Many women say that, although her father Shaykh Mohamed Salah ben M'Rad had combatted Tahar Haddad's work, Bchira Ben M'Rad was sincere in her own fight for women's rights.

After being awarded for several years, the B'Chira Ben M'Rad Prize was discontinued, having succeeded in its aim of giving impetus to a feminist dynamic, and with other institutions setting up similar awards. CREDIF, in coordination with the Tahar Haddad Club, founded the Zoubeida Bchir (1938–2011) Prize in 1995 in honour of the first Tunisian woman to publish a poetry collection, *Hanin* (*Nostalgia*). This prize, which aims to encourage research in literature, poetry and science in both Arabic and foreign languages, is conferred every year on International Women's Day, and is also the occasion for CREDIF to produce its annual bibliography of women's writings, although it did not carry out any research on women and literature between 2001 and 2010. Other literary prizes are awarded to men and women, such as the Comar d'Or Prize, established in 1997 by Comar Insurance (Les Assurances Comar). An analysis of this award shows that women are less likely to receive it than men: it has been given to only fourteen women compared with forty-six men over the past decade, and only three Arabic-language novels written by women (by Massouada AbouBekr, Amel Mokhtar and Afifa Saoudi Essmiti)[3] have received the prize. Here we should mention the difficulties writers in Arabic encounter in getting their works distributed throughout the region. On several occasions I have heard women Arabic-language writers complain about the reception of their work in the Arab world and how difficult it is for their work

---

3 Tunisia counts a number of women novelists and poets writing in Arabic, among them Faouzia Aloui, Hind Azouz, Hayet BeCheikh, Massôuda Boubaker, Fadhila Chebbi, Fatma Ben Fdhila, Nefla Dhab, Rabiâ Firchichi, Hafidha Gara Bibane (Bint AlBhar), Fathia Hechmi, Rim Issaoui, Jamila Mejri (the first woman to hold the position of president of the Writers' Union, December 2008–January 2011), Souad Methnani, Amel Mokhtar, Halima Mosbahi, Aroussia Nalouti, Saloua Rachdi, Alya R'Haiem, Mounira Rezgui, Fatma Slim, Alia Tabaî, Najia Thameur, Emna Waslati, Wassila Zarrai, Dalila Zitouni, and many others.

to be distributed and discussed. Here, it is important to note that the French-language writing by women in Tunisia, although significant in volume and often winning awards, has no real presence in France, with rare exceptions such as the essay *Le Coran au risque de la psychanalyse* (2007), which enabled its author, Olfa Youssef, to be welcomed on French television programmes, although her works in Arabic led to controversy and she has not found a warm welcome on Arabic-language television in the region.

Also, women novelists cannot survive on the income from their writings and in only a very few cases do publishing houses, local or foreign, finance their publication. Only within the past few years have a number of French language departments in Tunisian universities shown an interest in the writings of Tunisian women. And university departments of Arabic literature show lower rates of women in the faculty than other departments. Also, censorship has affected publications in Arabic more significantly than those in French (Arvanitis 2007), which deprives youth of significant sources of imaginative expression. This phenomenon may account, in part, for the lack of reading by youth – girls and boys devote, respectively, 10 and 5 minutes to reading per day, numbers that decrease as age increases (Mahfoudh 2004). In general, students have very little access to today's Tunisian literature: of the 800 Tunisian titles published since independence (more than a third are poetry collections, some 150 are stories and novels), only fifty are part of secondary school programmes in Arabic (and only five of these are by women) (Chraiet 2013).

Throughout the decade of the 2000s, women pursued their productive work and made significant contributions. Jamila Mejri, born in 1951 in Kairouan, was elected president of the Tunisian Writers' Union in 2008 – the first woman to hold this position in an institution that was founded in 1971 and that has 400 members. Facing challenges related to the unrest that broke out in December 2010, she resigned in January 2011 (Allani 2010). Research units and laboratories emerged in the universities, leading to the recruitment of academics in the new universities throughout the country. National and international conferences were organised in literature and women literary critics began to focus on the literature of the Maghreb, with some dealing with women's literature. In addition, the number of titles published by women writers continued to grow, with Olfa

Youssef, Amel Grami, Raja Ben Slama and others publishing writings discussing interpretations of Islam. But there was also widespread misogyny affecting all women regardless of training, age or political orientation, and this devalued women's activities on all levels. For example, in 2004 Abdelwaheb Bouhdiba, director of Beit El-Hikma (a state institution at the highest level concerned with cultural and intellectual activities) and author of the introduction to the volume *Réel et imaginaire de la femme dans la littérature du Maghreb au XXème siècle* (edited by Hédia Khadar), a collection containing contributions by women academics attempting to dislodge stereotypes, writes in his introduction that the book would never have been published without the aim of encouraging women's literary production – saying, in effect, that the book did not deserve to be published on its own merits. This view is far from unique. Joseph T. Zeidan points out how, in Egypt, the well-known and widely published writer Abbas Mahmoud Al-Aqqad (who died in 1964) saw women as dependent and weak by nature, needing the guidance and supervision of men, and as disobedient because of 'their resentment of the way men had been their masters throughout history and that now they had enough and wanted revenge' (Zeidan 1995: 89, 90). Similarly, Taoufik al-Hakim attributed the absence of women in fields such as musical composition and architecture to their lack of capacity to think and to concentrate.

More recently, in 2008, an article vilifying women philosophers at the University of Tunis was published in *Le Temps*, an independent Tunisian newspaper, applying to these women epithets such as 'frivolous', 'a bitch in heat' (*'chienne mordue'*) and other such terms (Mosbah 2008a). However, Salah Mosbah denied authorship of this article in a 'right of reply' (2008b). And when Zeinab Ben Said Cherni responded in an article defending her colleagues, discussing the programme and philosophical orientation of each of them and how they were 'devoted to their teaching activities, carrying out their work assiduously and conscientiously, serenely, far from the stakes of power' (*'Dévouées à leurs taches d'enseignantes, elles mènent leur travail avec assiduité et conscience, sereinement, loin des enjeux de pouvoir'*), she disdained any mention of the article that provoked her response (Cherni 2008: 105).

We have seen that, at each of these stages, feminists, whatever their social and economic levels, were motivated by the desire to find solutions to certain urgent problems facing women. From the 1930s until 1955, women were subject to, among other things, early marriage, polygyny, divorce by repudiation, poverty and illiteracy, and they had no access to institutionalised healthcare. The promulgation of the PSC and the promotion of literacy and books contributed to the formation of new personalities and encouraged the mixing of genders in the schools, and consequently in public space, trends that continued into the 1970s and beyond. The demands of the new generation of feminists of the 1970s, who were graduates from the national universities, focused on the rights of women to be their children's guardian in divorce situations, to transmit their Tunisian nationality to their children in cases where the father was foreign, and to have inheritance rights equal to those of men – this last has not yet been achieved. These socio-juridical objectives correspond to a new psychological orientation that has encouraged women's confidence and self-esteem.

Here, the film *Dowaha* (*Buried Secrets*, Raja Amari, 2009) – the second feature film from a woman director, known for films in which sexuality and secrecy play important roles – corresponds to a turning point in Tunisia's socio-political history. The film tells the story of three women – Aicha, Radhia and their mother – who have been living for the past several years in an abandoned house that they leave only to sell in town the small handicrafts that they produce. When a young couple arrives to live in the house, the lives of these three women are shaken and they fear that their secrets will be uncovered, although the youngest of the three is attracted by the dynamic lifestyle of the young couple. The film ends with the young woman murdering those around her and leaving the environment that imprisoned her, with the flow of blood being Raja Amari's metaphor for achieving freedom. This may also be seen as a foreshadowing of the Arab Spring, which broke out with the self-immolation of Mohamed Bouazizi on 17 December 2010.

In this context, a new literature of denunciation emerged and a few publications by and press interviews with women who had been harassed and even sentenced to prison terms under the Bourguiba and Ben Ali regimes for having worn the hijab or for their political views enriched the literary and cultural scene. During this period around the time of the Arab Spring, the main feminist demands were related to achieving political parity, lifting Tunisia's reservations on the Convention on the Elimination of All Forms of Discrimination against Women (CEDAW), and enshrining women's rights in the new constitution.

In the next section, we will discuss how Tunisian women writers, after having witnessed and participated in advances in family law and being committed to social justice, brought the verve of their ancestral women oral poets back to life both before and after the Arab Spring, producing a literature of denunciation attacking the domain of formal politics in written forms that had formerly been dominated by men.

The literature of denunciation and the struggle for a new public morality

During the second phase, which began in the mid-1950s and was marked by Tunisia gaining its independence from France, the promulgation of the PSC and the spread of the book as an important cultural element, along with factors such as mass education, decreased mortality and so on, all contributed to women's psychological security, which was part of a new horizon. Strengthened by their new identity, towards the end of this second phase women authors shifted from writings that denounced and criticised domination in private space to a literature of denunciation that condemned social and political injustice, expressing a new consciousness in which ethics were central. Among these authors, the writings of Sihem Ben Sedrine are among the most remarkable – she was the first Tunisian woman to publicly denounce the corruption of Ben Ali and his clan, doing this from London, and she also denounced the support the West gave to this regime's rule over the population.

Sihem Ben Sedrine's struggle for human rights Sihem Ben Sedrine has long struggled against corruption and for women's and men's rights. This summary is based on her life story that I collected during the 1980s as well as on other sources. As a child she was affected by the lack of recognition given to the right to be different. She was the granddaughter of Mohammed Ben Ammar (1889–1972), a jurist and founder in 1946 of the Association of Tunisian Magistrates, and the niece of Ridha Ben Ammar (1926–79), who led the armed wing of the national liberation movement for the greater Tunis region from 1952 to 1956. In 1953, when she was three years old, her uncle

Ridha Ben Ammar was arrested; he and several other activists succeeded in escaping, taking refuge in Libya and then in Egypt. Upon independence he returned to Tunisia, was arrested in 1956, and was accused of being a member of the Youssefist group, led by the opposition figure Salah Ben Youssef, which the state claimed was plotting a coup d'état. In 1957 he was sentenced to twenty years of hard labour by the High Court. He was given amnesty in 1965 and Bourguiba offered him the post of Minister of National Defence, which Ben Ammar refused; later he was named honorary president of the Tunisian Human Rights League (Ammar 2012).

Sihem Ben Sedrine grew up among many brothers and sisters, and her father, a judge, while conservative, also believed very deeply in freedom, a belief that strongly influenced her development and her struggles against patriarchy, imperialism and dictatorship. She married Omar Mestiri, a journalist and human rights activist who himself came from a political family – he is the son of Zohra Chenik, mentioned above – and is the mother of three children. After studying philosophy at Toulouse University in France, where she frequented other political activists, upon her return to Tunis she joined the Tunisian Human Rights League (LTDH) in 1979 and in 1985 became a member of its Executive Committee. She joined the autonomous feminist movement and also joined the PDP (Parti democrate progressiste), a political party whose secretary-general was Nejib Chabbi, her husband's brother-in-law; she then chose to resign when she disagreed with its policies on democracy. She founded, along with more than thirty other figures, the National Council for Freedoms in Tunisia (Conseil National pour les Libertés en Tunisie or CNLT) and was its official spokesperson from 2001 to 2003, although the organisation was outlawed from 1999 to 2011. Her experience enabled her to be chosen as a media observer at the 2005 Lebanese elections.

She became a member of the Tunisian Journalists' Association (Association des journalistes tunisiens) in 1980, becoming responsible for their external relations in 1987. She worked for a number of well-known publications, such as the independent magazines *Maghreb* and *Réalités*, and the opposition publications *Le Phare* and *Al-Mawkif*, and she was a co-founder of the feminist magazine *Nissa*. She was editor-in-chief of *La Gazette touristique* and founded another magazine, *L'Hebdo touristique*. Among her publications we find a 'Women's agenda' ('Agenda femmes') in 1992 that traces the history of the autonomous women's movement in Tunisia and includes a useful list of addresses of women's associations in the Maghreb – this was seized at the printer's by the authorities, censured, and was not allowed distribution. After unsuccessfully applying, with Naziha Rajiba (known by her pen name of Oum Zied), for permission to publish the independent magazine *Kalima* in 2000, they set up an electronic version in 2004 which did not receive official authorisation. In 2008, she launched Radio Kalima on the internet and via satellite, which she believes contributed to the revolution that broke out in December 2010. Radio Kalima was officially authorised in 2011 but had several years of financial difficulties, and Sihem Ben Sedrine sold her shares in Radio Kalima in 2015.

As a result of her defending human rights and press freedoms, Sihem Ben Sedrine was the target, under Ben Ali's regime, of harassment by the intelligence services and by the state-controlled press, which called her a prostitute, hysterical and delirious, claimed she had sold out to Zionists and Freemasons, and circulated pornographic images on which her face was pasted, in an effort to break her psychologically. In May 2011, she brought a case against three journalists who had written articles insulting her. Chedlia Boukhchina, one of Ben Ali's advisers, proposed stopping all the harassment and satisfying her wishes if she would simply resign from the LTDH, a proposal Ben Sedrine rejected. Her passport was taken from her from 1994 to 2000. In 2001 she was arrested upon her return to Tunis after having appeared on a London television show to discuss the use of torture, the judiciary's lack of independence, and the corruption of the Ben Ali clan; she was defended by Radhia Nasraoui, another woman activist for human rights and against torture. She is cited along with Radhia Nasraoui as a woman political activist who posed difficulties for Béji Caid Essebsi when power was handed over to Prime Minister Hamadi Jebali in December 2011 – a handover that she denounced in an open letter addressed to the local press (*La Presse de Tunisie*, 4 November 2012). She received the Olof Palme Prize for human rights in Stockholm in 2013. Marie-Claire Servan-Schreiber, wife of the late Pierre Mendès-France (a moral paragon of the French left and former Minister of Foreign Affairs who had favoured Tunisian independence), joined the campaign in support of Ben Sedrine and intervened with President Ben Ali for her liberation. With all that her family had suffered – including loss of income, reduced freedom of movement and isolation from their children – Ben Sedrine's view was that the suffering of the Tunisian people under the Ben Ali regime was far greater than that of her own family ('Sihem Ben Sedrine', Dialogue with the Muslim World, 2003[4]).

After Ben Sedrine's period in prison, the Hamburg Foundation for Victims of Political Persecution, which works to support writers, offered her a one-year residential fellowship to aid her in writing a book, following which she published *Letter to a Disappeared Iraqi Woman Friend (Lettre à une amie irakienne disparue)* (Ben Sedrine 2003). This book shows a fine sense of observation and provides a moving analysis of the experience of societies under dictatorship. She describes how she arrived in Iraq after the Anglo-American invasion in 2003 to look for Nacéra, a woman engineer she had known ten years earlier who had helped her understand the impact of Saddam Hussein's totalitarian regime on Iraqi society. Unable to locate her in 'liberated' Iraq, she describes how, during this visit, she learns about the other countries of the region under totalitarian regimes – with common graves, highly equipped torture chambers, societal breakdowns while under the illusion of a mythical present and future (the myth of an Arab world renaissance in Iraq, of a North African economic dragon in Tunisia), societal brainwashing, and so on. The French newspaper *L'Humanité* reviewed this book, saying: 'Beyond what the author tells us, it is not only the Arab peoples who are addressed by the questions in this letter, by this cry of distress ... [it is] an appeal for thinking about bringing together all those who have no other choice than to rebel against the rule of the strongest.' And *Version Fémina* saw Ben Sedrine's text as showing 'Iraqis in a light that European special reporters will never be able to show'.

With Omar Mestiri, Ben Sedrine published another book, titled *Europe and its Despots (L'Europe et ses despotes)*, denouncing the European Union's policy which, since the Barcelona Declaration of 1995, has declared a 'zone of peace and stability' in the Mediterranean while, in fact, providing support for the totalitarian regimes in the

---

4 http://www.universalrights.net/heroes/display.php3?id=83.

southern Mediterranean (Ben Sedrine 2003). Tunis had become the Arab capital where Arab ministers of the interior met regularly with their European counterparts to pursue security policies that eased the way for terrorism while claiming to fight it. Her books and activities have gained her several prizes, including from the organisation Canadian Journalists for Free Expression, the 2004 International Press Freedom Award for her courage in defending and promoting press freedom, the Danish Peace Fund Prize in 2008 for her commitment to democracy, the rule of law and human rights in the Arab world, and, in 2011, the Alison Des Forges Prize for her commitment to human rights.

Ben Sedrine went into exile in 2009, returning to Tunisia only in 2011, to participate in the construction of a democratic state. While not sharing Islamist ideas and being opposed to Salafist views, she defended the rights of Islamists who had been marginalised, imprisoned or forced into exile by the Ben Ali regime. These balanced, ethical views towards the rights of all political actors have often cost her: for example, in the March 2011 elections for the High Commission for the Realisation of the Objectives of the Revolution, of Political Reform, and of Democratic Transition, she won only twenty-two votes out of 126, with the voters preferring figures who were less controversial – this also testified to the fact that the political outlook that dominated from 1987 to 2010 was still widespread. Attacks against Sihem Ben Sedrine continued when she announced her candidacy to become a member of the IVD, established by the Tunisian Constituent Assembly (Assemblée Nationale Constituante or ANC), and they continued even after she was named head of the IVD in 2014.

The new literature of denunciation in the context of the Arab Spring

New types of social movements During the first decade of the 2000s, new forms of social movements began to appear, showing an aspect of youth culture of which the wider culture was largely unaware: Tunisia had 800,000 Facebook accounts before the revolution and 2.5 million following it, in a total population of some 10.5 million, of whom many are still illiterate, and a Facebook page such as facebook.com/MaTunisie numbers some 771,000 fans. We should also note the emergence of blogs published in Arabic, French and

English. Clearly, we are in the presence of a new culture, one in which writing is approached in a new manner.[5]

In Tunisia, urban youth and the youth of the middle classes use the web to great effect, among them the cyber-activist Slim Amamou, a computer engineer whose parents are both doctors and who, after his arrest during the revolution, was freed and named a member of the first transitional Tunisian government following Ben Ali's flight on 14 January 2011 (he was a Secretary of State for Youth, a position he occupied for several months before resigning, and he willingly recognised the importance of the computer training that had been offered to youth by companies from abroad[6]); Azyz Amamy, a specialist in computer development and a poet; Hamada Ben Amor, nicknamed '*le Général*', the first rapper to oppose Ben Ali, whose song 'Rais el-bled' ('The country's president') is considered by many to be the anthem of the revolution (it was also sung in Tahrir Square in Egypt), and who *Time* magazine ranked among the 100 most important figures of 2011; and other bloggers who participated in the successful protest *Nhar Ala Ammar* in May 2010, demanding the removal of web censorship. Young women also took part in this movement, such as Amira Yahyaoui, who participated from Paris. Later, the attacks from the Anonymous collective contributed to the fall of the regime.[7]

Women bloggers Women citizens in urban areas of the Arab world, including young university teachers, pharmacists, dentists and journalists, enabled the spread of a kind of literature that over a very short period reached a wide audience and was very important in the Arab world. When the Saudi woman Raja al-Sanie, a dentist by training, published in Arabic her novel-blog *Banat ar-Riyadh* (*Girls of Riyadh*) in 2005 in Beirut, she no doubt did not foresee that this would introduce a new dynamic into the literary life of women in the region. In Egypt, women writing blogs about being unmarried experienced such success among web users that publishers proposed publishing these blogs: among others, in 2008 Al-Chourouq published the

5 http://www.opinion-internationale.com/2011/06/22/que-represente-facebook-en-tunisie-aujourd%E2%80%99hui%C2%A0_2242.html.
6 http://www.youtube.com/watch?v=npS6_13OhlE.
7 http://www.e-torpedo.net/imprimersans.php3?id_article=3395.

chronicle *Ayza atgawes* (*I Want to Get Married*) from a blog written by Ghada Abdel-Al (later adapted as a television series for Ramadan and, in Tunisia, as a theatre play), and *'Orz bi-laban li chakhsein* (*Rice Pudding for Two*) by Rehab Bassam, both of whom had been writing their blogs since 2004. In Tunisia there were several women among the bloggers, for example Imen Laâmari, who founded the Tunisian Bloggers Association (Association des bloggeurs tunisiens); also Henda Chennaoui, called Hendoud, Emna Ben Jemaa, Sana Sbouai, Lilia Weslaty, Hana Trabelsi and Amira Yahyaoui, who is also president of the al-Bawssala Association, founded in 2011. Together with some other associations and individual Tunisians, Amira Yahyaoui registered a complaint in August 2012 with the Administrative Tribunal against the Constituent Assembly for its lack of adherence to the transparency of information statute that was laid out in the law decree no. 41 of May 2011.

Among the figures in this movement, Lina Ben Mhenni, an academic and instructor of English at the University of Tunis, played a pre-eminent role. This role was similar to that played by Halima Jouini, a Tunisian activist for women's and human rights since the 1980s, a member of the ATFD, and to whom Mounir Baaziz devoted a documentary, *A Life of Saw's Teeth* (*Une vie en dents de scie*), testifying to the struggles of women activists who, although victims of physical and psychological violence, pursued their fight against dictatorship and its various forms of violence. Lina Ben Mhenni internalised the basics of the 1980s women's struggle – a struggle for equality with men and for freedom – and she belongs to the new generation nourished by the internet.

Lina Ben Mhenni was born in 1983. Her mother is a secondary school Arabic teacher and her father is an activist, employed in the Ministry of Transport, who spent several years in prison and was tortured for his opposition to Habib Bourguiba. Despite weak health – she had a kidney transplant in 2007 – she participated in 2009 in the world games for people with transplants, held in Thailand and Australia, and won a silver medal in the walking race. She won a Fulbright scholarship to spend 2008–09 in the USA. Her blog, written in the three languages of Arabic, English and French, is one of the few blogs to carry the author's real name. Among her actions over the internet, she conducted a campaign for her close friend when he was arrested. Her blog was censored by the Ben Ali regime and her material – computer and cameras – was stolen. She calls herself a cyber-dissident against censorship and torture and pursues her activity in support of democracy, denouncing the excesses of the transitional governments of Béji Caid Essebsi and Hamadi Jebali put in place following the revolution.

With the popular uprisings in the interior regions of the country following Mohamed Bouazizi's self-immolation on 17 December 2010, Lina Ben Mhenni went to Sidi Bouzid, to Regueb, and to Kasserine – all places where the repression of protest was violent – and she became a reporter, distributing photographs of those wounded and killed in the events as well as collecting the testimony of the martyrs' families. Her blog served as a main source of information for a number of foreign journalists, for she recounted what she observed on the ground, following in the tradition of women of the 1980s in their struggle against censorship and contributing to the youth movement that aided the Tunisian revolution via blogs, mobile phones, YouTube and Facebook.

The wider Tunisian public discovered Lina Ben Mhenni when she was nominated, to general surprise, for the 2011 Nobel Peace Prize, for her blog *Tunisian Girl: Blogueuse pour un Arab spring* and as a representative of the Arab Spring. A short book of about thirty pages based on her blog and with the same name, *Tunisian Girl*, was published in France by Indigène Editions and translated into German and published as *Vernetzt Euch!* by Ullstein-Verlag in 2011. After her nomination for the Nobel Prize was announced, she faced a number of criticisms from both within Tunisia and abroad. Among these, Bouthaina Sha'aban wrote that 'Meherzia Laâbidi and Lina Ben Mhenni are two sides of the same coin ('*Meherzia Laâbidi et Lina Ben Mhenni sont deux faces de la même médaille*'[8]). The Muslim intellectual Tariq Ramadan criticised both Ben Mhenni and the Western media for presenting her as a muse of the revolution, whereas, in his view, she did not represent those who were behind the revolution and she was not among those who had received training in communications technology.[9] In the event, the Nobel Prize was awarded to another woman activist in the Arab Spring – the Yemeni

8 http://www.tunisie-secret.com/photos/Meherzia-Laabidi-Lina-Ben-Mhenni_gp19918424.html.

9 http://www.youtube.com/watch?v=XImD4P82GFY.

Tawakkul Karman, the first Arab woman to win a Nobel Prize – and to the Liberians Ellen Johnson Sirleaf and Leymah Gbowee. As for Lina Ben Mhenni, in 2011 she received the prize for the best blog in a competition organised by *Deutsche Welle*.

Women and rap music In parallel with these forms of writing, we also hear the emergence of women's voices in rap songs. When rap music emerged in the Arab world, it was basically a masculine form of expression among youth, gaining momentum and continuing after the Arab Spring. This expressive form continued to be controversial, sometimes leading to the arrests of listeners, as in the case of the song *Boulicia Kleb* (Jelassi 2013), and imprisonment of singers such as Kafon and Weld El 15. In this domain, since the Arab Spring, we are now hearing women's voices, extending into the present the practice of Arab women using poetry in song to express their visions, with themes that are socio-political and/or concerned with gender issues. Among women rappers who have become important in public space, we can cite Mayam Mahmoud, the first Egyptian woman rapper, who wears the hijab. She says she was strongly influenced by her mother teaching her poetry, and she sings about rape, abused women and sexism, as in her song 'I won't be the shamed one'. Sultana, a Moroccan, sings about illiteracy, poverty and domestic violence, with one of her songs entitled 'Why do you call me a whore?' Some of her songs pushed for changing the Moroccan law on rape, following the suicide of Amina Filali, who committed suicide after having been forced to marry her rapist, and these legal reforms were introduced as a result of an outpouring of protest after her death (see Chapter 5 by Sadiqi).

In Tunisia, Shayma, who wears her hair in braids, African style, has worked closely with well-known Tunisian rappers such as DJ Costa and Balti. As with the other women rap singers in the region, she sings texts of a socio-political character, and some of her songs' themes overlap with those of Mayam Mahmoud and Sultana.

In 'My brother', she sings about her arrested brother and the difficulties this creates for her family. In 'Factory girls' she deals with societal representations of factory girls, addressing issues such as sexual harassment and rape; this song was in part a response to the widely seen 2008 Ramadan television serial *Sayd Errim* (*The Gazelle Hunt*), a drama directed by Ali Mansour with a screenplay by Rafika

Boujday that won a number of awards, and that portrayed women factory workers as lacking morals. In her song 'Humiliated', she sings about children born out of wedlock, a theme that was the focus of a broad debate in Tunisia in 2011, when Souad Abderrahim, a newly elected delegate to the National Constituent Assembly (ANC) and a member of the Nahdha party (of moderate Islamist orientation), was questioned on Radio Monaco about the rights of single mothers. Her response did not support single mothers and led to a broad debate about the rights of women and children and to a widespread mobilisation among professionals caring for abandoned children, lawyers and women's organisations. Another song deals with the rape of a woman by policemen, based on a true incident that occurred in September 2012 when a young woman was raped by two on-duty policemen. The lawyers for the policemen appeared to attempt to tarnish the victim, suggesting her responsibility for the crime, emphasising the fact that the young woman was not a virgin, claiming that she had regular sexual activity, and so on. The young woman, following her rape, suffered from depression and post-traumatic stress. She published her testimony, under the pseudonym Meriem Ben Mohamed, in France in 2013, with the title *Coupable d'avoir été violée* (*Guilty of Being Raped*).

Rap music, as an element in youth counterculture, gave Shayma a way to be in sync with her age group, to share the worries and hopes of the women of her generation, and to denounce the violence that made them targets.

Conclusion

In this discussion I have highlighted the social, cultural and political aspects of the context in which a feminist literature or a literature of denunciation emerged in Tunisia. First, we have seen that it took several decades after the marginalisation of women oral poets and storytellers for women writers to appear, but now the number of women authors is increasing. The theme addressed by feminists in the 1980s was sexual oppression, whereas in the 2000s they address social and political questions. In addition, we see that women writers are more frequently publishing their autobiographies and letters, or documents and biographies of women in their family who became active in public space (Baccar 2012; Bournaz and Ben Laïba 2013; Medimegh 2007).

Second, the promulgation of the PSC contributed to the spread of a new culture and a new identity from the 1960s onwards, but these were not sufficient to provide answers to the questions that women of all social classes were raising, leading to tensions that filmmakers such as Selma Baccar, Moufida Tlatli and Raja Amari gave expression to. Following the deposition of President Habib Bourguiba in 1987, and again after Ben Ali left power with the revolution of 14 January 2011, women feared that the PSC would be attacked by a growing Islamist movement with its variety of tendencies, signs of which were seen in 1985 when there were calls for a referendum on the PSC, and again in 2012 with the debate over whether the new constitution should refer to women's 'complementarity with men' or to 'equality' between men and women. Many Islamist women believed that a number of the PSC's inadequacies were not being addressed – in this they were in agreement with many feminists, but, under Bourguiba and Ben Ali, they had not been allowed to publicly articulate their arguments in this direction, due to censorship and other limits on expression. And some groups of feminists believe that the PSC has now been superseded by the new constitution, since any discrimination against women would be against the constitution.

During the debates over writing the new constitution and the questions on 'complementarity' or 'equality', the hijab began to appear in online commentary as marking a division between social classes. Those who wore the hijab were referred to in online comments and in demonstrations as *Harza*, a woman who washes others in the *hammam* – a profession among the lowest in the hierarchy of activities. This term also resonated with the first name of Maherzia Laâbidi, a member of the Nahdha party and vice president of the Constituent Assembly. On the ground, the absence of discussion over inclusiveness, over how groups with different orientations might come to mutual understanding and move forward, went along with a weak representation of women in decision-making positions.

Finally, the third aspect concerns the literature of denunciation before as well as after the Arab Spring in Tunisia. This literature is instructive regarding old and recent socio-political conflicts, and we see how women writers such as Sihem Ben Sedrine, Lina Ben Mhenni and Shayma Saeed, from different environments and different generations, were affected by violence and how, later, they approached conflicts, how they responded when faced with injustices affecting the entire society. We have also seen that, whereas for the women writers of the 1980s the book and international solidarity networks were essential, for those of the 2000s mastery of communications technology provides one of the foundations of an expansion of freedom. The nomination of Lina Ben Mhenni for the Nobel Peace Prize for the book growing out of her blog, and the success greeting rap songs seen on YouTube that denounce violence against youth and women, show that a corpus that expresses denunciation of the authorities in power deserves to be taken into account in analyses of the political and cultural situation in Tunisia.

These creative works produced by a new generation of women authors who write or sing without complexes, and the importance of their demonstrating their participation in a culture that is global and universal, contribute to the construction of a humanist feminism and a transnational modernity.

References

AFTURD (2006) *Égalité dans l'héritage: Histoire, droits & sociétés*. Tunis: AFTURD.

Allani, F. (2010) 'La situation de la femme créatrice est, aujourd'hui en Tunisie, idéale'. Interview with Jamila Mejri. *La Presse*.

Ammar, F. B. (2012) 'Justice transitionnelle? Cas du militant "Ridha Ben Ammar" ou l'histoire oubliée'. Babnet Tunisie, 14 September. Available at http://www.babnet.net/festivaldetail-54217.asp.

Arebi, S. (1994) *Women and Words in Saudi Arabia: The Politics of Literary Discourse*. New York: Columbia University Press.

Arvanitis, R. (2007) *Towards Science and Technology Evaluation in the Mediterranean Countries: Final Report*. Bondy, France: ESTIME (Evaluation of Scientific, Technology and Innovation capabilities in MEditerranean countries).

Baccar, A. (2012) *Rafia Bornaz. Militante tunisienne sous le protectorat français*. Tunis: Sahar.

Badran, M. and Cooke, M. (eds) (1990) *Opening the Gates: A Century of Arab Feminist Writing*. Bloomington: Indiana University Press.

Bakalti, S. (1990) 'L'enseignement féminin dans le primaire au temps de la Tunisie coloniale'. *Revue de l'Institut des Belles Lettres Arabes*, 249–73.

Béji, H. (1982) *Le désenchantement national*. Paris: Maspero.

Ben Sedrine, S. (2003) *Lettre à une amie irakienne disparue*. Collection Cahiers libres. Paris: La Découverte.

Benattar, C., Sebai, E.-H. and Ettéalbi, A. (1905) *L'esprit libéral du Coran*. Paris: E. Leroux.

Berrada, M. (2008) 'Women's Writing in Greater Maghreb' in Ashour, R., Ghazoul, F., Reda-Mekdashi, H. and Mcclure, T. M. (eds) *Arab Women Writers: A Critical Reference Guide 1873–1999*. Cairo and New York: American University in Cairo Press.

Binous, J., Harzallah, F., Hamzaoui, S., Ben Romdhane, H., Mahfoudh-Draoui, D. and Tahar-Baklouti, L.-V.

(1992) *Tunisiennes en devenir. Vol. 1: Comment les femmes vivent.* Tunis: Cérès.

Bourdieu, P. (1993) *La misère du monde.* Paris: Le Seuil.

Bournaz, A. B. and Ben Laïba, M. M. (2013) *Mongia Mabrouk Amira: Une tunisienne qui a su donner un sens à sa vie.* Tunis: Sahar.

Bresillon, T. (2015) 'Ibtihel Abdelatif, Présidente de la commission femmes à l'IVD'. *Inkyfada*, 10 July.

Cherni, Z. B. S. (2008) 'Les femmes philosophes en Tunisie'. *Rue Descartes*, 61(3), 105–10.

Chraiet, A. (2013) 'Une goutte d'eau dans l'océan'. *La Presse de Tunisie*, 24 March.

Di Falco, P. (2007) *Le goût de Tunis.* Paris: Mercure de France.

Jelassi, N. (2013) 'Un étudiant arrêté à Hammamet pour avoir écouté la chanson de Weld El 15 dans sa voiture'. *Webdo*, 27 October.

Krifa, A. (2008) 'Modes et limites des résistances à la domination du genre dans les écrits de romancières tunisiennes'. *L'année du Maghreb, CNRS Editions*, IV, 383–97.

Labidi, L. (1987) *Qabla, médecin des femmes.* Tunis: UPPS.

Labidi, L. (1989) *Çabra Hachma. Sexualité et tradition.* Tunis: Dar Ennawras.

Labidi, L. (1998) 'Discours féministe et fait islamiste en Tunisie'. *Confluences* 27.

Labidi, L. (2003) *Romancières sénégalaises à la recherche de leur temps.* Tunis: Sahar.

Labidi, L. (2009a) *Joudhour al-harakat al-nisa'iyya: riwayaat li-shakhsiyyaat tarikhiyya.* [*Origins of Feminist Movements in Tunisia: Personal History Narratives.*] Tunis: Imprimerie Tunis Carthage.

Labidi, L. (2009b) *Qamus as-siyar li-lmunadhilaat at-tunisiyaat, 1881–1956.* [*Biographical Dictionary of Tunisian Women Militants.*] Tunis: Imprimerie Tunis Carthage.

Labidi, L. and Zghal, A. (1985) *Génération des années 30: la mémoire vivante des sujets de l'histoire.* Tunis: Université de Tunis, Centre d'études et de recherches économiques et sociales.

Mabrouk, A. (2001) *Sombre histoire de cellules folles.* Tunis: Alyssa-Editions.

Mahfoudh, D. E. A. (ed.) (2004) *Etude sur le budget temps des femmes et des hommes.* Tunisia: MAFFEPA.

Mamelouk, D. M. (2010) 'Redirecting Al-Nazar: Contemporary Tunisian Women Novelists Return the Gaze'. PhD thesis, Georgetown University.

Medimegh, A. D. (ed.) (2007) *Lettres à Lili. Correspondance d'amour à Tunis. 1943–1944.* Tunis: Cartaginoiseries.

Mernissi, F. (1992) 'Préface' in Binous, J. E. A. (ed.) *Tunisiennes en devenir. Comment les femmes vivent.* Tunis: Cérès.

Milani, F. (1992) *Veils and Words: The Emerging Voices of Iranian Women Writers.* Syracuse NY: Syracuse University Press.

Mosbah, S. (2008a) 'La philosophie des couples'. *Le Temps*, 17 November.

Mosbah, S. (2008b) 'Right of reply'. *Le Temps*, 17 November.

Nazli, H. (2010) *La Princesse Nazli Fadhel en Tunisie. 1896–1913.* Tunis: Editions Sagittaire.

S'kiri, S. (1997) 'Voices of the Marginalized in Tunisia narrative'. *Research in African Literatures (Arabic Writing in Africa)*, Autumn, 3.

Said, R. (1970) *La politique culturelle en Tunisie.* Paris: UNESCO.

Shaaban, B. (2009) *Voices Revealed: Arab Women Novelists, 1898–2000.* Boulder CO: Lynne Rienner Publishers.

Smith, J. C. (2000) 'L'École Rue du Pacha, Tunis: l'enseignement de la femme arabe et "la Plus Grande France" (1900–1914)'. *Clio: Femmes, Genre,*

Histoire, 12.

Sraieb, N. (1993) 'L'idéologie de l'école en Tunisie coloniale (1881–1945)'. *Revue du monde musulman et de la Méditerranée*, 68(1), 239–54.

Tlili, B. (1974) *Études d'histoire sociale tunisienne du XIXe siècle*. Tunis: Université de Tunis.

Yazbek, S. and Weiss, M. (2012) *A Woman in the Crossfire: Diaries of the Syrian Revolution*. London: Haus Publishing.

Youssef, O. (2007) *Le Coran au risque de la psychanalyse*. Paris: Albin Michel.

Zarrouk, R. (2005) *L'amour maternel triumphant*. Tunis. Self-published.

Zeidan, J. (1995) *Arab Women Novelists: The Formative Years and Beyond*. New York: State University of New York Press.

Zmerli, S. (1906) 'L'instruction de la femme musulmane'. Presentation to the Congrès de l'Afrique du Nord, Paris.

5 | THE MOROCCAN FEMINIST MOVEMENT (1946–2014)

Fatima Sadiqi

Introduction

In this chapter I address the fight and struggle of educated urban women within a social movement that interacts with the other two social movements in the country, namely the Islamist movement and the Amazigh (Berber) movement. This does not mean that uneducated, mainly semi-urban and rural women are passive; on the contrary, these women have always expressed their agency through other means, such as oral poetry, community service, art and other means (see Sadiqi et al. 2009; Sadiqi 2014). The Moroccan feminist movement has undergone multiple changes over the past seventy years, and, in the process, has engaged with the issue of women's rights in different ways. This chapter seeks to contextualise the development of the women's movement in Morocco and outline the ways in which it has changed over time.

The women's movement has historically been divided between the secularist trend, which will be described in detail here, and the Islamic trend, which has been a more recent outgrowth. The secularist trend of the women's movement evolved under colonialism and largely represented upper-class, educated women.

During the second wave of the secularist women's movement, during the 1980s and 1990s, women's organisations began to abound and pushed for change to family law, incorporating a greater range of economic classes into their constituency. In many ways, the third wave of the women's movement had its roots in the second wave; however, it expanded its reach through social media, allying itself with the Amazigh activist movement, although its focus remained in urban areas. In contrast, the Islamic women's movement's origins lie in the response to the secularist women's movement, and, in particular, in the Islamist movement's efforts to attract women as supporters. This chapter discusses the evolution of these movements, as well as their ideologies, and compares them, elaborating on the ways in which they interact in the present day and their prospects for the future.

Thus, the Moroccan feminist movement is almost seventy years old. It was born in the heat of nationalist struggle against the French colonisers (1912–56), suffered under state building, gained in maturity with globalisation and political Islam, and emerged in the 2011 Moroccan Spring as a central player in policymaking in Morocco. Born through a document demanding the abolition of polygamy in 1946, the movement developed into a complex social movement in which activists, academics and politicians combine their efforts without always converging. Today, the Moroccan feminist movement is at the forefront of Arab feminist movements. When the movement was born, patriarchy was strong; today, with women's education and access to salaried jobs in the public spheres of authority, patriarchy is increasingly weakened. This movement is characterised by change and continuity, resilience and a capacity to adapt to the paradoxes of tradition and modernity, as well as urban and rural life, amid the turmoil of politics and economic crisis, persistent female illiteracy, and poverty. Conscious that Islam per se was not the problem, but rather the way Islam was used in politics, and that the legal traditions of Islam on which the family was based were man-made, the founders of the Moroccan feminist movement have steadily and over decades – from 1946 to 2014 – made legal rights the backbone of their demands.

This chapter addresses the genesis of the Moroccan feminist movement, with a focus on contextualising its development, comparing its trends, assessing its achievements and failures, and gauging its future. The broader aim of this chapter is to show that women in North Africa confront patriarchy and other sources of authority in various ways. To address these issues, the chapter is organised as follows: it documents and historicises the major trends of the feminist movement, evaluates those trends, and then elaborates on the present and the future.

Two main feminist trends

Broadly speaking, two main feminist trends can be singled out in Morocco: a secular and an Islamic trend. As their names indicate, the major difference between the two resides in the way in which Islamic law is translated into family law. The difficulty of 'Islamicising' secularist thought or 'secularising' the Islamic camp is real and is significantly affected by the conservative–modernist tension that characterises Moroccan society (Sadiqi 2016). The recent post-Arab Spring developments, which, among other things, uncovered a stark failure of political Islam to provide gender equality, further preclude any genuine convergence of the two trends.

The secular trend The notion of secularism in Morocco necessarily includes a dose of religion, since the king is the highest political and religious authority. As such, the secular trend seeks to improve, not replace, sharia law. The secular feminist trend dates back to 1946, when the first women's association was created – Akhawat Al-Safaa. This was the first women's voice in the public sphere. It stemmed from the Parti Démocratique de l'Indépendence (PDI or Democratic Party of Independence), in which the Akhawat Al-Safaa women had male relatives. In addition to demands for the independence of Morocco, these urban and elite women sought to promote girls' and women's education and provide charity to the families of the martyrs. These goals and strategies were dictated by the imperatives of the then colonised Morocco: the struggle for independence (with pervasive nationalism), the promotion of written Standard Arabic (in contrast to the 'dialect' or spoken Arabic) in the face of colonial French, the respect of Islamic tradition (in the face of French 'modernity'), and the promotion of urban ideology (maintenance of a class system). The feminist aspect of this association resided in its women's personal and communal aspirations and their public speeches, of which only one survives; this was called 'al-Wathiqa' ('The Document') and it is the first written text by a woman in modern Morocco (Sadiqi et al. 2009). This text embodied three main demands: the abolition of polygamy, dignity at home, and dignity outside the home. The nature of these demands and the attraction modernity held for their class position these pioneer women as 'secular'.

The Akhawat Al-Safaa feminist spirit and message continued after the independence of Morocco and has developed up to the present day in parallel with the ups and downs of the Moroccan society and state. The postcolonial neo-patriarchy (a mixture of modernity, state feminism and patriarchy) as well as globalisation and Islamisation have had an impact on postcolonial, secular feminism. With the advent of the new millennium, state Islamism, sophisticated technology and the recent uprisings in the region, secular feminism has adjusted to the new developments and has attempted to bridge the generational gap. In the process of doing so, it seems to have experienced some kind of renewal with the emergence of two new players on the public scene: youth culture and Amazigh activism (which is related to a centuries-old, women-related, marginalised language, which became an official language after the recent uprisings).

Post-Akhawat Al-Safaa secular feminism has witnessed three major waves: the pioneers or first wave (from 1946 to the end of the 1970s), the second wave (1980s and 1990s) and the third wave (2000s to the present). Although they share secularism as a common tenet, the three waves differ in their overall historical and socio-political background. Together, they constitute a continuum that has regenerated itself from within and that has been having a profound impact on Morocco's politics and gender policies. This was made possible partly by the fact that secular feminist thought was grounded in universal human rights and avoided religion without dismissing it. For example, patriarchy and not Islam was constantly defined as the source of oppression. Without supporting sharia as the main source of legislation, secular feminists have been keen to include civil law and the resolution of human rights conventions, as adopted by the United Nations, as other frames of reference. Like any social movement, secular feminism ranges from extreme to moderate attitudes towards Islam: radical secularists privilege rationality, consider religious texts as inherently anti-women, and highlight modernity as the sole path to guaranteeing women's rights. As for the moderate trend, they focus more on international human rights conventions than Islam as a basic reference, and when they address religious issues, they focus on *maqasid al-shari'a* (goals of sharia law) more than sharia itself and encourage the re-reading of the religious texts in the light of social changes in society. Moderate secular feminists fluctuate between seeing Islam as valid for all times and places and using Islamic principles to justify a modernist approach.

The first wave was constituted by the first generation of women who benefited from education and, more importantly, who communicated their thoughts in the public sphere of authority. Most of these feminists belonged to the urban upper and upper-middle classes and were aware of the fact that, although they belonged to well-off families, they did not have the same opportunities and choices that their male counterparts enjoyed.

The larger socio-political context that characterised the first wave was marked by a combination of state building and post-colonialism, which reinforced the 'modernity-tradition' cohabitation in the lives of women. Within their families and communities, these women felt privileged in comparison to the women of lower classes and rural areas, but, at the same time, they knew that they lacked status when compared with the male members of their class. For example, after independence, many women had husbands positioned in various chambers of power, with the prospect of marrying younger women. They also felt crippled by oppressive legislation. Indeed, the first family law, promulgated during the November 1957 to January 1958 legislative session, obliged women to obey their husbands, who could repudiate them at will and without justification. These women were aware that, on the one hand, French colonisation deeply disrupted Moroccan traditional modes of living, while, on the other hand, the Moroccan and French modes were doomed to coexist and interact. Much as they felt the heavy burden of tradition, they also understood that women were significantly instrumentalised in accommodating the competing sets of paradigms that the two modes and lifestyles brought about.

For example, during the struggle for independence (1912–56), both the nationalists and the colonisers capitalised on women in implementing their opposing agendas. The former saw in women the gatekeepers of tradition and, hence, restricted their roles to ensuring family cohesion and bringing up 'appropriate' future citizens. The latter, on the other hand, saw in the female elite a guarantee for the dissemination of Western norms, values and lifestyles. Women's status and appearance served both agendas in different ways; whereas the women's *djellaba* and *litham* were adopted as signs of nationalism and authenticity, Western attire was adopted as a measure of the spread of modernity. A *djellaba* is a long garment that covers the whole body, with a hood that may be used to cover the head as well, and is the Moroccan national attire. It was first used by men, then by both sexes. As for the *litham*, it is a piece of cloth that women put over their nose and mouth.

In spite of the central position of women in both the nationalist and the colonialist agendas, neither of these were genuinely interested in the education, let alone promotion, of women for their own well-being. The pioneer secular feminists were caught between these two powerful poles of tradition and modernity and endeavoured to make the best of both. The first wave saw in tradition a comforting anchor of identity, and in modernity a path to emancipation, salaried work and self-esteem. Although the use of Arabic was maintained, the general tendency of this political strain leaned more towards the use of French because it facilitated the expression of taboo topics and allowed a space for free expression for many of these early feminists. French also allowed these women to inscribe themselves in an interesting nascent Moroccan Francophone literature, which, although couched in French, transmitted a Moroccan content, often manifested in local imagery, folk culture and values.

To publicly voice these concerns, women of the first wave wrote journalistic articles on the need for girls' education, the need to balance tradition and modernity, the need for legal reforms, and the need for women's access to politics. They continued the pre-independence call for the education of girls. Indeed, Malika Al-Fassi published an article entitled 'On young women's education' in the Arabic magazine *Majallat Al Maghrib* (*Morocco's Magazine*) under the pseudonym of *Al-Fatat* ('The Young Girl') as early as 1935. Besides the education of girls, the first Moroccan journalists called for 'unveiling with decency' as an 'answer' to the political climate of the time. Along the same line of thought, Zahra Chraibi published an article on the theme in Arabic in the mainstream *Al-Alam* newspaper (see Sadiqi et al. 2009).

In addition to journalism, scholarship, political engagement and activism were used by the first wave activists. However, the nature and discourse of the first wave started to change as a result of the dramatic global events that marked the end of the 1970s and the beginning of the 1980s: the success of the Iranian revolution in 1979, the downfall of the Soviet Union in 1989, and the gradual emergence of the US as the sole superpower. Political Islam was brought about by the first event, bolstered by a weakening of the leftist ideology at the time of the second event, and globalised with the third one.

It was political Islam that impacted the second wave of secular feminism. The main change in this wave was partly located in the female 'newcomers' to the movement: younger, educated urban women from lower social classes, some with rural backgrounds. This made the then feminist community more heterogeneous class-wise and more discursively polyvocal. The strategies used by the second wave of secular feminism were twofold: on the one hand combining politics and activism, while on the other utilising scholarships and journalism.

In matters of politics and activism, the second wave feminists quickly realised that their issues and demands had never constituted a priority in Moroccan national history, nor in the ideologies of the country's formal post-independence political parties (Daoud 1993; Naciri 2008). As a result, young university women entered leftist (then opposition) parties en masse. The political climate of the time was conducive to militantism within leftist parties and organisations as a way to express anger with an authoritarian regime and a class-based oppressive social system that excluded growing masses of poor and illiterate populations. King Hassan II's regime was particularly oppressive in the 1970s and at the beginning of the 1980s, especially after the failure of the two military coups that marked the beginning of the 1970s. The feminists of the time were torn between their feminist commitments and their political allegiances. The male-dominated and hierarchical structure of the leftist parties, as well as their focus on broader national issues, pushed feminists to organise themselves in independent women's associations (non-governmental organisations or NGOs) without discarding their leftist orientation. The first such association was L'Association démocratique des femmes marocaines (ADFM or Democratic Association of Moroccan Women), which developed from the Communist Parti du Progrès et du Socialisme (PPS or Progress and Socialism Party) in 1985. In 1987, L'Union de l'action féminine (UAF or Union of Feminine Action) developed from L'Organisation de l'Action Démocratique et Populaire (OADP or Organisation of Democratic and Popular Action). The creation of these two NGOs marked not only the birth of women's activism in the public sphere of power, but also the subsequent feminisation of this sphere as hundreds of feminist associations of various sizes followed suit. This, in turn, played a significant role in the democratisation of the public sphere. When the Socialist Union for Popular Forces took power in 1998, the second wave feminists gained considerably in visibility and decision making, not only in numbers (more than five women were promoted to the executive body of the party) but also qualitatively, by pushing women's issues to the forefront of national politics. Further, in their strategies, they both criticised and supported the governments of their time. They criticised the government for deprioritising women's issues, while at the same time supporting it in the face of growing Islamism. The actions of the two pioneering associations expanded from social services to consciousness raising, which made them into serious mobilising forces. They offered psychological, medical, and legal assistance to women victims of violence, as well as literacy classes and legal knowledge to large numbers of beneficiaries in urban areas. They also put pressure on the state to reform family law along CEDAW (Convention on the Elimination of all Forms of Discrimination Against Women) principles.

In 1992, UAF spearheaded the One Million Signatures campaign to reform the family, which led to the first reforms of this law in 1993. The main substantial changes in the 1993 reforms were that a father would no longer be able to compel his daughter to marry, a mother was ensured legal guardianship of her child, and a woman must consent to marry by signing a register witnessed by officials appointed by the Minister of Justice. Although disappointing in other ways, these reforms stripped family law of its 'sacred' aspect and, as such, constituted a symbolic breakthrough. As a reaction to the 1993 reforms, a coalition between the first socialist government, which came to power in 1998, and political parties and women's associations led to the *Plan pour l'Intégration des Femmes dans le Développement* (*The Plan for Integrating Women in Development*), also known as 'The Plan'. This plan was spearheaded in 1999 by the then socialist Secretary of State for Social Protection, Family and Children, Mohamed Said Saadi. The main demands of the Plan included a rise in the minimum age of marriage for girls to eighteen, the prohibition of matrimonial guardianship, the registration of children born outside wedlock under their mother's name, the legalisation of all types of divorce, the abolition of polygamy, and the division of accumulated wealth between spouses upon divorce.

The political and activist endeavours of the second wave of secular feminists were reinforced by a combination of scholarship and journalism. Much of this literature was aimed at deconstructing Morocco's gendered history and highlighting marginalised voices, including many women's voices. Women's legal rights, the veil and public freedom were at the heart of this multilingual literature (in Arabic, French and, to a lesser extent, English). However, like the first wave, the second wave of Moroccan secular feminists did not address Amazigh issues despite the secular nature of the latter. These issues had to wait for the third wave.

The third wave of secular feminists grew from a rather complex socio-political context in which four major factors intersected: identity, Islamism, globalisation and new technology, and the uprisings in the region. It is a more versatile and complex wave in terms of class, level of education, affinity to Islam, language, gender, strategies and internationalisation. More lower-class and multilingual youth, both male and female, are making their feminist voices heard. The use of Moroccan Arabic and Amazigh for texting, Facebook, Twitter and other social media facilitated this, and the images of the revolutions in the region added more fuel.

Of the four factors that shaped this wave, the most spectacular one was identity politics, which 'transformed' Amazigh from a marginalised to a fully fledged official language in the new 2011 constitution. In a parallel way, and significantly, the new constitution also recognises equality and parity between the sexes (Article 19).

Men and women enjoy, equally, the rights and freedoms of a civil, political, economic, social, cultural and environmental character, as announced in this article and in the other provisions of the constitution, as well as in the international conventions and pacts duly ratified by Morocco, and, in respect of the provisions of the constitution, of the constants (*constantes*) and the laws of the kingdom. The state works for the realisation of parity between men and women.

As a result of this constitutional article, a new body called the 'Authority for Equality and the Fight against all Forms of Discrimination' was created to ensure that women's rights are safeguarded. As an offshoot of this 'Authority', the Forum on Parity and Equality was created to ensure the implementation process of Article 19. Also, a new section of the constitution called 'Libertés et Droits Fondamentaux' ('Liberties and Fundamental Rights') includes Articles 32 and 34, with statements concerning the rights of women, children and the disabled; Article 21, which prohibits sexism; Article 59, which safeguards these rights and liberties during states of emergency; and, most importantly, Article

175, which states that these rights cannot be retracted in future constitutional revisions.

The fates of the Amazigh (Berber) and women have always been parallel. The two groups were marginalised during the Protectorate and state-building period, and they have almost synchronistically invested in the public sphere of authority. Feminist consciousness is increasingly congruent with Amazigh consciousness, since the two share secularism as a guiding tenet. This has translated into reciprocal networking on the ground. Hence, the secular feminist Spring of Dignity Network, a coalition of twenty-two secular feminist associations, originally created in 2008 but reinvigorated in the aftermath of the uprisings in the region, supports the Amazigh movement's own initiative of One Million Signatures to implement the new constitution. Furthermore, cultural rights have been added to secular feminist demands, and Tifinagh (Amazigh alphabet characters) are now systematically included in secular feminist slogans.

The third wave has also redefined the feminist stance with respect to Islamism, which is now part and parcel of the government. Indeed, the Islamist Parti de la Justice et du Développement (PJD or Justice and Development Party) won the 2011 elections and took power for the first time in the modern history of Morocco. Disillusioned by the failure of mainstream national parties and attracted by the Islamist 'corruption-fighting' slogans, many young and less secular Moroccans gave this Islamist party a 'pragmatic' rather than a religious vote. However, after a couple of years, the Islamists proved to be just like the other parties, failing to deliver on issues such as employment, and, as a result, their failures have somehow 'demystified' political Islam. This disillusionment with political Islam in Morocco was further intensified by the failure of the Muslim Brotherhood in Egypt and the pragmatism of Moroccan youth. Another factor that greatly neutralised the impact of Islamism in Morocco was the fact that democratic transition in the country took place long before the uprisings in the region, and activism as well as the policies targeting women's roles and rights were part and parcel of this transition, as shown in the previous sections. The recent (and unexpected) victory of the secularist camp over the Islamist one in Tunisia is a further blow to political Islam in Morocco.

In addition to identity politics and Islamism, new technology, an offshoot of globalisation, has had a huge impact on the third wave.

By facilitating communication and democratising the linguistic landscape through the use of Moroccan Arabic or Amazigh (mainly written in the Arabic and Latin scripts), or a mixture of both, for emails, Facebook, Twitter, YouTube, mobile phone texting, blogs and street advertisements, the new social media affected the third wave of secular feminists in significant ways. Internet-based tools allowed a quick and relatively unregulated sharing of information, which appealed to the youth of this wave.

Finally, the 2011 uprisings in the region affected Morocco by leading to the 20 February Movement. This movement did not demand a regime change, as was the case in Tunisia, Egypt and Libya, but it certainly gave renewed vigour to, among other movements, the feminist secular movement. On 20 February 2011, crowds gathered across Morocco asking for more legal, civil and cultural rights, as well as freedom and dignity. The king responded quickly, and within two weeks, important constitutional reforms were announced. These reforms were approved in a referendum on 1 July 2011, by 98.5 per cent of voters.

The main strategies that the third wave of secular feminists have used include (virtual) activism, scholarship and journalism. With respect to activism, the core ideas of the second wave re-emerged with the third one. For example, March 2011 saw the creation of the 'Spring of Feminist Democracy and Equality', a coalition of a thousand organisations working for human rights and the rights of women, which presented a list of demands to the Advisory Committee for the Revision of the Constitution. Among their demands was the state's commitment to combat all forms of discrimination against women, and to ensure gender equality (a 50 per cent quota for women) in all fields, including decision making. They also demanded that the constitution recognise the principle of the indivisibility of human rights, so that women could enjoy their civil, political, economic, social, environmental and cultural rights. Finally, they demanded that the constitution enshrine the primacy of international law over national law. Thanks to their pressure, most of these demands were satisfied in the 2011 constitution.

Women's post-2011 legal gains were not, however, matched by similar advances at the social and political levels. For example, in the parliamentary elections of 2011, there were only sixty-seven women MPs elected out of 395. Admittedly, this was a step forward compared with previous elections, where only thirty women MPs were elected; however, it was expected that at least a third of seats would be allocated to women. More significantly, there was a drastic decline in the number of women ministers, from seven in 2007 to only one in 2011. This was somewhat remedied by the inclusion of five more women in the second version of the Islamist government in 2013. Four of the five new ministers were appointed only as deputy ministers and not full ministers, which implies that women are still not judged able to lead ministries. An MP described these new deputy ministers as the 'harem' of the government. This new incarnation reduced the space of the Islamists in decision making, since they now need to share more power with other parties.

The third wave of secular feminists also gained more strength in fighting violence against women. Thus, for example, the March 2012 suicide of the sixteen-year-old Amina Filali, who swallowed poison after being forced to marry her rapist, pushed the Equality Now association to issue an act demanding legal reforms to strengthen punishments for sexual violence and to prevent child marriage. This association demanded the revision of Article 475, which allowed the rapist to marry his victim, a minor, in order to avoid punishment. These demands were advanced in defiance of the silence and inertia of the Islamist-led Ministry of Solidarity, Women, Family and Social Development. The Equality Now Act led to national dialogue and heated debates in parliament, and, finally, in February 2014, Article 475 was revised, precluding the exemption of the 'kidnapper' from punishment if he marries his victim and raising the sentence in such cases to thirty years of prison: a great victory for secular feminist civil society.

As for virtual activism, it may best be illustrated by the role of women in the 20 February movement, created in the context of the uprisings in the region. This movement was partly started by a young woman, Nidal Hamdache Salam,[1] who initiated a Facebook forum discussion on the political and socioeconomic issues in contemporary Morocco. The separation of the executive, legislative and judiciary, individual freedoms, secret detention centres, the corruption of state elites, nepotism, clientelism, regular violations of human rights and

---

1 See https://www.mamfakinch.com/printemps-marocain-le-role-des-femmes-par-osire-glacier/ (accessed 4 October 2016).

personal freedoms, as well as unequal access to education, healthcare and work were discussed in this forum. Videos calling on people to demonstrate in big cities followed, and the movement materialised in large demonstrations on 20 February 2011. Hamdache coordinated the Youth Commission of the Moroccan Association for Human Rights and was instrumental in mobilising youth. It is reported that more than 50 per cent of the protesters in the movement were women.

Even after the king's speech of 9 March 2011, when substantial reforms of the constitution were announced, the 20 February movement continued to demonstrate. Its main demands addressed the fact that members of the commission in charge of the reform of the constitution were appointed by the king and were not democratically elected by Moroccan citizens. Such demands were instrumental in changing the Moroccan political scene. Ups and downs in the intensity of the movement followed, but, regardless of its fate, there is no denying that it brought people onto the street and united them across age, class and gender. It is important to note that the struggle of the third wave was robustly supported by associations that the second wave started. For example, the ADFM issued a report in support of maintaining women's rights when the new constitution was being written (see ADFM 2012).

Islamic feminism Although the expression 'Islamist politics' makes sense, 'Islamist feminism' does not because it is contradictory. In other words, while a feminist discourse may be Islamic, Islamist discourse cannot be feminist. Islamic feminism is an intellectual endeavour, which denotes an awareness of gender power dynamics that privilege men and that are enshrined in family and society as part of Islam. As such, it is mainly concerned with women's rights, gender equality and social justice from within an Islamic framework (Badran 2005, 2008). Islamic feminism is often geared towards using gender as an analytical tool to produce *Ijtihad*-based (progressive interpretation of the Qur'an) reforms that offer new women-friendly interpretations of the sacred texts. It is thus anchored in the discourse of Islam as put forward by the Qur'an (Holy Book) and the Hadiths (Sayings of the Prophet). Islamic feminism has triggered a substantial body of literature in non-Muslim majority democratic countries (Barlas 2002; Cooke 2001; Mahmoud 2005; Mir-Hosseini 2006; Moghadam 2009; Wadud 2006).

In Morocco, Islamic feminism is a relatively new reality that has emerged in the heat of the 1990s ideological crisis over the woman issue. According to Meryem Yafout (2008), Islamic feminism started in the 1970s, but the developments were not homogeneous enough to create a genuine movement at that time. However, the later debates in the 1990s around the reform of family law involved the modernists (feminists and democrats in general) and conservatives (traditionalists and Islamists in general) in opposition. The scale of the debates was large and involved the entire nation, transcending parliament and making their way to the street, the university, the mosque, and the home. The first peak of this ideological confrontation was the political turmoil and social anarchy that followed the above-mentioned 1992 One Million Signatures campaign to reform family law. At that time, cushioned by the support of the monarchy, the left, the state and secular feminists were gathering considerable momentum but also faced fierce resistance from the Islamists. In the midst of this turmoil, the male Islamist leaders of the time realised that the success of their project depended on their ability to 'curb' the female secular feminists by proposing a 'new' brand of 'female veiled Islamic feminists'. Two such female feminists were Bassima Hakkaoui (current Minister of Solidarity, Woman, Family and Social Development in the current Islamist government) and Khadija Messala, a member of the Islamist group in the parliament.

The second peak of the confrontation between modernists and conservatives was the socialist government's plan to integrate women in development, noted above. The Plan provoked a number of *fatwas* (religious decrees) condemning feminists as atheists (hence eligible for death) and depicting them as 'enemies of Islam' in mosques, as well as in cassettes distributed on the street and in public spaces. In addition, bearded men would stand at roundabouts making gestures to unveiled female drivers that they needed to cover their heads, and some women were openly confronted on the streets for not wearing the veil. The Plan itself was demonised as lacking an Islamic reference, and a march was organised on 12 March 2000 to condemn it. In parallel, and along with the male Islamist leaders' 'push' for veiled women's visibility in the public sphere, more Islamist associations were created and the Forum Azzahrae pour les Femmes Marocaines (Azzahrae Forum for Moroccan Women) was founded in 2002 as an umbrella network covering these associations. On 16 May 2003,

Moroccan extremist Islamists killed forty-four people in a terrorist attack in Casablanca. Most of the victims were Moroccan, but some foreigners were among the victims. The confrontation between the modernists and the conservatives cooled off after these attacks, the subsequent state crackdown on the Islamists, and moderate Islamists' decision to participate in the government.

These events show that Islamic feminism was initiated and largely instigated by male Islamist politicians' tactics to counter secular feminists who were gaining considerable momentum. The Islamists saw in this Islamic feminism an arm of their ideology that would both counter the then sweeping trend of the secular feminists and earn them more followers, especially among women, most of whom were illiterate. The veil was heavily instrumentalised during this period. The international scene, especially the first Gulf War, accelerated the spread of Islamist ideology among the Moroccan population. In addition, large portions of older educated middle-class women embraced a form of Islamist ideology, veiled, and performed pilgrimage to Mecca to make up for their guilt-related feelings due to absence from the mosque. This particular phenomenon was enhanced by the rapid spread of 'modern preaching' by the young Egyptian accountant Amr Khalid. It is important to note that, generally speaking, the veil does not mean the same thing for men and women in Morocco. Whereas most veiled women see their veiling as a token of emancipation from male control, most Muslim men see in it a sign of obedience.

Gradually, female Islamic feminists started to appear on the scene, first to support the political Islamist project and later to challenge the paternalism within this movement. The majority of Islamic feminists acted more as politicians than feminist scholars. This was largely the result of the fact that the Islamists succeeded to a great extent in collectivising a larger segment of laywomen to endorse the ideological viewpoints of the Islamist movement.

There are two types of Moroccan Islamic feminists: the moderate PJD feminists and the more extremist Justice and Benevolence (JB) Association feminists, both of whom align with the political ideologies of their respective parties. For both types of feminists, the biological difference between men and women leads to different social statuses and different rights, and hence equity, and not equality, should be their target. For these feminists, gender justice is perceived in terms of equity (difference based on biological difference), and not equality (similitude). This perspective maintains and reproduces the complementarity of sexes, and the division of sexual labour. For Islamic feminists, it was not a question of applying equality to Islam, but of applying correctly the textual predispositions to equity within Islam. In other words, the question to explore was not the extent to which textual predispositions were egalitarian, but how male Muslims had never ceased to betray them since the Umayyads of the seventh century. While secular feminists talked about how insufficient Islam-accorded rights were, Islamic feminists spoke only about the non-application and violation of these rights. It was not a betrayal of the ideal of equality that was at stake, but a rupture with the imperative of equity. That is why neither equality in inheritance, nor equality in the number of spouses (polygyny), nor equality in the choice of a spouse (the right of a Muslim woman to marry a non-Muslim) were debated from an Islamic perspective. In a sense, equity was presented as the legal and legitimate inequality of rights and seemed to be founded on a rejection of individual autonomy, as a woman was first and foremost a wife and a mother (the pillar of the household and the first vector of values). All in all, the project of Islamic feminists in Morocco was a moral order doubled by the traditional political patriarchy founded on sexual discrimination.

Both the PJD and the JB count large numbers of female feminist members. These women share a number of characteristics: a strong belief that Islam provides women with rights, an adherence to the veil, work within the ideological tenets of the party or association with which they are affiliated, a belief in complementarity (instead of equality) between men and women and between rights and obligations, and a tendency to consider women's problems within the whole context of the family, and not as individual matters. However, there is a difference between the two groups: the JB women are more vocal and outspoken than the PJD ones. A reason for this may be that the JB association is not recognised by the state, hence the apparent erasure of gender and class in its discourse. However, the death of Sheikh Yassine in December 2012 created a gender issue within the association, and, as an outcome, his daughter, Nadia Yassine, who was also the mouthpiece for women's issues in the association, has been distanced from politics. While these female Islamists refute the idea that women in conservative parties are silent, they also present

Islam as the only source of women's rights. The main channels that Moroccan Islamic feminists use to disseminate their thoughts and ideas are preaching, activism, and to a certain extent scholarship.

The topics of preaching revolve mainly around how a believer should live and practise his or her religion. For example, Islamic feminists both advise women on how to practise their faith and, at the same time, disseminate the socio-political perspective that Islam has become misguided due to political interests and misogynistic readings. As for activism, it is largely composed of the organisation of religious gatherings and study groups to empower women and to allow them to transform their roles in their families. The inspiration they get from the lives of the Prophet and his companions is very positive for most women. As far as scholarship is concerned, it includes a reading of the Qur'an from a feminist point of view.

In addition to the PJD and JB Islamic feminists, two other types of Islam-based feminism are found in Morocco: 'self-based' and 'state-based'. While the latter is widespread and may include feminists from the PJD party or the JB association, the former is rather restricted to a few women and is independent. The two types are also characterised by non-affiliation to a unifying Islamist movement or association. Both start from using the Qur'an and Hadiths to support equality between the sexes and to underline the egalitarian and universal message of Islam. An example of self-based feminism is Asma Lamrabet, a pathologist and writer. Although she wears a 'modern' veil, Lamrabet does not see the veil as mandatory. According to her, by focusing on the veil, theologians reduce women to 'bodies' and de-emphasise the fact that Islam is a religion of equality, knowledge and compassion, values deemed by her as more important than the veil. Furthermore, Lamrabet leans towards more involvement in female *ijtihad* and the production of fatwas.

As for state-based Islamic feminism, this appeared in the aftermath of the 2003 terrorist attacks in Casablanca as a state attempt to control and monitor the religious field in order to eradicate terrorism, and as a way of developing a positive international image of Morocco. To achieve these goals, in 2005 the state, through the Ministry of Endowment and Religious Affairs, created the Islamic association Munaddamat at-tajdid Al Wa'y Al-Nisaa'i (Organisation of the Renewal of Female Consciousness), with the benediction of the moderate Islamists and the *Ulamas* (religious leaders). The main mission of this association was the 'nesting' of an 'Islamised' version of feminism, which would channel the shared interests of the state and its allies and ensure their positioning as 'democratic' and 'open' vis-à-vis the national and international community. The Ministry of Religious Affairs was also in charge of training and supervising the first cohort of female religious preachers or guides (*Murshidat*) in 2005, a pioneer move in the history of Morocco (Ennaji 2011). This move was facilitated by the status of the king as *Amir al-Muminin* (Commander of the Faithful). The *Murshidat* programme was geared towards reviving Islam's tolerance and moderation, fighting radicalisation, and underlining the religious legitimacy of the Moroccan regime. To enter the programme, the would-be *Murshida* needed to be under forty-six years of age, hold a BA degree or an equivalent diploma with high grades, and succeed in the entrance exam (which consisted of an interview in which she needed to prove that she had memorised half of the Qur'an). Since 2005, the programme has been training fifty women each year, and the courses include Islamic affairs, psychology, sociology, computer skills, law and business management, as well as Islamic history and geography, Qur'anic recitation techniques, the art of preaching, and communication.

Upon graduation, the *Murshidat* are assigned tasks that include guiding women (and men) in their religious practices in mosques, as well as in various public institutions, such as prisons, youth clubs and hospitals. This move is revolutionary in itself, since Moroccans in general, and Moroccan women in particular, often find it difficult to seek religious guidance from men on intimate things pertaining to their lives from men. When addressing mixed audiences, the preachers share their interpretations of the Qur'an and Hadiths, but when addressing all-female audiences, they also give advice on private, and sometimes intimate, issues such as how to dress in private and public spaces, how to interact with men in those spaces, and how to deal with sexual problems.

The state also encouraged women to participate in religious lectures during Ramadan (*al-Durus al-Hassaniyya*), in the local scientific councils (*Majalis al 'ilmiyya*), and in the *Rabitat* – councils where twenty out of seventy *Ulamas* are women. Furthermore, *'alimat* (women religious leaders) have been integrated into the regional delegations of the Ministry of Religious Affairs and Habous (state-owned property), where they direct family units. The state endeavoured to keep a balance and to control ideologies, and therefore appropriated some Islamic feminism (Pruzan-Jørgensen 2010). State-instigated Islamic feminism may also be viewed as a response to increasing demands from religiously based women's activists in recent years (Eddouada and Pepicelli 2010).

Given their nature, both the self-based and state-based Islamic feminist initiatives were welcomed by the secular feminists for three main reasons: they draw on the Sufi (rather than the legal orthodox) Islamic heritage in Morocco, they include the principle of equality, and they introduce change in gender relations within a powerful public space, namely religion.

A comparison of secular and Islamic feminisms

In this section, I focus on mainstream Islamic feminism and do not include the state or individual Islamic perspectives. Secular and Islamic feminist trends in Morocco are products of specific contexts in which historical, social, political and international factors intersect. Hence, while secular feminism was to a large extent a product of the leftist ideology, where the political use of religion was de-emphasised, Islamic feminism was the product of an Islamist ideology in which the political use of religion was placed at the forefront. The ideological opposition of these two perspectives makes the two trends intrinsically divergent. In other words, although Islam is in a sense part of both trends, it is not instrumentalised in the same way, hence this is a core difference that gives rise to other divergences, namely on issues of reference, goals, perspective on tradition, religious identity, equality versus complementarity of rights, the gender issue, and knowledge production.

With respect to reference, secular feminists privilege *maqasid al-sharia* (goals of sharia), international conventions of human rights, and universal values. As for Islamic feminists, they privilege the sacred texts: the Qur'an and Sunna. The bone of contention between the two is that, while Islamic feminists resist Western values and acknowledge Islam as the sole source of inspiration for any reform, secular feminists highlight universal values and lean towards an interpretation of the sacred texts that is based more on human rights. This contention is also rooted in the ambiguity that surrounds the way in which sharia and *fiqh* are used. While sharia is more inclusive and refers to regulations and rules that emanate from the sacred Qur'an and the Hadiths, *fiqh* refers to a set of non-sacred regulations and rules that are produced by Muslim scholars. As such, *fiqh* is open to *ijtihad*. It is for this reason that most secularists refer to the goals of sharia that allow changes in *fiqh* according to the changing conditions of women in real life.

The issue of universality is linked to attitudes towards the West. Many Islamic feminists refute the 'universality' of women's secular rights and see these as representations of a particular, not universal, Western point of view – one that contradicts and challenges Islam. This view is linked to the Islamist ideology that opposes modernity and, in doing so, confuses the West with modernity: it takes the West, which may be defined as an incomplete historical manifestation of modernity, for modernity itself.

As far as goals are concerned, while secular feminism targets women's rights, Islamic feminism uses preaching, charity and global activism for the purpose of advancing the Islamist movement, not women's rights. For example, the way in which the secularists and Islamists address women victims of violence on the ground is particularly revealing. Secularist listening centres were created in the aftermath of the Vienna 1993 international convention; their main aim was to fight violence against women through legal action. Whereas secular feminists use 'listening centres' to increase women's awareness of their rights as citizens, Islamic feminists use 'family consulting centres' to reinforce the values of the Islamist project, including solidarity and a justification of polygamy.

The Najma Centre, set up by the secular network Anaruz (the National Network of Centres for Women Victims of Violence in Morocco), was initiated by the secular Democratic Association of Moroccan Women (ADFM), and encourages abused women to speak about their traumatic experiences. The centre also created a free telephone hotline that provides legal help and counselling to women victims of violence. Women victims of violence can either file a complaint with the court or, if they can afford it, hire a lawyer to handle the case. The Islamic counterpart of listening centres, the family consulting centres, were created by a network of Islamist feminine associations called Mountada Azzahrae li Al-maraa Al-Maghrebiya (Azzahrae Forum for Moroccan Women), which covers sixty associations that focus more on the family as an institution than on women as individuals. The main services that these consulting centres offer for free are family reconciliation, psychological and legal instruction promoting family values as the only guarantee for a stable society, and encouragement of youth to seek marriage as a shield against child abuse and sexual harassment. These endeavours are further supported by fieldwork, lecturing, seminars and training programmes on family solidarity. These family centres also reach out to courts and schools to disseminate their ideas. In their strategies, the centres often invoke the Qur'an and divine laws as tools to curb human instincts. The secular and Islamic centres therefore have divergent agendas. While the former emphasise legal action in accordance with the core aims of the secular feminist movement, targeting patriarchal legal Islam, the latter stress family and social solidarity in accordance with the political Islamist ideology which tolerates (and often thrives on) such patriarchy.

The third issue on which the secular and Islamic feminist discourses diverge is tradition. While seen as versatile, dynamic and fluid by secular feminists, at least by the third wave, Islamic feminists generally associate tradition with 'old' practices that counter 'true' Islamic teachings. At the same time, secular feminists tend to combat traditional practices and reject them as acts that diminish women in and outside the family, Islamic feminists stress women's traditional roles as wives and mothers and support a heavy system of proscriptions on how women should behave in and outside the home, with an emphasis on the segregation of the sexes in public spheres. Furthermore, while secular feminists are more vocal in advocating 'progressive' change in women's behaviour and practices, Islamic feminists focus more on 'protecting' the 'threatened' family values.

With respect to religious identity, Islamic feminists highlight cultural identity as an unambiguous Islamic identity, whereas secular feminists generally consider this notion almost obsolete. For the latter, religious identity is part of women's multiple identities, and highlighting religious identity is reductive and crippling as it complicates the treatment of gender inequality, injustice and patriarchy. This is also often seen as highlighting the male establishment as the supreme authority. The focus on religious identity by Islamic feminists makes the discussion of women's issues outside religion almost impossible. This is generally seen by secular feminists as a way of reducing a woman's multiple identities to her religion.

As for the issue of equality and complementarity, the Islamic trend capitalises on men and women having complementary roles in the family, in the sense that a woman may choose specific roles in the family alongside her fundamental roles of wife and mother, and a man may choose other roles in addition to his fundamental role as breadwinner and head of the family. In other words, for Islamic feminists, women's rights are equal to but not similar to men's. Rather than seeing men and women as equal and similar, they are seen as complementary, as having different roles, possibilities and obligations. Islamic feminists' views on complementarity are often challenged by various non-married women such as widows, divorcees, single women and single mothers. Furthermore, Islamic feminists' stance on equality is ambiguous and misleading; hence, while some of them label secular women's rights activists 'un-Islamic', others underline the 'just' and 'equal' nature of Islam. This renders the Islamic feminists' standards and measures of equality rather shaky (Abou El Fadl 2003). Knowledge production in Western countries, where Islam is not state law and where individual freedom is guaranteed, produces an equality-based Islamic feminism; however, this type of equality does not constitute part of Moroccan Islamic feminism.

As for the use of gender as an analytical tool, it is more problematic for Islamic than for secular feminists. The former are not sympathetic to the use of 'gender' as a tool because it disregards differences and complementarity between men and women. Indeed, CEDAW has become the main 'arena' of controversy between the two trends over the utility of the gender category. For Islamic feminists, CEDAW is associated with 'Western individualistic approaches' that seek to make gender relations equal, in contradiction to the Islamic view that considers the family, and not the individual, as the primary entity to be protected. Islamic feminists generally oppose the gender approach on these grounds and often refer to it as 'international interference in Moroccan internal affairs'.

Finally, knowledge production is a domain in which divergence between secular and Islamic feminists is attested. Unlike the former, Islamic feminists lack scholarly rigour and border on political Islam propaganda in their writings. For example, Nadia Yassine's ambivalent attitude to the family law (*Mudawana*) reforms, as reported in the press, is polemical and self-contradictory: in 1999 she was staunchly opposed to any legal reforms, and in 2004 she stated that the laws needed to be more aggressive.

In sum, there are deep and substantial divergences between secular and Islamic feminist trends. While Islam is a reality in Moroccan society and culture, and while politicians may have reached a certain compromise, secular feminism cannot converge with Islamic feminism. The two are poles that cannot meet discursively; otherwise they would have to constitute one discourse.

Concluding remarks: an alternative?

It is important to note that neither the secularist nor the Islamic trend addresses the Amazigh issue per se in spite of the fact that this language is closely related to the third-wave women's movement. This is due to the fact that, geographically, secular and Islamic feminist centres that fight violence against women are concentrated in urban areas, especially the cosmopolitan Rabat and Casablanca. In a sense, both secular and Islamic feminist trends generally represent rural women as 'passive beneficiaries', or 'reasons' for securing national and international funding. Within the post-2011 constitution context, the absence of the Amazigh dimension weakened the Islamic feminist trend and called for a more inclusive secular feminist trend that is rooted in the Moroccan context while keeping a door open to progress. Only this broader-than-Islam approach can neutralise the attacks of the conservatives on secular feminism.

References

Abou El Fadl, K. (2003) 'Islam and the Challenge of Democracy: Can Individual Rights and Popular Sovereignty Take Root in Faith?' *Boston Review*, April/May.

ADFM (2012) *Rapport des ONG de défense des droits des femmes au Maroc au titre du 2e Examen Périodique Universel (EPU) Soumis au Haut Commissariat des droits de l'Homme.* Available at http://lib.ohchr.org/HRBodies/UPR/Documents/session13/MA/ADFM_UPR_MAR_S13_2012_Association DemocratiquedesFemmesduMaroc_F.pdf (accessed 6 October 2016).

Badran, M. (2005) 'Between Secular and Islamic Feminisms. Reflections on the Middle East and Beyond'. *Journal of Middle East Women's Studies*, 1, 6–28.

Badran, M. (2008) *Feminism in Islam: Secular and Religious Convergences.* Oxford: OneWorld Publishers.

Barlas, A. (2002) *'Believing Women' in Islam: Unreading Patriarchal Interpretations of the Qur'ān.* Austin: University of Texas Press.

Cooke, M. (2001) *Women Claim Islam: Creating Islamic Feminism through Literature.* New York: Routledge.

Daoud, Z. (1993) *Féminisme et politique au Maghreb: 1930–1992.* Paris: Maisonneuve et Larose.

Eddouada, S. and Pepicelli, R. (2010/1) 'Morocco: Towards an Islamic Feminism of the State'. *Critique internationale,* 46, 87–100.

Ennaji, M. (2011) 'Women's NGOs and Social Change in Morocco' in Sadiqi, F. and Ennaji, M. (eds) *Women in the Middle East and North Africa: Agents of Change.* London: Routledge.

Mahmood, S. (2005) *Politics of Piety: The Islamic Revival and the Feminist Subject.* Princeton, NJ: Princeton University Press.

Mir-Hosseini, Z. (2006) 'Muslim Women's Quest for Equality: Between Islamic Law and Feminism'. *Critical Inquiry* 32 (Summer), April/ May, 629–45.

Moghadam, V. (2009) *Globalization and Social Movements: Islamism, Feminism and the Global Justice Movement.* Lanham MD: Rowman & Littlefield.

Naciri, R. (2008) 'The Fight for Reform Has Given Much Power to Women's Organisations'. Presented at the 11th International Forum on Women's Rights and Development, Association for Women's Rights in Development (AWID), Cape Town, South Africa.

Pruzan-Jørgensen, J. (2010) 'New Female Voices within the Islamist Movement in Morocco'. *IPRIS Maghreb Review,* October/November, 15–18.

Sadiqi, F. (2014) *Moroccan Feminist Discourses.* New York: Palgrave Macmillan.

Sadiqi, F. (ed.) (2016) *The Center: An Emerging Post-Spring Space for Women's Rights.* New York: Palgrave Macmillan.

Sadiqi, F., Nowaira, A., El Khouly, A. and Ennaji, M. (2009) *Women Writing Africa. The Northern Region.* New York: Feminist Press.

Wadud, A. (2006) *Inside the Gender Jihad: Reform in Islam.* Oxford: OneWorld Publishers.

Yafout, M. (2008) 'Femmes au sein des mouvements islamistes: facteur de modernisation'. Doctoral Dissertation. Rabat, Morocco: Réseau d'excellence des centres de recherche en sciences humaines sur la Méditerranée.

6 | WOMEN'S RIGHTS AND THE WOMEN'S MOVEMENT IN SUDAN (1952–2014)

Samia Al Nagar and Liv Tønnessen

Introduction

This chapter attempts to integrate Sudanese women's history into Sudanese political history, in light of the changing political contexts that Sudan has faced in the post-independence period. In particular, the chapter charts the development of the Sudanese women's movement, from the creation of the Sudanese Women's Union in 1952 to the present day, focusing on ways in which the political context of Sudan has altered and changed these movements. During this time, it is argued, the main emphasis of political debate surrounding women's rights has shifted from the public sphere, including women's role in politics and economic activity, to the private sphere, focusing on family law, divorce, female genital mutilation and child marriage. Since independence, the women's movement has fragmented into different groups, displaying divisions along generational and ideological lines. Most significant of these cleavages, however, has been that between Sudanese secularists and Islamists, who argue in favour of women's rights with a religious rather than a human rights orientation.

Relying on the long-standing engagement of the authors with Sudanese civil society activists with different ideologies and perspectives, this chapter uses interviews as well as secondary literature to chart these developments. It concludes by pointing to the challenges facing these debates in the context of the current political landscape within which the women's movements of Sudan operate.

The political history of Sudan is generally written from a male perspective, and accounts of the Sudanese women's movement are isolated from the larger historical literature. This chapter attempts to situate the evolution of the Sudanese women's movement within this wider historical context. It looks at the shifting foci and strategies for legal feminist action by the women's movement during different military and democratic regimes in Sudan, with a particular emphasis on the latest period of Islamist rule starting with the *coup d'état* in 1989. It is argued that the main emphasis of the women's movement has shifted from women's rights in the public domain, tackling issues such as education, political and economic rights, to challenging women's 'private' rights within the family, by taking up issues such as child marriage, divorce rights and male guardianship. This is partly related to the fact that the earlier women's movement did not call for equality within the family. It is also related to the codification of the Muslim Family Law in Sudan in 1991 for the first time in Sudan's history. While sharia has regulated women's rights in marriage, divorce, custody and inheritance since before independence, this area of law was regulated through judicial circulars formulated by religious scholars, with little or no interference by political authority. By making family law the state law, it also opened up this area of intervention for political contestation. Women activists today are claiming that 'private' rights are pivotal in order for women to fully enjoy their citizenship rights. They are doing this by pointing out the paradoxical treatment of women's legal status within Sudan's laws: for example, while Sudan's constitution from 2005 guarantees a woman's right to become a president, she needs her husband's permission to work outside the home, according to the 1991 Muslim Family Law.

This chapter examines how the Sudanese women's movement has strategised to push for law reform in light of democratic and non-democratic periods of Sudanese history. Although the history of the women's movement in Sudan is rich and long, women have not been able to introduce many pro-women legal changes. Exclusion from political decision making is a factor; however, more importantly, this chapter highlights that the women's movement is fragmented along political lines and polarised along secular–Islamic divides. This has hampered the effectiveness of the movement for adopting legal feminist action.

The analysis in this chapter depends on in-depth interviews and group discussions conducted between 2010 and 2014 by the authors, focusing on law reform and the history of the women's movement. The chapter also relies on secondary literature (books, reports, chapters) on the Sudanese women's movement, much of which has been written by women activists themselves. In the history of Sudan studies, most scholarly accounts of the political development of the country, by both Sudanese and international researchers, are blind to the role played by Sudanese women. Literature is therefore scarce. This chapter is part of an ongoing research effort to critically analyse the history of the women's movement. It relies on our long-standing engagement with women activists from different political parties and ideologies.

Theoretical considerations and regional trends: a framework to understand the Sudanese women's movement

Women's movements, like other social movements, work for social and legal change. To understand the strategies and actions of women's movements, it is important to analyse them against the specific context in which they emerge. That means taking into consideration the political, economic, cultural, religious and social factors that influence the movements' aims or goals and strategies vis-à-vis society and the state. Specifically, the movement's relationship with the state is imperative when it comes to pushing through legal changes. According to Htun and Weldon (2012: 560), 'a *strong, autonomous feminist movement* is both substantively and statistically significant as a predictor of government action to redress violence against women'.

Women's movements in the Middle East and Northern Africa are influenced by both an international human rights agenda and the expansion of Islamic and Salafist influences, which are doctrines that place women's rights within an Islamic frame. These conflicting trends have led to polarisation between secular and Islamic approaches to legal reform, particularly within the area of family law. The women's movement has thus remained divided in many locations in the Middle East and Northern Africa. There are, however, many activists in the region who have started the processes of harmonising feminism and Islam, looking beyond the secular–Islamic binaries (Arenfeldt and Golley 2012: 27). These efforts, often termed Islamic feminism, argue that gender equality and justice as enshrined in international human rights are inherent in Islam. Thus far, legal feminist actions have materialised in Tunisia, Egypt, Turkey and Morocco, but under strict state control. The region is best described as lacking democracy even after the so-called Arab Spring. This leaves limited room for a truly independent women's movement. A complicating factor has also been that political and religious elites have attempted to sideline claims for gender equality as 'Western' and 'alien' to local culture and religion. At the level of society, patriarchal attitudes about women's participation in politics and civil society still prevail. Women activists often run the risk of being accused of 'shaming' their families. These tendencies are also at play in the Sudanese context.

The chapter views women's movements as 'de facto feminist praxis' (Misciagno 1997). Consequently, we start with a perspective that 'the meaning of feminism has changed over time and from places and is often disputed' (Rupp and Taylor 1999: 364). As we go through the history of Sudanese women's movements, we see changes in aims and in strategies. The strategic options available to women activists are shaped by three factors: 1) the existence of a unified women's movement capable of making political demands; 2) existing patterns of gender relations that influence women's access to, for example, arenas of political decision making; and 3) available gender ideologies and how women deploy them to further law reform (Okeke-Ihejirika and Franceschet 2002: 441).

We employ the concept of feminism analytically, meaning that those women's groups who do not necessarily identify as feminist can be viewed as having contributed to legal feminist action. Adoption of a broad definition may be necessary for Sudan in order to consider a broad range of activists, including those groups that do not have an explicit feminist agenda (Grey and Sawer 2008: 5).

The Sudanese women's movement (1952–2014)

The beginnings of a women's movement The history of the Sudanese women's movement started during the colonial period. The policy of the colonial administration was to be sensitive towards traditional and Islamic perspectives on Sudanese women's situation. While they introduced civil law, the area of family law remained within the realm of sharia law (Fluehr-Lobban 1986). Colonial rule reinforced patriarchal structures rather than enabled Sudanese women to challenge them. For example, it put in place restrictive laws on women's right to work outside the home.

The nationalist period of the late 1940s and early 1950s saw the rise and fall of a number of women's organisations and unions. These included the Women's Club, formed in 1944 in Gezira; the

Young Women's Cultural Association, established in 1947; and the Society for the Prosperity of Women (*Jam'iyyat Tarqiyat al-Mar'a*), which was founded in Omdurman in 1947 and was closely associated with the Mahdi family. In addition, women members of the Communist Party organised the League of Sudanese Women (*Rabitat al-Nisa' al-Sudaniyyat*) in 1946, the same year in which the Sudanese Communist Party was established and made women's emancipation part of its main goals. Also, the Union of Sudanese Women Teachers was formed in 1949; in 1951 it changed into a trade union for Sudanese women teachers and submitted a memorandum demanding an increase in the number of girls' schools and an improvement in conditions of service for women teachers. They put equality of wages on the agenda as well as a reform of the labour law that discriminated against married women (Kashif 1984). The union was later amalgamated with the men's teachers' trade union to form a unified trade union of teachers.

Although the interests of these associations supported limited legal changes, there was a growing awareness of the importance of collective organisational activities for changing women's situation. It is important to note that they encountered opposition from traditional and religious groups, which said that women should not participate in public life. The traditional sects, Ansar and Khatmiyya, which later became the two biggest political parties – the Umma and the Democratic Union parties respectively in post-independence Sudan – did not promote women's issues at this point in time (Kashif 1984; El Bakri 1995; Mahmud 2008). The first political party to open up to women members was the Sudanese Communist Party in 1946 (Hale 1986).

The divisions between women's organisations mirrored sectarian politics at the time (Hale 1986). These women's groups reflected the political landscape, and their political space to act depended largely on the political party or the sect's relationship with the colonial rulers. While the Ansar sect, rooted in Mahdism, had a good relationship with the colonial regime, the Communist Party and women's groups faced a more constraining environment. As a result, the development of these women's groups and associations largely reflected the formation of competing political parties and ideologies at the time. The tensions between these political parties were also reflected in the women's groups, with leadership struggles and factional disputes.

The establishment of these women's groups has been regarded as a pragmatic move, orchestrated by the political parties to expand their membership base as 'part of their attempt to influence the educated middle classes by appearing champions of [the] cause of women' (El Bakri and Kamier 1983: 13). This history shows that the polarisation of today's women's movement in Sudan has its roots back in the period before Sudan's independence.

The women's organisations reflected particular class interests. They were based in urban centres and run by the educated middle class. In fact, membership of the organisations was open only to educated women. Thus, they had limited understanding of poor rural women's needs (Al Sanausi and Al Amin 1994). This helps explain why most of the organisations were ultimately dissolved. According to El Bakri and Kamier (1983):

> The basis of these organisations lay largely in the urban middle classes, which meant a general lack of understanding of the real needs of rural women or even of poor urban women, let alone women in remote parts of the country such as the south. They were relatively isolated also from other political groups, such as trade unions, which represented different interests from those of traditional political associations, and which did have specific tactics for change. By the 1950s, and with the intensification of the nationalist movement, a need was once again felt for a new organisation for women which would raise their standard and promote their participation.

In 1952, as a response to the need for a broader membership with more independence from political parties, a handful of women founded the Women's Union (*al-Ittihad al-Nisa'i*). Those women were: Fatima Talib Ismaeil, Khalda Zahir Sarour al Sadat, Jajja Khasif Bedri, Azziza Meki Osman Azrag, Nafisa Abu Bakr al-Mileik, Mahasin Geilani al-Sayed, Thuraya Umbabi, Umsalama Sayed Abd al-Latif, al-Naeim Adam and Nafisa Ahmed El Amin. With the heightened activities of the nationalist movement, educated women realised the need for a new organisation for women to enhance the participation of women in the intensified activities for independence. This 'was a political turning point in the women's movement' (Al-Amin and Magied 2001: 5). The Union's objectives included political and economic rights, the promotion of educational and health services, poverty reduction, and raising awareness. Some prominent Muslim Brothers opposed the formation of the Union (Al-Amin and Magied 2001). However, the Union was supported by male academic scholars, journalists, leaders in political parties, and leaders in the civil service who had either secular, nationalist or leftist agendas. It was also influenced by socialism, regionally and internationally (Abdelal 2003; Ibrahim 1962). This was reflected in the Union's campaign for equal pay for equal work, long maternity leave and other needs of urban female workers. It thus remained urban-based and detached from the poor and rural women's needs, although some members, mostly teachers, formed branches outside Khartoum in Wad Medani, Kosti, El Obeid, Atbara and Port Sudan, and also in South Sudan in Malakal, Wau and Juba. These branches focused mostly on adult literacy, kindergartens and primary schools. However, it largely remained a centralised organisation without organised bases outside Khartoum, according to Fatima Al Gadal, a member of the Communist Party and the Women's Union (Al Gadal n.d.: 9).

Most of the founders were Communists, however, and some had helped to form the Union. Again, it was a group of educated women and literacy was made a condition of membership. Thus, the membership of the Union was dominated by women teachers, nurses, government officials, students, and very few housewives. Political rights were high on the agenda of the Union; already in 1953 the leaders approached the British administration demanding women's participation in elections (Abdelal 2003). Because of this, the Union also suffered from internal conflicts. In 1952, Neimat Alzain had a different view about the Union's approach and therefore formed an organisation in Khartoum, Women's Advancement Association in Sudan, which attracted some educated women, but the organisation stopped functioning with her death in 1957. Another division in the Union came with the defection of two other leaders, Suad El Fatih and Sorya Umbabi, who developed an Islamist orientation. At that time, they were against granting women political rights equal to those of men. These divisions in the Women's Union are reflected even in today's landscape of women's movements in Sudan. Although women's political rights are championed by all political parties, the division between the secular or Marxist approach and the Islamic approach to women's empowerment remains a significant cleavage among contemporary women activists. The Union also faced opposition from some women who tried to form parallel organisations. The women of the Mahdi family were against the Union and thus formed the Women's Cultural Advancement Society in 1952 with very limited objectives for literacy and raising awareness of women's issues. In 1953, some Sudanese and British housewives formed the Women's Cultural Association, with the aim of providing social and religious education in addition to some charity activities. According to Kashif (1984), the latter association was intended to attract housewives away from the Women's Union. Although theoretically and constitutionally there is no link between the Women's Union and the Sudanese Communist Party, according to Sondra Hale (1986), in reality it was organised along the principles of the Communist Party. This connection did not become less pronounced after several prominent members left because of ideological disagreements.

By 1955, the Union was publishing *Sawt al-Mar'a* (*The Woman's Voice*), which was considered to be one of the most progressive publications in Sudan's history and 'played a profound role in raising awareness on women's issues' (Mahmud 2008: 62). It was a platform for the free exchange of ideas, calling for women's rights and liberation. Unlike the Union, the magazine took forceful stands on a range of issues, from neo-colonialism to female genital mutilation (FGM). The general trend of the magazine was leftist. In an interview, Nafisa El Amin, one of founders of the Women's Union explained: 'The Union was trying to fight against harmful practices in weddings and funerals, but it did not consider female genital mutilation as it is a culturally sensitive issue and we were careful to preserve the confidence of people.'[1] Fatima Ahmed Ibrahim was a regular contributor to the publication and the leading spirit behind the Union. The Union also initiated a weekly radio programme from Omdurman radio station under the title 'The Corner of the Sudanese Women'.

A first experience with democracy (1956–58)

The British recognised the importance of the Sudanese involvement in the government during the decolonisation process and created an Advisory Council for the Northern Sudan (ACNS). It

---

1 Interview with Nafisa Ahmed El Amin, Ahfad University, 8 October 2012.

was composed mainly of representatives from the two largest Islamic organisations in Sudan, the Ansar and the Khatmiya, which became the bases for the two largest political parties in post-independence Sudan, the Umma Party (UP) and the Democratic Unionist Party (DUP). The ACNS participated in the Sudan Administration Conference, which defined the steps towards national independence and self-government and resulted in the creation of a legislative assembly in 1948. Agreements signed in 1952–53 defined the process of bringing an end to colonial rule. Britain granted Sudan independence in 1956, handing over political power and control of the army and civil service and management of economic resources to the UP and the DUP. These political parties had a traditional outlook on women's issues and showed no political will in terms of putting women's emancipation on the agenda in post-independence Sudan.

In 1957, the Women's Union held an important conference attended by all political parties. At the conference, it presented its memorandum or programme for the advancement of women's situation, demanding rights to political and economic participation, equality in wages, and family protection. The political parties approved the following demands: equality in pay for working women, maternity leave, an increase in education opportunities for girls, and improved health services for women and children. But only the Communist Party approved of the demand for women's political rights. The political environment thus remained conservative, and it gave little room to women to address sensitive issues. This was exacerbated at the societal level. Only educated women were allowed to vote in the first elections in 1956, and no women were elected to the first National Assembly.

The Union realised that it was not a viable strategy to allow membership only to literate women, and therefore opened it up to all Sudanese women. Union members worked intensively to diversify and increase the membership among grassroots, illiterate women as well as among female graduates. The activities of the Union at the community level included setting up literacy classes, sewing workshops and day-care centres, supporting rotating credit associations, and the formation of housewives' organisations. The strategy of the Union was 'to respect tradition and religion to win the confidence of the people'. According to Nafisa Ahmed El Amin: 'We used to cover half of our faces when going out in public to ensure our commitment to tradition and religion.'[2] According to Sondra Hale (1996: 171), the Union's activities did not reflect efforts to work on the substantial changes needed in grassroots women's conditions. Although the involvement of women in public political activities was an integral part of the Union and an extension of the Communist Party programme, it was not 'related to the women's private lives, their undervalued domestic labor, domestic violence and female circumcision'. There was little consciousness raising on the subject of the oppression of women, and the Union's activities reinforced rather than challenged traditional gender relations. It did not address issues relating to family law. Instead, it regarded these as a private matter outside the realm of politics. Generally, the Union's views on women's rights within the family were not progressive: it did not advocate gender equality within the family. Additionally, it was very careful not to directly criticise sharia or the religious scholars or interpretations. Both nurses and teachers, often through trade unions, continued to put working women's rights on the agenda together with the Women's Union. Although important, these issues did not reflect the concerns of most Sudanese women, who worked in agriculture and the informal sector.

In 1957, the Union tried to call all active organisations for a meeting to discuss whether women could come together as a unified movement. Many organisations, however, refused, because they feared the dominance of the Union and the strong influence of the Communist Party (Kashif 1984). It was particularly difficult to bridge the ideological differences that started to emerge between the Communists and the Muslim Brothers. The Sudanese Muslim Brotherhood, which was originally founded at the end of the 1940s as an independent student organisation at the University of Khartoum, was gaining strength, particularly among students. It was initially called the Islamic Liberation Movement (Harakat al-Tahrir al-Islami) before being renamed the Muslim Brotherhood (Ikhwan al-Muslimin) in 1954. The primary aim at the time was to educate and preach the 'real understanding of Islam, to adopt its teachings and to oppose the atheistic materialism of communism among students' (Zain al-Abdin 2008: 3). It started to present itself as an alternative to the Communist movement and attracted some female students and former leaders of

2 Interview with Nafisa Ahmed El Amin, 8 October 2012.

the Women's Union, including Suad al-Fatih. The Muslim Sisters established the *Al Manar* magazine in 1956 and the *Al Ghafla* magazine in 1957 to present women's issues from an Islamist perspective. The intention was to promote an Islamic alternative for women to the one offered by *The Woman's Voice* of the Union (El Affendi 1991).

The Abboud military regime (1958–64), the October Revolution, and a second experiment with democracy (1964–69)

In 1958, the first military regime took over. General Ibrahim Abboud banned the constitution and dissolved all political parties, trade unions and organisations, including the Women's Union. Although the Union was dissolved, the magazine *The Woman's Voice* continued to operate. The Union also continued to work through housewife cooperatives and with student members at the neighbourhood level. The regime attempted to form an alternative body, the Sudanese Women's Council, but it failed. The regime was ousted by a popular revolution in 1964.

Women participated extensively in the popular October Revolution in 1964. The most concrete result for women was the extension of universal suffrage in Sudan, a political right neither the colonial nor the first post-independence regimes had offered. Al-Amin and Abdel Magied (2001: 11–12) wrote:

> Women, together with other sectors of the society, went out
> of their homes under the leadership of the Sudanese Women's
> Union in a manner that had not been witnessed before.
> They were exposed like their fellow men to different sorts of
> harassment and dangers including gunfire from live ammunition.
> A great number of them were wounded ... This increased the
> vigour of the popular revolution ... the distinguished role played
> by women in bringing about the downfall of the first military
> rule, pushed women's issues to the forefront of the agenda ...
> Women gained full political rights and took part for the first time
> in Sudanese history in the general election.

Following the revolution, the Union's activities resumed. The Muslim Brotherhood also established a new women's organisation called the Patriotic Women's Front (El Affendi 1991). Following women's right to vote, the traditional political parties started to form women's branches to attract the female vote.

In the period of political opening following the October Revolution, important developments included the increase in the number of women in the labour force and the appointment of the first woman judge, Ihsan Fakhri. Also, there was an increase in the number of women in the universities and their prominent participation in cultural and political activities within the university. In addition, there was even an initiative to form an association for university women students in 1964. The Sudanese Women Journalists Association was formally registered in 1968. Youth and women benefited from the opportunities to organise during this brief transition to democratic rule. The youth were active, particularly women university students. Another development was the emergence of organisations with religious orientations, such as the Women Believers Society, founded in 1961, which focused on religious education and whose leader was very active in the public arena.

The Union took the opportunity given by the democratic space and intensified its advocacy for women's rights. In 1965, women gained not only the right to vote, but also to be elected to office. Women exercised their political rights during this period, participating in the 1965 election, and one woman made it to parliament. Fatima Ahmed Ibrahim, a Communist and leader of the Women's Union, was the first woman to be elected to Sudan's National Assembly. Thuriya Umbabi ran for the Islamic Charter Front, the political wing of the Muslim Brotherhood, but failed to gain a seat.

Activism against economic discrimination outside parliament and the loud voice of Fatima Ahmed Ibrahim inside parliament resulted in a decree in 1968 for equal pay for employees with similar qualifications. This, however, was implemented only for women in the civil service and teachers. The Union continued to be active in advocacy for national issues and democracy and thus distanced itself from the needs and interests of its membership. The late 1960s witnessed a decline in its popularity (El Bakri and Kamier 1983: 15). Also, there was a growing generational gap. Fatima Ahmad Ibrahim published an article in *The Woman's Voice* criticising the girls who followed fashion and were wearing short dresses. Some members defended the right of youth to choose.[3] Many objected to the conservative line put in place by Fatima Ahmed Ibrahim,

3 See *The Woman's Voice* [*Swat Al Maraa magazine*], 1968, issue no. 110.

emphasising conformity to Islam. Some were starting to advocate for a secular approach, stating that the Union should also start to address sensitive issues such as family law and FGM. According to Anis (2001: 53):

> In light of women's revolutionary base in civil society and most
> of all its association with the Sudanese Communist Party, there
> is no doubt the WU, as reflected in practice suffered from
> lack of ideological socialist innovation, leadership paralysis
> and a debilitating hierarchal set up that were not conducive to
> empowering women beyond generic political objectives.

Lastly, this period witnessed another attempt to coordinate a unified women's movement. In 1967, the government approached the active organisations, aiming to create an alliance. However, the Women's Union and some of the organisations linked to it refused to participate. The alliance was registered and continued to work until it dissolved in 1970, but it had no real impact on women, as it was formed only to present women's demands in a meeting of Arab heads of state in 1967. The women's movement remained divided along party political lines, and the different groups were not able to come together to agree on a common agenda.

The May revolution and the military regime under Nimeiri (1969–85)

Gafaar al-Nimeiri came to power through a *coup d'état* in 1969 and established a one-party state. This is often referred to as the May regime, which shut down the democratically elected parliament. It first advocated for a radical transformation, following socialist ideology, and established the Sudan Socialist Union (SSU) to encourage popular participation, resolve the problem of the ongoing war in the south, and reform the economy. The programmes of the regime gained the support of the Sudanese Communist Party (SCP) and the Women's Union. One of the first acts regarding women undertaken by Nimeiri and his Minister of Justice, Babiker Awadalla, was to abolish the presence of police enforcement of 'house obedience' (*bayteta'a*). 'House obedience' stipulates that a woman who leaves her husband's house without his permission will be brought back to the husband's house by the police. Thus, the use of the police to enforce a wife's obedience was abolished in 1969. This was one of the few achievements within the area of family law, but it did not challenge the idea of a woman's obedience to her husband.

The Women's Union had pointed to the injustice and repressive character of the police-enforced obedience of wives on numerous occasions.[4] This reform was popular and the Woman's Union organised demonstrations in support of the government's actions that were favourable to the status of women (Fluehr-Lobban 1986). During the first years of his reign, Nimeiri put women's issues on the agenda, partly because women were 'a major constituent in the process of mobilizing and gaining support of the masses. Nimeiri decided to focus on what the previous government had missed, and that included the implementation of women's rights' (Khalid 1995: 190).

Ideological differences between Nimeiri and the Communist Party emerged, and the latter attempted a coup in 1971, after which the party was dissolved and the Union was banned. However, the Union leadership was divided, and some of its leaders decided to continue with the regime, which created its own machinery for women, the Sudanese Women's Union (SWU), which dominated all women's activities and was led by former Union leaders.

The SWU was considered a branch of the SSU and was expected to follow the general framework of the state party, and thus it remained under the strong influence of the President. This is confirmed in an interview with Nafisa Ahmed El Amin, one of the leaders of the Union: 'All decisions are controlled by the President.'[5] This 'effectively means that all women would serve SSU interests first and women's issues would take a second place' (Khalid 1995: 187). The leader of the women's committees in the SSU and SWU's representative in the SSU were chosen by the President, and the secretary-general of the Union was nominated by the President. The SWU's effectiveness in taking an independent political stance or in criticising government policies was greatly limited by its intimate, dependent and subordinate relation to the SSU and the government. Thus, the SWU 'isolated most educated, progressive and committed women, who did not wish to be involved in a structure inhibiting

4 *The Woman's Voice*, 1968, issue no. 108.
5 Interview with Nafisa Ahmed El Amin, Ahfad University for Women, 8 October 2012.

democratic expression and perpetuating the existing status quo' (El Bakri 1995: 207).

By law, the SWU was the only legitimate women's organisation and thus there was no opportunity for other women's groups to work. Therefore, during the sixteen years of military rule, few forums were open to women. The SWU remained the only political, social and cultural organisation for women for almost a decade, and its activities were addressed by specialised government offices. Membership of Nimeiri's union was open to all women above sixteen years of age. A 25 per cent women's quota on local government councils was approved.

The support of the new state-sponsored union was legitimised by the legislative gains achieved during Nimeiri's rule. Most of these gains had been on the Union's agenda since independence. One of the most important was the enactment in 1973 of the Public Service Ordinance, which entitled women to equality with men regarding wages, pensionable services, and any other benefits. Also, working women were given the right to two months' maternity leave, one hour per day of baby care, in addition to four years of leave without pay when accompanying their husbands abroad (Al Nagar 1986).

During the second period of Nimeiri's regime, he underwent a complete ideological shift. As early as 1977, the influence of the Muslim Brotherhood had become apparent. The Muslim Brotherhood became more active in the recruitment of women, and its ideological leader, Hasan al-Turabi, published a pamphlet in 1973 with the title *Women between the Teachings of Religion and the Customs of Society*, advocating a reinterpretation (*ijtihad*) of women's rights in Islam. While the Muslim Brotherhood had earlier been against the political and public participation of women, Turabi promoted and encouraged it within an Islamic frame. Still, the Muslim Brotherhood continued to put forward a view that was conservative on women's rights, in which the role of women as mothers and wives was emphasised. The shift from socialist to Islamic ideology left its mark on the women's movement, particularly after 1983 when the September Laws were introduced. Nimeiri introduced *hudud* penalties under which, for example, *zina* (adultery and fornication) was criminalised. Implementation was harsh.[6] The Muslim Brothers took this political opportunity, supported the state,

6 Interview with Suad Ibrahim Eissa, Khartoum North, 7 October 2012.

and gradually dominated the political scene, including the area of women's issues. The SSU leaders were against the September Laws, as noted by Nafisa Ahmed El Amin, but they were not able to influence the President, who at that time was under the influence of the Muslim Brothers. The Muslim Sisters and socialist unionists were fighting for political recognition, and this might be the reason why the President himself dissolved the Women's Committee of the SSU (Khalid 1995).

The SWU leadership was not only challenged internally by the Muslim Sisters, but also by the underground work of the Union. Although the Union continued to exist as an underground organisation, this signified a severe curtailment of the range of its activities and membership. Still, many educated women who were against the dictatorship of the SSU and the influence of the Muslim Brothers continued their work. The magazine *The Woman's Voice* continued to operate, but 'the only focus was to overthrow the regime. They did not target women's issues holistically.'[7] Thus, the SWU had to deal with two forces that represented conflicting ideologies. The SSU continued to dominate women's activities in the public and political arenas until 1979. At that time, a few non-governmental organisations (NGOs) were allowed to function, one of which was the Babiker Badri Scientific Association for Women's Studies. With the growing influence of the Islamists, however, women started to form their own Islamic women's organisations. One prominent example is *Raidat al Nahda*, which was registered as a charity organisation. These organisations emphasised women's familial and domestic roles. The Islamist groups worked among secondary school and university students and were able to attract many female students. The Islamists' support base was mainly in urban areas among the middle class.

The military regime of Nimeiri did bring about legal changes during its first years, such as the right to leave from work to accompany one's husband, but these did not necessarily challenge prevailing patterns of gender relations. There was no programme for legal reform beyond women workers' rights. Rather, it conformed to the ideals of a patriarchal household. The SWU women have been highly criticised in Sudanese public discourses and activists today

7 Interview with Nour Muhammed Uthman, Omdurman, 13 October 2012.

remain critical, especially since they did not tackle sensitive issues within family law facing Sudanese women. According to Balghis Badri:

> These women were either anti or passive on certain issues. They could have made Nimeiri pass laws. They were not there for the critical things: FGM, the family law … They did not do something substantial. Within the family law, they did not have anything. I do not consider it a movement. It was dissolved after the regime. They could not revive it again.[8]

Also, the gains made for working women were achieved only in the formal sector, ignoring women working in the agricultural and informal sectors (Al Nagar 1986). Despite the fact that the SWU had the state machinery at its disposal and could expand throughout the country to benefit women more widely, it remained an urban middle-class phenomenon. The SWU started to lose support, precisely because it was viewed as an organisation by and for the urban middle class. 'The leadership of the SWU did nothing to deal with issues confronting the majority of women. Instead they limited themselves to the interests of women from [the] middle class, to which most women leaders belonged' (Khalid 1995: 191).

The 'April Uprising' and a third experiment with democratisation (1985–89)

The 1985 uprising came as a result of political suppression, ongoing war in the southern parts of the country, the deteriorating economic situation and the imposition of the September Laws. A national strike paralysed the country and in April 1985 a group of army officers overthrew Nimeiri and established a Transitional Military Council to rule the country. A National Alliance for Salvation was established and included professionals, urban workers, political parties and trade unions. The Alliance signed a charter with a minimum agenda and led the demonstrations and strikes that peacefully ended the era of the May regime. Women participated as members of the professional unions in the preparations for the general strike. Many of them took part in demonstrations. It is important to note that housewives led

8 Interview with Balghis Badri, Ahfad University for Women, 15 October 2012.

some demonstrations, held secret meetings in their homes, and helped to protect the people attending the meetings. However, gender issues were not raised during the strike, being considered of secondary importance in relation to political issues (El Bakri 1995). The Transitional Military Council prepared for elections the following year. The UP, led by Sadiq al-Mahdi, won the popular vote in the 1986 elections, but it also incorporated into its coalition government the National Islamic Front (NIF), headed by Hasan al-Turabi, which gained 20 per cent of the votes. It was not long before the 'modern forces' that had actually led the uprising were isolated from the decision-making processes, which were dominated by a conservative Council of Ministers and the Military Council. The situation was not friendly to women, as they were not represented on the Council of Ministers. They were excluded from the National Alliance as well, since they did not constitute a political party and had no separate trade union. A move for reserving seats for women in the parliament was not approved, based on the argument that it was 'undemocratic' and might raise the demands for seats for other categories, such workers and farmers (El Bakri 1995). Islamic laws that were restrictive to women were not abrogated; instead, a restrictive decree was stipulated, giving women in the civil service only two-thirds of the male officials' housing allowance. In addition, a women's committee was instituted in the department responsible for passports and immigration to enforce restrictions on the travel of women abroad (El Bakri 1995).

The most prominent achievement of the women's movement during the period from 1986 to 1989 was the establishment of women's sectors in most political parties and the representation of women in the top positions in some parties and in key ministries. However, the famine of 1984–86 and the floods of 1988 overshadowed feminist claims to further rights. Sudanese women participated in the 1985 World Conference on Women held in Nairobi and debated the strategies adopted by the conference. However, no initiatives were taken to debate or advocate for the Convention on the Elimination of all Forms of Discrimination Against Women (CEDAW), although at that time, in 1986, Sudan ratified the International Covenant on Economic, Social and Cultural Rights, and the International Covenant on Civil and Political Rights. These conventions gave women several important rights as equal citizens. According to Balghis Badri:

The Sudanese women's movement did not take advantage of the right times of history. Like after the popular revolution in 1985, we signed the convention for political and civil rights, but not CEDAW. We missed our chance.[9]

Sudan, along with the US, Somalia and Iran, has still not ratified CEDAW.

The experiences during the May regime resulted in a continued fragmentation of the women's movement (El Bakri 1995). After the April 1985 uprising, the Union resumed its activities, but excluded the supporters of the May regime. Whereas previous conflict within the Union, especially in its earlier days, had been between the left and the right (especially the Muslim Brothers), during the May regime the conflict was between different factions of the left.

Earlier conflicts had been over issues such as whether women were to be granted political rights and whether such rights were un-Islamic. The new conflict did not relate to the women's movement or its role in Sudanese society. It was concerned with larger ideological issues relating to the extent of support that was given to the May regime. This conflict was damaging to both the women's movement and the left in general (El Bakri 1995: 206).

The developments during the May regime made it difficult, if not impossible, for the Union to be an inclusive organisation and an umbrella for women's groups in Sudan. After Nimeiri, there were at least four categories of women activists: the Islamists, the Communists, those who had supported the May regime, and the rest of the activists, some of whom were members of other political parties. These groups did not interact or cooperate at all.

The principal challenge faced by the Union after the April uprisings was how to transform itself to cope with the changing situation of women. The Union continued carrying out the same activities as before, holding charity fêtes and literacy classes, organising talks on International Women's Day, and mobilising women during elections (Al Gadal n.d.; El Bakri 1995). The ideology of the Union considered the family as an important institution in society, but still its leaders did not tackle issues of inequality, domestic labour burden, or subordination of and violence against women. It did not put family

9 Interview with Balghis Badri, Ahfad University for Women, 15 October 2012.

law on the agenda, and it did not challenge the patriarchal patterns of gender power relations. According to Asha al-Karib:

> Their approach accommodated culture. They did not challenge the dominant discourse at that time, but worked within it. It was a tactical methodology not to challenge the status quo. They never thought outside of the box. For example they did not challenge the family law. This is my critique ... They did not manage to keep up with changes nationally and internationally. They stopped in terms of their thinking/concepts. Their framework froze. Their aspirations were not progressive enough for the women activists seeking gender equality and were too progressive for those who did not believe in equality. Yet it was still claiming to be the guardians of women's rights. As a member I tried to breach this wall and said 'let's move forward' let's move past the dogma of the past ... they did not challenge the discourse. They respected the patriarchy of the family. To some extent, they still talk about it. They do not challenge male guardianship. They did not provoke the system and went for gradual change as a strategy, but they did not think beyond that theoretically. That is problematic ... They put emphasis on enjoying rights women have gained rather than pushing for equality. The Union never accepted the idea of gender equality. They addressed women's issues as part of a context through a class analysis. They did not know what feminism is.[10]

There was a growing generational gap emerging and an opposition to the conservative leadership of Fatima Ahmed Ibrahim. The Women's Union's position was still to conform to traditions and culture, despite vast developments in society, including women's entry on a large scale to universities and the workforce. Issues relating to marriage, sexuality and virginity, which are of great importance to young Sudanese women, were not raised at all by the Union (El Bakri 1995). Fatima Ahmed Ibrahim did not identify FGM as a harmful practice, despite pressures from younger activists. She stated in an interview: 'If we eradicate FGM will it eradicate women's illiteracy or do we get equality as a result? How did FGM constrain women

10 Interview with Aisha Al Karib, Khartoum, 10 October 2012.

from education and work?' (in Mahmud 2008: 146). In the words of Nour Muhammed Uthman:

They [the union] lost their vision and grew out of touch with the international developments. They still maintained the same programme despite vast demographic and social changes. With time, they lost members. The youth did not identify with the movement because of their dinosauric attitudes. They did not manage to bridge generations.[11]

The period of political liberalisation also saw the rise of sixteen women's NGOs, and women activists negotiated issues of building a coalition umbrella for different women's civil actors, including political parties. Nonetheless, their activities remained scattered. Prominent among these organisations was the National Women's Front (NWF), the Islamic counterpart of the Union, which was closely associated with the Muslim Brothers (known at the time as the National Islamic Front). The front was led by two Muslim Sisters who, at a very early stage, had defected from the Union, since they considered that granting women political rights was against Islam. Another organisation, the National Alliance of Women, was formed by the women's sector of the UP in 1985 to represent the interests of Sudanese women, because they considered that the Union represented the Communist Party. The Alliance was to be the official voice of Sudanese women nationally and internationally. It attempted to create special constituencies for women in the 1986 election, but that idea – and the Alliance itself – never came into being.

Most of the writings on women during this period have neglected the Islamic discourse of the Republican Brothers (*Ikhwan al-Jumhuriya*), which was very progressive on women's rights, including on the issue of family law. The Republican Sisters started to be active on issues related to family law as early as the 1970s. They arranged debate forums and issued publications on Islam and divorce, polygyny and women rights in sharia law. Their discourse mirrors the recent discourses by Islamic feminists such as Ziba Mir-Hosseini and Sisters in Islam. However, they were not well received by the Union or by the Islamists. Their leader, Mahmoud Muhammad Taha, was executed for apostasy in 1985 for his controversial interpretations of

11 Interview with Nour Muhammed Uthman, Omdurman, 13 October 2012.

Islam, including on the issue of family law. (For more information on Taha's and the Republican Sisters' stance on family law, see Al Nagar and Tønnessen 2015.[12]) The importance of the Republican Brothers and Sisters was not in their vast popular support base, but in the gender ideology they represented. They made available a completely new way of thinking about the question of Islam and women's rights, one that emerged from within the country, Islam and the culture itself. Still, neither the women within the Union nor the Islamists made use of this discourse to argue for reform. On the contrary, the Islamists objected to the frame of equality and considered the Republicans as a potential political contender for the female vote. The Union, although losing members fast, insisted on an approach that conformed to tradition and it did not agree with the position on equal rights within the family.

The Revolution of National Salvation: a military Islamist regime (1989 onwards)

The period from 1989 to the present has been characterised by the rule of an Islamic political party holding power after a military coup that overthrew a democratically elected government. The Islamist regime undertook the codification of Islamic law to reconfigure women's rights, roles and gender power relations according to a particular – and, in the eyes of many observers, strict – interpretation of the Qur'an.

The Civilisation Project (*al-Mashru al-Hadari*) initiated by the Islamist state in 1989 set out to 'civilise' Muslim women under the umbrella of Islamism through mechanisms that included legislation, indoctrination, education and the use of violence. The Civilisation Project highlights structural shifts in gender relations. In the state's

---

12 Taha's interpretation of Islam is based on the Qur'anic distinction between the verses revealed to the Prophet Muhammad in Mecca and those revealed after his flight to Medina – the first and second messages of Islam respectively. Taha wrote his most famous book in 1967, *The Second Message of Islam (Al-risala al-thaniya min al-Islam)*, stressing that the first message revealed in Mecca is superior to the second message revealed in Medina. The Mecca verses are universal and have everlasting application. In demonstrating the historicity of the second message and its limitations, Taha focused on the specific issue of women's rights and he argued for gender equality before the law (for more information on Taha's work, see An-Nai'm 1996).

effort to implement the project, Muslim women have borne a heavy burden in representing authentic Islam in cultural, political and social spaces. The project standardised women's dress, appearance and movement in order to homogenise women as righteous Islamic and pious citizens (Nageeb 2004).

The gender ideology, which Islamists refer to as *insaf* or gender equity, builds on the idea that women should be active participants in the public sphere: getting an education, working and participating in trade and politics on condition that they behave and look pious, moral and chaste. At the same time, in the private sphere, the man is designated the main decision maker and the guardian and protector of women and children (Tønnessen 2011).

This ideology is reflected in codifications of sharia (Nageeb 2004; Tønnessen 2011; Al Bashir 2003). During the early 1990s, the Islamist state imposed new restrictions on women through law, particularly on movement and dress. The Passport and Emigration Act of 1994 stipulated that women needed the written approval of a male guardian (husband, father or brother) in order to travel. In December 1991, the hijab became the official dress code for women by presidential decree. In terms of laws introduced by the regime that significantly changed women's legal rights, the Muslim Family Law (1991) is central. The core elements of this law are the following: the age of consent for marriage is puberty; a woman needs a guardian (*wali*) to validate her marriage; the man is the breadwinner of the family (Article 51); a man can deny his wife the right to work outside the home, even in cases where he himself fails in his financial obligation (Articles 91 to 95); a man is allowed to marry up to four wives, although he has to treat all his wives justly (Article 51(d)); a husband can divorce his wife outside the court by unilateral repudiation; and the husband has the right to take his wife back if he revokes the divorce within the *idda* (a waiting period of three months after the divorce). In addition, a wife can obtain a divorce in court only under certain conditions stipulated by the law: 1) if the husband fails to fulfil his financial obligation to support her (*nafaqa*); 2) if her husband has more than one wife and she can prove that her husband does not treat all his wives justly; 3) if her husband has a defect she did not know about before marriage; 4) if her husband suffers from an incurable mental illness; 5) if her husband is impotent; 6) if he behaves cruelly; 7) if he is abroad for more than one year; and 8) if her husband is sentenced to prison for more than two years. The wife can also obtain a divorce if a judge declares her to be disobedient to her husband (Articles 151–203). The wife is entitled to financial maintenance (*nafaqa*) for up to six months after a divorce, and her husband is the financial provider for their children even when they are under the custody of the mother. The father is financially responsible for his daughters until marriage and for his sons until they provide for themselves. The mother has custody of her daughters until they are nine years old and of her sons until they are seven. However, if the woman remarries, the father will automatically get custody of the children. The inheritance laws are in accordance with classical sharia; a woman inherits half the amount of property that her brother(s) inherits.[13] For more detailed information about the law, see Tønnessen (2011).

Family law has emerged as a contested piece of legislation in contemporary Sudan. It builds on the principle of male guardianship (*qawama*) within the family, effectively denying women rights equal to those of men. The Islamist gender ideology builds strongly on this concept of *qawama*, in which women and men have different and complementary roles and responsibilities within the family because they are born biologically different. In the Muslim family, the ideal man is the protector, provider and decision maker of the household, while the ideal woman is the obedient caregiver and nurturer. This is the essence of *qawama* (Tønnessen 2011).

While women's civil rights have been regulated by sharia law since before independence in 1956, they were codified for the first time under Islamist rule in 1991. Before 1991, Muslim family law developed through judicial circulars issued by the religious clergy (*ulema*). The new law reversed rights previously enjoyed by Sudanese women. For example, legally, a woman needs a male guardian (a father, brother or uncle) to contract her marriage. This follows the practice of the Maliki School and revokes a judicial circular from 1960 based on the precepts of the Hanafi School, according to which a woman can contract marriage herself without a male guardian. Another prominent example relates to child marriages. According

13 *Qanun al-'Ahwal al-Shakhsiyyalil-Muslimin* (Muslim Family Law), Khartoum, 1991.

to the 1991 law, a judge can affirm a marriage for a girl who shows signs of puberty, often interpreted as the age of ten. This law revokes a judicial circular stating that the legal age of marriage is eighteen (Fluehr-Lobban 2012: 139). While the judicial circulars did not provide women with equal civil rights to men, they were regarded as 'an enlightened and liberal interpretation' of family law (Fluehr-Lobban 1993: 117). With the codification of the law, women's civil rights became the domain of politics rather than religion alone. From being part of the authority of the religious scholars, they became open for political contestation. Rather than opposing the religiously learned establishment's understanding of sharia, the law represented a political regime's particular interpretation of it (Tønnessen 2011). Paradoxically, the Islamist regime then facilitated more debate on women's rights within family law, including new actors such as women's rights activists. The codification of the law and the fact that it was considered regressive to women's rights in certain areas were in themselves significant for the shift in focus in this period of Sudan's history.

To implement its Islamisation project during the initial years of its rule, the regime banned the activities of all political parties, and all NGOs were dissolved and forced to register again and go through security screening, since many were considered to be affiliated with the oppositional political parties. Generally, all non-governmental groups worked with some caution during this period, as their activities were monitored closely by security. In 1990, the government established the Sudanese Women General Union, the International Muslim Women's Union and the International Women's League, all three with their headquarters in Khartoum. These institutions constituted the state policy mechanism or national machinery concerning women's rights. Disregarding an overall gender ideology, the structure had similarities with the authoritarian state feminism implemented during the reign of Nimeiri. These organisations concentrated their activities on literacy training, handicraft lessons and teaching the Qur'an, but they also served a political purpose in mobilising for the war in the south of the country before the peace agreement was signed in January 2005.

The period witnessed a decline in civil society activism, since organisations with views on gender conflicting with those of the government were suppressed. When Sudan transitioned to civilian rule with the establishment of the National Congress Party in 1995 and the holding of elections in 1996, however, a gradual process of civil activist revival started. Some space was opened up; many pro-governmental NGOs were established, but some that had been considered 'anti-government' or 'independent' also gained permission to register. The government even permitted some NGOs to participate in the Beijing Platform of Action in 1995, together with government representatives. As a consequence of a shift in international discourses on development, the international community started to show considerable interest in gender equality, initiated collaborations with civil society organisations, and made resources available for some of the women's groups (other than the SWU), facilitating independence from the state and from the traditional political parties. This meant that women were no longer restricted by conservative political parties' ideologies. Some independent NGOs took the opportunity afforded by this limited space and collaborated with a peace initiative supported by the Netherlands Embassy; this brought together diverse groups from war zones, civil society organisations and the government and initiated a dialogue on peace and women's role. For example, the Sudanese Women Empowerment for Peace (SuWEP) was established in 1997 and formally registered by 2001. Another example is the Women in Development network, established in 2000. A regional network, the Southern Initiative for the Horn of Africa (SIHA), was also registered.

The period after 1996 witnessed the adoption and intensified advocacy of issues of gender equality and human rights by independent women's and human rights organisations. A focus on the equality of rights for men and women was considered to be in opposition to the official state ideology, particularly its ideology concerning equality in the family. This represented a break with the earlier periods of women's activism, with the notable exception of the Republican Sisters during the 1970s, which had addressed gender inequalities mostly in the public sphere. Issues relating to violence against women, women's civil rights, FGM and reproductive rights were put on the agenda. With assistance of the international community, some of the active organisations, such as Mutawinat, the Babiker Badri Scientific Association and the Gender Center, engaged in reviewing Sudan's laws, informed by a human rights perspective. Forums on women's human rights were organised and generated debates on discriminatory laws such as the Muslim Family Law, the Khartoum Public Act and criminal law.

These organisations and other women's groups increasingly started to advocate against the discriminatory laws of the Islamist government. It was clear that their views on gender justice were qualitatively different from those of the government. The preliminary initiatives calling for reform and gender equality were integral to the debates on CEDAW, human rights and the Beijing Platform of Action's recommendations. Initially, the regime was tolerant of such debates, which were supported by the international community in Sudan. Later, the Sudanese Women General Union, a government-supported NGO, led a debate on CEDAW that included civil society. After several sessions of discussions of the content of CEDAW and reservations for Sudan, the government stopped these activities, having deemed CEDAW to be against sharia and Sudanese culture. One of the conservative Islamists, renowned for speaking against family planning in parliament and a former adviser to the President on women's affairs, publicly stated 'CEDAW over my dead body.' The debate over CEDAW made clear the growing polarisation between civil society and the government. There were particularly sharp disagreements over Article 16, which concerned equality in the family (Tønnessen 2011). While both the Islamist government and civil society agreed on the importance of women's equal rights to work, education and political rights, they very much disagreed on women's equal rights in the family. While the Islamists put an emphasis on *qawama*, civil society called for equality (Tønnessen 2013).

After the signing of the comprehensive peace agreement that ended the long-standing war in the south in 2005, a lot of international funding has gone to women's groups and there has been an explosion in the number of NGOs working within the area of women's rights. There is no accurate information on the number, but in 2000 there were about 100 active organisations and in 2006 officials estimated the number to be over 2,000 in all states of Sudan. We have never seen so many actors working to better the Sudanese women's situation as at the present time. According to Balghis Badri:

Now we are present in all spheres ... Although this regime is restrictive, there have never been so many women NGOs and there has never been so much awareness. There is more engagement. We have had more exposure to the international community; we have started to learn and see; we have started to mature during this repressive regime. We are ready![14]

There has been a shift in the international discourse on women in development, and particularly on women in armed conflict, after the adoption of United Nations Security Council Resolution 1325 in 2000. This has meant an increasing influx of international aid to women in countries affected by war, focusing particularly on women's inclusion in peacebuilding and political decision making as well as on violence against women. Despite the outbreak of war in Darfur, the east of Sudan and more recently on the border between the south and the north, many women's groups have been undertaking different activities. Some of the NGOs, particularly in the war zones, have engaged in development or relief activities. Others have concentrated their activities on the grassroots, whether microfinance, literacy training or awareness raising.

After the arrest order of President Omar Al Bashir from the International Criminal Court (ICC) for war crimes and crimes against humanity in Darfur, the space for independent civil society in Darfur and beyond has been somewhat limited. Many international organisations were expelled and national organisations shut down because (according to the government) they provided information to the ICC. Women's groups have been affected by this as well. Most recently, Salmmah Women's Resource Centre was shut down in 2014 after its leader, Fahima Hashim, appeared as a speaker at the Global Summit to End Sexual Violence in Conflict in London.

In spite of these developments, civil society continues to be vibrant against all odds. But it is not united in its goals and strategies for change. While some activists (strategically) engage and cooperate with the government, others deliberately do not, arguing that they will not risk giving an authoritarian government legitimacy. This is despite the fact that critical actors within the government have advocated for some political opening and law reform; among these is the former Minister of Social Welfare, Amira Al Fadil.

14 Interview with Balghis Badri, Ahfad University for Women, 15 October 2012.

A considerable number of activists and some Islamist women have been working on issues of women's rights and law reform, particularly family law. This has been undertaken with a specific focus on child marriage and violence against women, as well as rape and sexual violence in conflict zones (Tønnessen 2014). In addition, it has included efforts focused on reproductive health and attempts to criminalise FGM in the National Child Act (2010), as well as political rights including a mobilisation for a 25 per cent women's quota in the national and state legislative assemblies in the 2008 National Election Act (Tønnessen and Al Nagar 2013; Abbas 2010). Some of the political parties, particularly the UP, have also been active in these debates. It is also important to mention that there are some reformists within the government who are also putting critical issues on the agenda. The peace agreement and the 2005 interim national constitution enabled a critical debate to emerge. Because of the bill of rights in the new constitution, a review of Sudan's laws to conform to the constitution was inevitable.

The groups within civil society and political parties that work for feminist legal action agree on the goal: namely equality in rights and protection from violence. While some activists are secular at heart, others are part of an Islamic movement or more traditional political parties. Within the context of an Islamic state, many groups frequently employ religious arguments to argue for legal reform. Interestingly, many contemporary activists refer to the Islamic framework given by Mahmood Muhammed Taha and the Republican Sisters to argue for equality within the frame of Islam. This is partly a pragmatic move, intended to counter the government attempts to sideline them as 'Western' and thus foreign to the Sudanese culture and religion, whereby they try to abolish the distinction between opposition to the state and opposition to Islam. It is also partly an Islamic feminist project, which genuinely believes that gender equality is part and parcel of religious sources. Nahid Muhammad Hassan (in Tønnessen 2011: 205) explains:

> With a secular frame of argument you are excluded from the debate. We need to deal at the level of Islamic interpretations and go back to the roots of Islam and defend women's rights from Islam. For this reason the campaign is tough. They try to exclude us ... They are afraid of women's liberation.

Of these initiatives for legal feminist action, only the mobilisation for the 25 per cent women's quota has been successful thus far (Tønnessen and Al Nagar 2013). In the mobilisation for the quota, women from the government and civil society were able to come together across political divides. This was partly facilitated by the fact that the gender ideology of the Islamists is open towards women's political participation. In fact, they encourage it, but from a different perspective than many civil society actors in that they emphasise Islam rather than international human rights. Many Islamist women argued for women's political participation, referring to women's and men's biological differences and the need to have both 'soft' and 'hard' elements included in decision making.

This mobilisation across divides also happened on a different occasion during this regime, when the governor of Khartoum issued a decree in 2001 forbidding women from working in jobs rendering direct services to men, such as economic activities in the market. Soon, over twenty 'independent' organisations engaged in joint efforts to raise a constitutional case against the governor. The Sudanese Women General Union followed the organisations' path and separately raised a constitutional case. Again, women's right to work is central to the Islamist doctrine and the Union had the approval of the ruling party to pursue the case.

Interestingly, the fact that the only feminist legal action to be enacted in the period after the peace agreement related to women's public (and not private or civil) rights is symptomatic of the history of the women's movement in Sudan. Advocacy for women's public rights does not meet much political or religious resistance. In contrast, when it comes to mobilisation for law reform within what is regarded as the private sphere – for example the eradication of child marriages and the criminalisation of FGM – the counter-mobilisation has been strong, not only within the ruling political party but also outside it. After the signing of the comprehensive peace agreement, not only have women's groups come to the surface to demand rights, but also more conservative groups such as the Salafists have become more active. In particular, they are quick to respond on sensitive issues including family law and FGM, because these issues are more directly related to Islamic scripture. They often deem advocates of woman friendly law reform as apostates of Islam who have been seduced by the 'West'. For example, international support for the efforts to criminalise FGM was presented in this black-and-white frame as a neo-colonialist attempt to Westernise Muslims. In this case, President Bashir had turned to neo-conservative rhetoric (at the expense of women's rights) and to the Salafists for support, particularly after increased national and international pressure following the Arab Spring, internal demonstrations, renewed conflict at the border, and an arrest order hanging over his head from the ICC. The events are described by someone loosely involved in the process in the following manner:

> We attempted to insert an article, Article 13, in the National Child Law. But it was dropped by the President. He was under pressure from the ICC. He started to talk to the Salafists who advocate the Sunna circumcision. They say it is Islamic. Against this backdrop, the criminalization of FGM was portrayed as an intrusion from the West; That the National Council for Child Welfare, a government institution, was working for the UN ... The 'no' came from the supreme leader himself.[15]

Additionally there has been little mobilisation, cooperation or dialogue between women in the government and women in civil society on these issues. Both sides agree that, ideologically and politically, their positions are in conflict (Tønnessen and Al Nagar 2013).

Despite the lack of de facto law reform with regards to sensitive issues such as FGM, there is a vigorous debate that has not been seen in Sudan before. This is important in itself, because it has put gender equality on the national political agenda. What is also notable is that many women activists are employing Islam in these efforts. This is in contrast to the strategy of conformity to religion, for which the Women's Union previously stood.

Conclusions

Viewed from a historical evolutionary perspective, the feminist scene in Sudan can be characterised by some form of solidarity across political party and sectarian lines at the time of its formation in 1952, but it was soon politicised and co-opted by political parties. Long periods of military rule, which banned the activities of the women's

---

15 Interview with Samira Amin Ahmed, Khartoum, 22 October 2012.

movement, radically limited its room for manoeuvre. These military regimes created their own state machineries, top down, without much genuine inclusion of women's groups or oppositional political parties. Because of the strong link between women's groups and political parties or state parties during the last few decades leading up to the present day, the political engagement of women in Sudan has suffered from polarisation. One of the most prominent cleavages has been between groups associated with 'Islamism' and groups that are considered 'secular'. It should be noted that Sudanese secularism has never been anti-religion. The Women's Union and the Communist Party emphasised conformity to Islam, culture and tradition, rather than confrontation and transformation. In terms of diversity, the women's movement also suffers from generational gaps, an urban–rural rift and class differences, although the Islamist–secularist divide has been the most central for explaining the lack of broad mobilisation of women making demands for feminist legal action vis-à-vis the state.

Under the Islamist regime, there has been an explosion of women's groups at the same time as there has been a growing polarisation between Islamist women's groups and women's organisations in civil society. The latter have been calling loudly during the last decade for the reform of Sudan's discriminatory laws. Many of these groups have received funding and support from international donors, something that has enabled some sort of independence from political parties and the state. In the wake of the comprehensive peace agreement in 2005, the Islamist women in government have also started to engage with the cause of legal reform. This was necessitated by the bill of rights in the new constitution; all laws were to be reviewed and reformed to be in congruence with the 2005 constitution. Islamist women initiated the attempt to criminalise FGM in the National Child Act (2010). The attempt failed at the national level, but it succeeded at the state level; five states have now criminalised FGM. Women successfully mobilised across ideological divides for the 25 per cent women's quota in the National Election Law (2008). This was a rare occasion when women in government and women in civil society came together to make a demand vis-à-vis the state to expand women's political representation. The debates on the reform of family and criminal laws are much more polarised. These initiatives were undertaken separately by each group, and the Islamists' stance remains conservative when it comes to issues relating to marital rape, divorce rights, polygyny and male guardianship.

It is evident that the agenda of women's groups has changed since earlier periods in Sudan's history. In addition to women's political rights and female workers' rights, it now includes issues relating to family justice, rape and sexual violence. This is also related to shifts in the international discourse on women's rights. Activists have moved beyond a line that emphasises conformity to Islam. Rather, the discourses used now challenge Sudan's Islamic laws by seeking alternative and feminist interpretations of religious texts. In their opinion, Islam and a human rights framework are in harmony, not in conflict. However, they shy away from directly engaging in religious interpretations themselves and rely on others, inside and outside Sudan. In doing so, they avoid fully adopting the standpoint of the Republication Brothers and Mahmoud Muhammad Taha, an ideology that put gender equality within an Islamic frame and even tackled the most controversial issues such as women's equal inheritance.

Despite the 25 per cent reserved seats for women in national and state legislative assemblies, the legal reform initiatives inside and outside government have had limited success in the period since the peace agreement. The failure in making reform a reality can be attributed to several factors, including the increased political influence of Salafist groups that have blocked laws to expand women's rights, for example the criminalisation of FGM. After the indictment of the President by the ICC, President Bashir has turned to these groups for support at the expense of women's rights. Another factor is the limitation of the state's gender ideology. While it is open to women's equal rights in the public sphere, its emphasis on male guardianship within the family effectively hinders feminist claims for legal change. Also, the patriarchal structure of the ruling party effectively limits room for manoeuvre for those seeking reform from within. For example, the women elected to the National Assembly on the women's quota are predominantly among the conservative voices, not those advocating legal reform. Finally, the strong polarisation between women in government and women in civil society constrains any efforts to make feminist legal demands vis-à-vis the state.

References

Abbas, S. (2010) 'The Sudanese Women's Movements and the Mobilization for the 2008 Legislative Quota and its Aftermath'. *IDS Bulletin*, 41, 100–8.

Abdelal, M. M. (2003) *Sudanese Women and Political Work: Fifty Years of Struggle for Women's Rights and Democracy.* Khartoum: Salmaah.

Al Amin, N. A. and Magied, A. M. (2001) 'A History of Sudanese Women Organisations and the Strive for Liberation and Empowerment'. *The Afhad Journal: Women and Change*, 18, 2–24.

Al Bashir, N. (2003) 'Islamist Women's Politics and Gender Activism: A Case Study from Sudan'. PhD thesis, University of Vienna.

Al Gadal, F. (n.d.) 'Sudanese Women Movement'. Manuscript.

Al Nagar, S. E. (1986) 'Participation of Women in Labour Force in Khartoum, Sudan'. Thesis, Department of Anthropology and Sociology, University of Khartoum.

Al Nagar, S. E. (2003) 'Women Movement in Sudan: Experiences and Challenges'. Beirut: United Nations Economic and Social Commission for Western Asia.

Al Nagar, S. and Tønnessen, L. (2015) 'Women's Equal Rights and Islam in Sudanese Republican Thought: A Translation of Three Family Law Booklets from 1975, Produced and Circulated by the Republican Sisters'. Sudan Working Paper 5. Bergen: Chr. Michelsen Institute. Available at http://www.cmi.no/publications/5605-womens-equal-rights-and-islam-in-sudanese.

Al Sanausi, M. and Al Amin, N. A. (1994) 'The Women Movement Displaced and Rural Women in Sudan' in Nelson, B. and Chowdry, N. (eds) *Women and Politics Worldwide.* New Haven CT: Yale University Press.

Al Turabi, H. (1973) *Women between the Teachings of Religion and the Customs of Society. [Al- Mar'a bayna Ta'alim al-Din wa Taqlid al-Mujta'ma].* Jeddah: Al-Dar al-Su'udiya li al-Nashr wa al-Tawzi'.

Anis, A. I. M. (2001) 'Charting New Directions: Reflections on Women's Political Activism in Sudan'. MA thesis, Mount Saint Vincent University, Halifax, Canada.

An-Nai'm, A. (1996) *The Second Message of Islam.* Syracuse NY: Syracuse University Press.

Arenfeldt, P. and Golley, N. A.-H. (2012) *Mapping Arab Women's Movements: A Century of Transformations from Within.* Cairo and New York: American University in Cairo Press.

Badri, B. (2006) 'Moslem Feminism in Sudan: A Critical Review'. Paper presented at the Conference on Islamic Feminism, Barcelona, Spain.

El Affendi, A. (1991) *Turabi's Revolution: Islam and Power in Sudan.* London: Grey Seal.

El Bakri, Z. B. (1995) 'The Crisis in the Sudanese Women's Movement' in Wieringa, S. (ed.) *Subversive Women: Historical Experiences of Gender and Resistance.* London and Atlantic Highlands NJ: Zed Books.

El Bakri, Z. B. and Kamier, E. M. (1983) 'Aspects of Women's Political Participation in Sudan'. *International Social Science Journal*, 35(4), 605–23.

Fluehr-Lobban, C. (1986) *Islamic Law and Society in the Sudan.* London and Totowa NJ: F. Cass.

Fluehr-Lobban, C. (1993) 'Personal Status Law in Sudan' in Bowen, D. L. and Early, E. A. E. (eds) *Everyday Life in the Muslim Middle East.* Bloomington and Indianapolis: Indiana University Press.

Fluehr-Lobban, C. (2012) *Shari'a and Islamism in Sudan: Conflict, Law and*

Social Transformation. London and New York: I. B. Tauris.

Grey, S. and Sawer, M. (2008) *Women's Movements: Flourishing or in Abeyance?* London: Routledge.

Hale, S. (1986) 'The Wing of the Patriarch: Sudanese Women and Revolutionary Parties' in *Middle East Report* No. 138, *Women and Politics in the Middle East*, pp. 25–30.

Hale, S. (1996) *Gender Politics in Sudan: Islamism, Socialism, and the State*. Boulder CO: Westview Press.

Htun, M. and Weldon, L. (2012) 'The Civic Origins of Progressive Policy Change: Combating Violence against Women in Global Perspective, 1975–2005'. *American Political Science Review*, 106(3), 548–69.

Ibrahim, F. A. (1962) *Tariqnuila el-Tuharur. [Our Road to Emancipation.]* Unpublished.

Kashif, H. (1984) *The Women's Movement in Sudan*. Khartoum: University of Khartoum.

Khalid, T. A. (1995) 'The State and the Sudanese Women's Union 1971–1983' in Wieringa, S. (ed.) *Subversive Women: Historical Experiences of Gender and Resistance*. London and Atlantic Highlands NJ: Zed Books.

Mahmud, F. B. (2008) *The Ideological Direction of the Sudanese Women Movements. [Al Itijahat Alfikriya fi Alharaka Al Nisaeeia Alsudanya.]* Khartoum: Azza House for Publication and Distribution.

Misciagno, P. S. (1997) *Rethinking Feminist Identification: The Case for De Facto Feminism*. Westport CT: Praeger.

Nageeb, S. A. (2004) *New Spaces and Old Frontiers: Women, Social Space, and Islamization in Sudan*. Lanham MD: Lexington Books.

Okeke-Ihejirika, P. E. and Franceschet, S. (2002) 'Democratization and State Feminism: Gender Politics in Africa and Latin America'. *Development and Change*, 33(3), 439–66.

Rupp, L. J. and Taylor, V. (1988) 'Forging Feminist Identity in an International Movement: A Collective Identity Approach to Feminism'. *Signs*, 24(2), 363–86.

Tønnessen, L. (2011) 'The Many Faces of Political Islam in Sudan: Muslim Women's Activism for and against the State'. PhD thesis, University of Bergen.

Tønnessen, L. (ed.) (2013) *Between Sharia and CEDAW in Sudan: Islamist Women Negotiating Gender Equity*. Abingdon and New York: Routledge.

Tønnessen, L. (2014) 'When Rape Becomes Politics: Negotiating Islamic Law Reform in Sudan'. *Women's Studies International Forum*, 44, 145–53.

Tønnessen, L. and Al Nagar, S. (2013) 'The Women's Quota in Conflict Ridden Sudan: Ideological Battles for and against Gender Equality'. *Women's Studies International Forum*, 41, 122–31.

Zain Al Abdin, A. (2008) 'Islamic Movement in Sudan. From Muslim Brotherhood to the ruling National Congress'. Unpublished paper presented at the conference 'Islamic Political Parties, Movements, Conflict and Democracy', The Hague, Netherlands.

7 | THE WOMEN'S MOVEMENT IN TANZANIA

Aili Mari Tripp

There have been three major historical influences on contemporary women's mobilisation in Tanzania, especially after 1990: 1) the women who participated in the independence movement and their leaders, such as Bibi Titi; 2) the role of the first president Julius Nyerere and his egalitarian ideology of African socialism or *ujamaa* that was embodied in the Umoja wa Wanawake wa Tanzania (UWT) women's union that was tied to the ruling party during the one-party era; and 3) the third impetus that came from the international women's movement, starting with the 1985 United Nations (UN) Conference on Women in Nairobi and the mobilisation that took place leading up to the 1995 UN Conference on Women in Beijing.

This chapter looks at these influences on the women's movement that emerged in Tanzania, many of which have parallels in other African countries. It also looks at two of the many areas in which the women's movement made a mark and that also reflect some of the African influences on global feminism: namely, women's participation in politics and gender budgeting (the process of analysing national budgets for gendered impacts).

Women during the struggle for independence

Women activists were integral to the movement that brought independence to Tanganyika in 1961. The Tanganyika Council of Women (TCW) was formed in 1951 by colonial women and taught household management skills, embroidery, childcare and hygiene to local women. Initially, in 1954 the Tanganyika African National Union (TANU) drew on the TCW and its related Women's Club movement to increase its base of support. This changed soon afterwards when Bibi Titi and her colleagues became involved in the independence movement.

Bibi Titi, who had been a lead singer in a coastal woman's dance group, Bomba, became critical to the recruitment efforts of TANU as she energised large segments of the population behind the cause of independence through her charismatic speeches. She helped expand the party's membership by recruiting large numbers of women in particular to join the party. Within a span of three months in 1955, TANU's membership jumped from 2,000 to 5,000 as Bibi Titi toured the country and rallied the crowds. She and other women carried out door-to-door canvassing and, thus, women came to form the backbone of the independence movement (Geiger 1987, 1997; Peter 1999; Meena 2003). TANU's early female leadership, interestingly, emerged from women who did some farming and sold *pombe* (beer), fish, firewood, and *vitumbua* and *maandazi* pastries. They were mainly Muslim coastal women like Bibi Titi, who had a few years of primary education. Other early leaders included such women as Hadija Swedi, Binti Kapara, Halima Khamisi, Kibuyu bint Saleh, Binti Fundi Mkono and Rehema bint Seleman (Geiger 1987).

Bibi Titi started by mobilising the women's *ngoma* dance groups, building up their self-confidence. She addressed their lack of education and talked about how independence would change that. Unlike the men's groups at the time, which tended to be formed on the basis of ethnicity, region or religious affiliation, the women's dance groups were nationalistic in orientation and were not formed along particularistic lines. TANU emphasised that women and men needed to work side by side for independence, and this greatly appealed to these early women activists (Geiger 1987).

As one of Geiger's informants explained:

The women had no say. We had nothing to say, and whatever we might have wanted to say, we had to follow ... We had no freedom at all. We were considered useless people. A woman was regarded as a useless person because she was a woman. That's why we put in more effort, after learning the saying 'all people are equal,' we understood well what that was supposed to mean and we said 'we shall see if all people are equal; we must cooperate if this saying is to become true'. (Geiger 1987: 19)

The women Geiger interviewed suggested that women were more supportive of TANU than the men at the time. For the civil servants, this might have been because they feared losing their jobs as civil servants were not allowed to join political parties. Most men, however, were not civil servants, but as Geiger speculates, they were likely to have experienced more direct and coercive control by the colonial state. 'Men were afraid and we were not,' was the most common way in which women explained the difference to Geiger. And so women bought and hid TANU cards for men, thoroughly relishing their role as 'protector' (Geiger 1987: 21). It is also possible that they were also able to elude surveillance more easily because they were mostly Muslim women, whom the colonial authorities considered harmless, given their many biases against them.

Bibi Titi first chaired the Women's Section of TANU. In 1965 it became the Women's Union, Umoja wa Wanawake wa Tanzania (UWT) and Bibi Titi was its first chair. She was also a member of the Legislative Council. Although Bibi Titi and Nyerere were the best known pro-independence leaders at the time, she fell from grace when she openly disagreed with Nyerere's 1967 Arusha Declaration, outlining the country's socialist orientation. In 1969, she and several others were arrested for treason and sentenced to life imprisonment. She maintained her innocence throughout and spent two years in prison until her term was commuted in 1972 without explanation. In 1984, Nyerere embraced her at an event in what was perceived as a public reconciliation. In 1991, during Tanzania's thirty-year celebration of independence, Bibi Titi was described in the party's paper, *Uhuru*, as 'A Heroine of Uhuru [Freedom] Struggle' and after her death a major street was named in her honour.

President Nyerere and the Women's Union

Like many party-affiliated organisations in Africa at the time, the UWT had little independence from TANU and its main purpose was to mobilise women to support the party. Its stated goal in its constitution (UWT 1962) was 'to foster the development of women in respect of economic, political, cultural, educational, and health matters'. The party nominated the final two candidates who ran for chair of the UWT. It is no surprise that many of the UWT's top leaders were relatives of leading party members: the early leaders included such women as Fatma Karume, wife of the Second Vice President, Sophia Kawawa, wife of the First Vice President, and Maria Nyerere, wife of the President. Any initiatives of the organisation had to be approved by the party. It was basically a branch of the ruling party through which the government transmitted its policies to women, and through women to the rest of the population, especially in the rural areas. The UWT's primary activities were developmental and welfare oriented: they organised literacy classes, cooperative agricultural projects, public health instruction, and nursery schools (Tenga and Peter 1996). At times, the UWT was plagued by infighting between the educated and less educated members and by a rivalry with the Young Women's Christian Association (YWCA), which was led by more educated women.

Although the autonomy of the organisation was constrained, it did manage to get key legislation passed, including the 1971 Law of Marriage, which abolished separate marriage laws for various confessional communities (Christians, Muslims, Hindus, and the so-called 'Natives'). With the new law, all marriages had to be registered and the age of marriage was set at eighteen years for men and fifteen years for women. Men could not divorce women on a whim or through the Islamic *talaq* pronouncement; they had to have grounds for divorce they could prove in court. The UWT also helped pass the Employment Ordinance (Amendment) Act of 1975, which gave women paid maternity leave regardless of their marital status. They also helped get a policy adopted in 1977 that allowed women to go directly to university after finishing national service without having to wait two years. This was aimed at preventing the possibility that women might become pregnant or married in those two years, thereby forgoing further education.

These reforms were supported by President Nyerere, who had an egalitarian orientation from the outset. Nyerere, who had helped usher in independence through the efforts of TANU, served first as the country's Prime Minister after independence, and then as its President after Tanganyika's unification with Zanzibar in 1964. As the only candidate, he was elected in 1965 and remained in power until his retirement in 1985, running every five years unopposed as the sole candidate of his party. TANU was renamed Chama Cha

Mapinduzi (CCM) after its merger with the Zanzibari Afro Shiraz Party in 1977. According to Nyerere, he formed the UWT because he felt it was important to provide a structure to organise women's interests. As he explained:

> I am the one who created UWT. It was 1965. We were working very hard after independence to give everyone a chance. But then all of a sudden there were so many women groups doing different things, not united, even fighting each other! I told them to unite. I united them under UWT!' (Tibaijuka 2016)

Early on, Nyerere recognised that women were discriminated against, particularly in the production process. Women worked the land but did not own it. As he explained:

> The truth is that in the villages women work very hard. At times they work for twelve or fourteen hours. They even work on Sundays and public holidays. Women who live in villages work harder than anybody else in Tanzania. But men who live in villages are on leave for half of their lives. (Arusha Declaration, 5 February 1967)[1]

Nyerere felt that for the country to progress, women would have to enjoy 'full equality with their fellow citizens who are men' (Chachage and Cassam 2010: 155). He stressed the importance of women and men having equal rights and supported girls' right to education. He introduced the drive towards universal primary education in 1974, and, as a result, Tanzania became one of the countries with the highest literacy rates in Africa. This benefited girls enormously, and today 65 per cent of females can read and the female-to-male literacy rate stands at 0.86, according to the World Economic Forum Gender Gap Index (see Table 7.1). Nyerere supported a 1976 UWT Lindi Resolution that argued that women should be allowed into institutions of higher learning directly after national service. His thinking influenced judicial rulings regarding women's inheritance and other such rights based on an application of the Marriage Law.

---

1 https://www.marxists.org/subject/africa/nyerere/1967/arusha-declaration.htm.

TABLE 7.1 Female education and labour force participation

	Percentage of female population	Percentage of male population	Female-to-male ratio (1.00 = equality)
Literacy rate	65	76	0.86
Enrolment in primary education	85	82	1.03
Enrolment in secondary education	26	30	0.87*
Enrolment in tertiary education	3	5	0.54
Labour force participation	90	91	0.99
Wage equality for similar work (survey)	n/a	n/a	0.65
Estimated earned income	n/a	n/a	0.93

Sources: World Economic Forum, Global Gender Gap Index 2015, http://reports. weforum.org/global-gender-gap-report-2015/economies/#economy=TZA; *http://www.epdc.org/sites/default/files/documents/EPDC%20NEP_Tanzania.pdf (accessed 23 October 2016).

Tanganyika was the first country in Africa to introduce a significant affirmative action programme in 1975, with fifteen women (8.3 per cent) holding seats in the parliament. In fact, this started even prior to independence. Ndigwako Bertha Akim King'ori was the first nominated woman to the Legislative Council in 1957 (Mwambulukutu 2013). The Legislative Council held elections in 1960 and of the sixty-one legislators, 10 per cent (six) were women.[2] All belonged to TANU, which won the election. Five women were elected and Lucy Lameck was appointed to the Council by Nyerere in 1960. She subsequently ended up being elected to the legislature and served for twenty years in all. Lameck was instrumental in introducing legislation on women (Akyeampong and Gates 2012). She was especially important in mobilising politicians and the public to accept that all children were Tanzanian children, regardless of the marital status of their mothers. She was a fairly independent woman and scandalised

2 See http://www.parliament.gh/content/431/41; Bibi Titi Mohamed, Sophia Mustafa, Lady Marion Chesham, Barbro Johansson and E. Markwalder as constituency MPs, and Lucy Lameck as a nominated MP (Yoon 2008).

the more conservative elite women by her independent behaviour at the time.[3]

Tanganyika had the highest percentage of women in parliament in Africa at the time, while in 1960 Ghana had ten women (8.7 per cent) filling specially elected seats in a parliament of 114 members. Their aim was to introduce them to political life. Thus, women's political participation was part of the Nyerere legacy of ensuring greater equality.

Salma Maoulidi argues that Tanzania's socialist aspirations may have opened up and regularised women's political participation earlier than in other African countries. She finds it remarkable that many of the women who

> rose up in the ranks were ordinary women from the lowest rungs of society, sometimes semi-literate but endowed with exceptional organising and oratory skills. Also an active, well-funded and devolved women's wing of the ruling party was an effective mobilising tool, such that the most visible political female face in Tanzania was often the chair or secretary general of the women's wing, instead of the first lady as is the case in other countries. (Maoulidi 2010)

The left-leaning influence on women's representation was evident in several of the early post-independence African parliaments beyond Tanzania, but subsequent statistical studies show that with time it faded as other non-left-leaning countries also adopted quotas (Hughes and Tripp 2015).

In spite of these aforementioned aspirations, women's political role was uneven, and women, particularly at the local level, were sometimes cut out of political life altogether and were not represented on various village committees. As Michaela von Freyhold described the situation in two *ujamaa* villages in Handeni: 'The men were represented on every institution of the village government, but the women did not have any representatives. Most of the decisions were taken by men and explained to the women and women accepted them' (von Freyhold 1979: 75).

3 Personal communication with Marjorie Mbilinyi, 23 October 2016.

International influences

As the country moved towards multipartyism in 1991, the Workers' Organisation and the Co-operative Movement became independent, but the UWT, along with the youth (Vijana) and parents (Wazazi) organisations, remained under party control (Tenga and Peter 1996). However, new heterogeneous organisations emerged that had their own leadership, own independent finances and own agendas and reflected new sensibilities and values. One reason for these developments, particularly after the 1990s, was that international influences and donor support began to shift to support such new organisations.

However, already in the late 1970s and early 1980s, feminist organisations were being formed in Tanzania. The Women's Research and Documentation Project had started in 1978 as an informal socialist feminist study group meeting in members' homes. Its goal was to promote the critical study of and research into the 'women's question' in Tanzania as it related to development at the local, national and international levels. In 1980 it was formalised as a study group of the Institute of Development Studies (IDS) at the University of Dar es Salaam. However, in 1982 it became an independent group because the IDS tried to appropriate its funds. At the time, its research represented some of the most cutting-edge gender analysis being carried out in Africa. It had a multidisciplinary orientation and was made up of university lecturers, curriculum developers, librarians, administrators, trade unionists, engineers, architects, lawyers and schoolteachers. It sponsored a delegation of women non-governmental organisations (NGOs) to the 1985 UN Conference on Women in Nairobi and they were the only Tanzanian group to get a workshop at the conference (Meena and Mbilinyi 1991; Shechambo and Mbilinyi 2015).[4]

The Tanzania Media Women's Association (TAMWA) was another early feminist organisation, formed in 1987 by women including Fatma Alloo, Edda Sanga, Leila Sheikh, Rose Haji and Ananilea Nkya.[5] Its formation was inspired, in part, by the UN Conference on Women in Nairobi in 1985, where women's mobilisation was seen as key to challenging patriarchal norms.

4 Also personal communication, Marjorie Mbilinyi, 23 October 2016.
5 Other early leaders included Valerie Msoka, Pili Mtambalike, Elizabeth Marealle, Rose Kalemera, Jamilla Chipo, Nellie Kidela and Halima Shariff.

There had been even earlier regional influences: for example, the East African seminar 'East African Women Look Ahead', held on 11–18 April 1964 at the Kenya Institute of Administration. This was one of the first efforts in the post-independence period to create interest in redefining women's roles in public life in East Africa. However, it was not until the mid-1990s that regional and even national networking began in earnest and a movement was formed to take on such concerns.

In Tanzania, as in Africa more generally, networks first formed nationally. The Tanzania Gender Networking Programme (TGNP), established in 1992, helped convene a network of women's organisations in Tanzania to prepare for the 1995 UN Conference on Women in Beijing. They held three workshops that were part of a process that was highly successful in galvanising the women's movement in Tanzania. TGNP was committed to catalysing and building a transformative feminist movement that networked at the grassroots, national, regional and international levels. In East Africa, a preparatory meeting was held in Kampala in 1993, and TGNP led the delegation of Tanzanian NGOs to this meeting, which brought together 120 leaders of women's organisations from Uganda, Tanzania and Kenya. They then made preparations for the Africa-wide 1994 UN All-Africa Women's Conference held in Dakar and the subsequent 1995 UN Conference on Women in Beijing (Kitunga and Mbilinyi 2009; Mbilinyi et al. 2003; Mbilinyi 2015; TGNP 1993).

The agendas that emerged from the national networks informed the regional and Africa-wide conferences, and in turn were taken to Beijing. Women delegates to the 1993 East African conference agreed that access to power was their top priority when asked to rank their preferences to determine overall strategic goals. The goals they settled on became the blueprint for activism in the years leading up to Beijing and beyond. In the process, new sub-regional networks were established to advance these objectives. For example, the Eastern African Sub-Regional Support Initiative (EASSI) was formed explicitly to facilitate linkage, collaboration, networking and information sharing between the different organisations and networks in East Africa. EASSI sought to promote, monitor and evaluate the implementation of the African and global platforms for action as they applied to the Eastern Africa sub-region (Tripp et al. 2009).

The process leading up to the UN Fourth Conference on Women in Beijing galvanised the women's movement throughout Africa. In a country such as Tanzania, it resulted in the formation of networks of organisations that had not existed prior to this time, in part because the women's organisations affiliated to a single party had predominated and there were few independent organisations. Because the Beijing process propitiously coincided with the political opening that occurred in Tanzania, this allowed the newly emerging independent women's organisations to take part in coalition building and networking with other organisations at the national, regional and international levels.

New women's rights mobilisation

New autonomous organisations emerged in the context of two events in Tanzania and Africa more generally. The first was a deep economic crisis, which resulted in the collapse of the formal economy. Price hiking (*ulanguzi*), hoarding, financial black markets and the overall informal economy had expanded in response to distortions created by state controls on the economy. Numerous structural adjustment programmes, starting in the 1980s, sought to address the crisis. However, they also led to a retreat of the state, which withdrew social and public services as well as agricultural supports and inputs along with consumer price subsidies. Privatisation and the liberalisation of the economy – including the liberalisation of trade, finance and prices – led to sharp drops in wages and increases in prices. Land was increasingly taken over by private mining, agricultural and tourist companies, creating new pressures on various populations. The problems were later compounded by the 2008 global financial crisis. These economic pressures created new difficulties for women as agricultural producers and as informal sector workers, who often served as the mainstay of the household. Those family members working outside formal employment (generally women, children, youth and the elderly) were contributing significantly more to the household livelihood in families that had previously depended on incomes from employment (Tripp 1997).

The other change at this time involved political liberalisation, which followed economic crisis and liberalisation. The hegemony of the ruling party that had begun after independence from British rule in 1961 began to dissipate. The changes were considerable. In the early

1990s, the ruling party, the CCM, separated from the government in a country where the party and government had almost become indistinguishable. Legislation was passed, moving the country from a single-party to a multiparty system, and the first multiparty elections were held in 1995. The CCM had dominated associational life and had significantly curtailed autonomous mobilisation. Associational life at the national level had been effectively crippled and was virtually non-existent. In the early 1990s, the trade unions and cooperatives were delinked from the party, although the UWT, Vijana youth organisation and Wazazi parents' organisation remained tied to the party. New political space opened up for civil society while new non-party and non-political space opened up for the first time.

Sensing the political liberation trends that were sweeping the continent, the CCM decided to open up the country, partly because they felt that there was a certain inevitability to the process and that it would eventually take hold in Tanzania. They also hoped that by jump-starting the process in Tanzania, they would be able to remain in control of it and the CCM would be able to remain in power. They also wanted to appease donors, who were increasingly pressuring the country to liberalise both economically and politically. Finally, they saw that opening up the political process would introduce an element of competition into Tanzanian politics and help revitalise the CCM, which had grown lethargic, complacent and non-reactive as the economy sharply declined. They felt that the political opening, if controlled properly, would not undermine the standing of the CCM – if anything, it would increase its popularity (Tripp 2000).

As mentioned above, TAMWA was one of the first feminist organisations to form in Tanzania. It started in 1987 as an organisation of media workers focusing on issues of violence against women in the home and in the workplace. It also looked at the phenomenon of schoolgirls who were impregnated by male teachers, yet were thrown out of school because of their pregnancy while the teachers remained in their jobs. TAMWA also addressed questions of legal literacy by forming a crisis centre in a working-class area of Dar es Salaam. To further publicise its concerns, it published its own magazine, *Sauti ya Siti*, and people such as Edda Sanga hosted radio programmes raising awareness around various issues including sexual harassment, teenage pregnancy, marital rape and violence, which until that time had been considered taboo.[6] At the time, the most important media that existed was a government newspaper, *Daily News*, the party newspaper (*Uhuru*), and one government-controlled radio station (Radio Tanzania Dar es Salaam). There was no television. Female media workers were only able to cover such topics as fashion, health and the management of the home. TAMWA thus began to tackle patriarchal practices within the industry itself.

TAMWA also became involved in advocacy around issues of sexual harassment. This was inspired by the death of Levina Mukasa, an engineering student at the University of Dar es Salaam who had faced sexual harassment from male students. There had been a widespread practice on campus that if a woman refused the sexual advances of a male student, she could be 'punched' or targeted for sexual harassment. A notice with the woman's name might be posted around campus and she would become the subject of widespread ridicule. After six months of such harassment, Mukasa committed suicide. TAMWA, along with other women's organisations, took up the issue and the practice was banned on campus (Myamba 2009). A Sexual Offences Special Provisions Act was also passed in 1998. As a result of the activities of TAMWA, TGNP and other organisations, women's issues are now taken seriously. Moreover, today there is considerably more coverage in the media of these concerns.

Soon after TAMWA was formed, many other independent women's organisations began to emerge. The variety of organisations gives a picture of just how heterogeneous the women's movement had become: it included a wide range of organisations covering issues from the environment to human rights and land rights, and there were welfare, professional, income-generating and credit associations. It included such organisations as TGNP, which also convenes the Feminist Activist Coalition (FemAct) of over forty NGOs in Tanzania. It included the Tanzania Women and Children Welfare Centre (TWCWC), the Centre for Widows and Children Assistance (CWCA), the Tanzania Women Lawyers' Association (TAWLA), Women in Law and Development in Africa (WiLDAF), Envirocare, the Women's Legal Aid Centre (WLAC), the Zanzibar Female Lawyers Association (ZAFELA), and many other such advocacy and women's rights organisations.

6 Interview with author, Edda Sanga, 7 February 1994.

Women's rights activists also participated in and were leaders of a variety of civil society associations, not just women's organisations. They played an important role in shaping land legislation through the Hakiardhi organisation, in influencing education policy through HakiElimu, and in human rights concerns through the Legal and Human Rights Centre, to give just a few examples.

Informal associations such as rotating credit organisations tied to women's expanding role in the informal economy had already been proliferating since the early 1980s in response to the economic crisis. The opening up of political space allowed for the creation of new women's rights and human rights organisations. Some welfare organisations sprang up in response to economic decline and the challenges of economic restructuring accompanied by state retreat. They emerged to provide public services and goods where the state proved inept and incapable. Weary of losing money to corruption, donors began to provide greater support to NGOs. In Tanzania, the main donors supporting women's organisations included the Swedish Embassy, the Danish International Development Agency (DANIDA), Irish Aid, the Norwegian Embassy, the UN Population Fund, UN Women, the UK Department for International Development, the Global Fund for Women, Mama Cash and the African Women's Development Fund. There are also local funds, including Women's Fund Tanzania.

As one leader of TAMWA put it:

What changed was psychological … Years of paternalistic state-led development had led to a prevalent attitude that if you want educational facilities, you wait for the government. If you want health services, you wait for the government. And then when that did not come, you blame the government. Economic crisis forced people to think for themselves. Economic crisis and political decontrol and loosening up stimulated people so much in terms of income-generation and in terms of real self-help efforts.[7]

Asserting associational autonomy

The struggle for associational autonomy became an important aspect of the early period of mobilisation, because the government

7 Interview with author, Pili Mtambalike, 1994.

tended to see activity outside the party/government ambit as anti-governmental, especially when it involved organisations engaged in advocacy. In many African countries at this time, NGOs, including women's NGOs, had difficulty becoming registered; in some instances they were de-registered or banned. Sometimes, the ministries of gender and women's party organisations feared competition for external funds. In other instances, they felt that their leadership of women's rights mobilisation was being sidelined as other organisations had more know-how, capacity and resources and a larger following. Some associations were accused of being too 'political' and of behaving like political parties. They were reminded that they should remain 'developmental' and avoid political objectives. For example, the Minister for Minerals and Energy told representatives of the Tanzanian Women Miners Association at their inaugural conference in 1997 to distance themselves from 'politics' and concentrate on economic, technical and commercial activities (Kivamwo 1997). In 1992, TAMWA held a public tribunal at which women testified not only about violence against women but also about how the legal system was corrupt and worked to women's disadvantage in such cases. The government objected because the tribunal suggested that the government was not working, but TAMWA refused to back down and saw the exposure as a way to challenge the legal system to get it to work better for women.[8]

In Tanzania in the 1990s, the registration of women's organisations went through the Ministry of Community Affairs, Women and Children. In the mid-1990s, the ministry was particularly fearful that TGNP would overtake its own efforts and those of the UWT. These tensions came to the fore when TGNP began to coordinate women's NGOs in advance of the 1995 UN Conference on Women in Beijing. Although these tensions put a damper on the early relations between TGNP and the government, today there is considerable cooperation. For example, TGNP, along with Women in Social Entrepreneurship, has cooperated in a Gender Equality and Women's Empowerment programme together with the Ministry of Community Development, Gender and Children. Similarly, other organisations enjoy good relations with government today. TAMWA, for example, has a good working relationship with

8 Interview with author, Pili Mtambalike, 7 February 1994.

the government of Zanzibar, particularly in programmes responding to gender-based violence (GBV).

The fate of Baraza la Wanawake Tanzania (BAWATA), which asserted its independence from the UWT in the 1990s, is suggestive of the perceptions and limits of mobilisation existing at the time. Ironically, the Ministry of Community Affairs, Women and Children had decided to form an NGO umbrella organisation that would include all women's groups in Tanzania, but that would still be under the control of the UWT. It was to be a so-called 'independent' NGO that could access donor funds, yet remain under the UWT's control. The organisation was led by Anna Tibaijuka, who was a strong supporter and member of the CCM. The founding congress was held in July 1994 at the University of Dar es Salaam, but the meeting was acrimonious because the UWT felt challenged by this new organisation.

The organisation was registered in May 1995. It was formed to encourage greater political participation on the part of women and to address questions of women's land ownership and inheritance, as well as women's access to education, health and water. However, the Ministry of Community Affairs, Women and Children and the Ministry of the Interior sought to ban it, claiming that the organisation had become too 'political'. In July 1996, BAWATA's activities were suspended due to allegations that it was organised like a political party with branches at the village level and that it was not holding meetings or submitting annual financial accounts to the Registrar of Societies. The government wanted the branches closed even though, according to Tibaijuka, these charges were fabricated.

BAWATA took its case to the Constitutional Court, where the case was defended by University of Dar es Salaam Professor of Law Issa Shivji. In 2009, BAWATA finally won its case; however, by then, the organisation had been destroyed because of the court case and because of intimidation and pressure directed at its leaders and their spouses.[9] Law professor Maina Peter explained what had happened in this way:

> Every sensible State knows that women are faithful voters. They
> normally register and actually go to vote. Unlike men who talk
> a lot and do little. They might even register only to forget to

9 Interview with Anna Tibaijuka, December 1997, Dar es Salaam.

vote on the elections day. Thus women are regarded as a safe and sure constituency and whoever controls them is guaranteed victory. By touching this sensitive area – BAWATA was seen as a mischievous lot. (Peter 1999: 11)

Women's rights activists in Tanzania have helped create global awareness of numerous concerns. Two examples are explored below that relate to women's rights activists' role in promoting women in politics and their participation in gender budgeting exercises.

Women in politics

African countries have been leaders in raising the issue of the importance of political leadership early on through strategies such as quotas: for example, women currently hold 64 per cent of legislative seats in Rwanda, the highest percentage in the world. As mentioned earlier, even before independence, TANU, the precursor to the present-day CCM party, had ensured that women were represented in the pre-independence Legislative Council and women were seen as integral to the independence movement. Tanzania adopted special seats reserved for women in 1975, before other African countries. Later, after the 1990s, it was also one of the few non-conflict countries in Africa to attain rates of female parliamentary representation above 30 per cent (Table 7.2).

Tanzania was a leader in other ways as well. About 20 per cent of African countries have female speakers of the house, which is higher than the world average of 14 per cent. Tanzania was one of these countries: Anna Makinda was speaker of the house from 2010 to 2015 after being deputy speaker from 2005 to 2010. Tanzania has done less well in ministerial appointments (three out of twenty after the 2015 election), but it has a woman Vice President, Samia Suluhu, who served as the only high-ranking woman minister in Zanzibar in Amani Abeid Karume's cabinet.

Today, women occupy 136 out of 372 parliamentary seats (36.6 per cent); of these, 113 are special seats reserved for women. In 2015, 238 women vied for constituency seats in parliament, 770 at the district level, twenty-nine for the Zanzibar House of Representatives and two for the presidency and vice presidency (Table 7.2).[10] At

10 http://www.unwomen.org/en/news/stories/2015/10/women-claim-their-space-in-tanzania-elections.

the local level, women must have at least one-third of the seats that are established by the parties. According to Maoulidi (2010), the profile of women running for office is changing. Until 2005 it was mainly middle-aged women who ran for public office, but today younger women are getting involved in politics as education, public service record and money are becoming more important qualifications than simply seniority. It should also be pointed out that Muslim women have been as engaged in politics as Christian or animist women in Tanzania. In fact, in Tanzania, it is interesting to note that, according to the 2015 Afrobarometer survey, the Muslim population overall favours women leaders (69 per cent) more than the Christian population (64 per cent) and people of other beliefs (68 per cent).

On occasion, women's organisations have sought to increase the number of women ministers. Pressure from women's rights groups for a female Minister of Finance resulted in the appointment of Hon. Zakhia Meghji during the ninth parliament. Today, the struggle continues with a fifty–fifty campaign to reach complete parity. In Tanzania, this campaign is led by the Feminist Activist Coalition (FEMACT) of TGNP and TAMWA.

TABLE 7.2 Women in parliament in Tanzania

Year	Number of parliamentarians	Number of women	Percentage of women
1970	205	8	3.9
1975	218	18	8.3
1980	239	23	9.6
1985	244	24	9.8
1990	255	28	11.0
1995	275	47	17.1
2000	295	63	21.4
2005	323	97	30.0
2010	357	128	35.9
2015	393	142	36.1

Source: Inter-Parliamentary Union, http://www.ipu.org (accessed 24 October 2016); IPU 1997; Yoon 2008.

Gender budgeting

Women's engagement in politics and participation in the legislature even prior to independence made Tanzania a leader in this regard, helping shape global norms. Another area in which it asserted leadership was in the adoption of gender budgeting, which was one way in which women's organisations addressed the negative impacts of economic crisis and structural adjustment on women.[11] Tanzania was one of the many African countries that borrowed the idea of gender budgeting from South Africa, which had adapted the practice from Australia in the mid-1990s. Most countries that initially adopted gender budgeting were Commonwealth countries, although the practice eventually spread to other countries in Africa and eventually from Africa to Europe and beyond.

Starting in the 1980s, cost-sharing policies in education and health had weighed heavily on women who took their children and other family members to clinics and who ultimately were responsible for the education of the children. Gender budgeting, which was initiated in 1997, became a way in which the gender impacts of the national budget were analysed, gaps between goals and committed resources were identified, and problems were addressed by ensuring that budgetary commitments and resources would be allocated to implementing those goals. According to Rusimbi (2002), research teams would include gender activists, academics (generally economists or sociologists) and government planners and budget officers from the National Planning Commission and Ministry of Finance (Kovsted 2008). They collected data and government participants provided hard-to-access data that was considered confidential. The researchers also used participatory methods through which to identify structural and social challenges. Research reports by the team were distributed to activist organisations, government departments and donor agencies. They were also shared through working sessions of public forums involving civil society, donors, policymakers, members of parliament and parliamentary committees such as the parliamentary finance and budget committees. The participants

---

11 These exercises go by different names, such as 'women's budgets', 'gender budgets', 'gender-responsive budgets', 'gender-sensitive budgets' and 'applied gender budget analysis' (Mushi and Edward 2010).

in these forums ranged from grassroots people to top government officials.

TGNP was a critical civil society actor that worked well with the ministries, particularly the Ministry of Finance, parliamentarians and parties on the gender-budgeting initiative (GBI) (Mushi and Edward 2010; TGNP 1999). In 2005, TGNP persuaded the National Bureau of Statistics to include a time-use survey as part of its Integrated Labour Force Survey in order to make women's unpaid work more visible. It also was able, for example, to increase the budgetary resources going to the Ministry of Water as a result of the GBI. It campaigned against the privatisation of water and promoted policies that helped poor women access water (Elson and Sharp 2010). TGNP's success in the GBI resulted in the programme being invited by government and donors to be part of the public expenditure review, which is responsible for ensuring increased transparency and accountability within government institutions. TGNP also participated in the Tanzania Assistance Strategy process, which seeks to coordinate government and donor programmes and budgets (Rusimbi 2002). Many of these decision-making forums were not generally open to NGOs.

TGNP was also a key participant in the Gender Macro-Policy Working Group, which involved women's rights organisations and activists within other NGOs, donor agencies and government ministries interested in advancing gender equality in the economy. They argued for gender equality by drawing on the language in government policies such as the National Strategy for Growth and Reduction of Poverty (Mkukuta), which referred to equitable delivery of social services and well-being for the poorest and most vulnerable groups as well as for the eradication of inequalities across region, class, age and other divides. TGNP also helped the government of Mozambique in launching their gender-budgeting project in 2005. This helped put TGNP on the map internationally in this area (Mushi and Edward 2010).

The examples of women in politics and gender budgeting illustrate some of the issues and strategies being adopted in Africa that have not only spread throughout the continent but have had impacts beyond Africa.

Goals and challenges of women's rights mobilisation

The main issues relating to gender equality in Tanzania have related to poverty, gender-based violence, employment and livelihood, land and property rights, and, more recently, women in politics and constitutional reform. For the past two decades, some of the main initiatives have been around reforming GBV legislation and policies and coming up with ways to enforce the legislation and create institutions, for example to address the Sexual Offences Special Provision Act of 1998. Coalitions have formed to revise the Law of Marriage Act, draft a domestic violence bill, establish family courts, and create a policy on reinstating pregnant schoolgirls. Laws and policies were adopted to reform property laws, allowing women equal rights to acquire, own and use land (1999 Village Lands Act No. 5). TAWLA coordinated the Gender and Land Group, which lobbied for gender mainstreaming in the Village Lands Act of 1999. There have been efforts such as the Education Sector Development Programme (2000–15) to increase female access to education. Feminist organisations have participated in the constitutional reform process. A few organisations, such as TGNP, have bravely spoken out for minority rights, such as the rights of LGBT people and sex workers. Led by the more recently established Women Development Fund, the Women and the Constitution coalition successfully lobbied for the insertion of women's rights issues in the revised constitution. The coalition has brought women MPs and other politicians together with civil society activists to advocate for legal reforms, with a focus on raising the age of marriage for girls from fourteen to eighteen, along with many other issues.

TGNP and other such organisations serve as resources on gender-related issues for ministries and parliamentarians. They provide input on the official CEDAW report,[12] prepare the shadow report on CEDAW, and advise on other policy reports and decisions regarding women and elections, gender quotas, and the introduction of gender-responsive budgeting. They carry out gender training for ministries and attend high-level ministerial meetings.

---

12 CEDAW is the UN's Convention on the Elimination of all Forms of Discrimination Against Women.

There are nevertheless many gaps that have yet to be addressed. Tanzania ratified the CEDAW treaty in 1986 but has yet to fully reconcile its laws with the treaty. A customary law of inheritance has yet to be abolished. Discriminatory provisions remain in the marriage law, for example permitting polygamy. The 1971 Law of Marriage Act provides for a minimum legal age for marriage of fifteen years for women and eighteen years for men, but it allows exceptions for girls aged fourteen years who have parental consent. The Citizenship Act of 1995 does not recognise children of Tanzanian women and non-Tanzanian spouses as Tanzanian citizens. The Law of Marriage Act says that no person can 'inflict corporal punishment on his or her spouse', but there are other gaps in legislation regarding violence against women. There is no law specifically addressing domestic violence, even though the Demographic and Health Survey (2009–10) found that 44 per cent of women had experienced physical and/or sexual violence in their lifetime. A Sexual Offences Special Provision Act (1998) deals with rape and incest and criminalises spousal rape, but only if the couple is legally separated. Sexual harassment in the workplace is prohibited in Tanzania (SIGI Index n.d.; CEDAW Task Force n.d.).[13]

Even with legislation in place, there are many issues that require stronger enforcement of the law. Violence against older women and widows who have been targeted as witches is prevalent in some parts of the country. The Legal and Human Rights Centre found that 2,585 killings of older women were reported between 2004 and 2009 in areas where the fear of witchcraft was evident, and, in 2012, 630 people were killed as a result of witchcraft accusations. Rape, female genital mutilation and domestic violence are common but rarely prosecuted. Child marriage persists (SIGI Index n.d.; CEDAW Task Force n.d.).

The problem of schoolgirl dropouts is related to pregnancy, sexual harassment, the long distance that girls have to walk to school, lack of sanitary pads, poor sanitation and lack of privacy in school toilets. In spite of progressive laws, women still face problems relating to health (Table 7.3), access to credit, and illiteracy. Their inability to claim their rights with regard to property and inheritance can be linked to the prevalence of customary laws and practices.

13 http://www.genderindex.org/.

TABLE 7.3 Women's health in Tanzania

Healthy life expectancy:	
Female	55
Male	52
Female–male ratio	1.06
Total fertility rate (children per woman)	5.2
Adolescent fertility rate (births per 1,000 girls aged 15–19)	128
Contraceptive prevalence, married or with partners, aged 15–49 (percentage)	34
Maternal mortality ratio (per 100,000 live births)	410
HIV/AIDS deaths per 100,000:	
Female	171.5
Male	210.3

Source: World Economic Forum, Global Gender Gap Index 2015, http://reports.weforum.org/global-gender-gap-report-2015/economies/#economy=TZA (accessed 23 October 2016).

The face of feminism in Tanzania today

Tanzania has been visible on the international stage, with numerous high-profile women's rights activists holding key positions in international institutions. Gertrude Mongella chaired the African Union's Pan-African Parliament as its first president from 2004 to 2009. Prior to that she was the Secretary-General of the Fourth UN Conference on Women in Beijing in 1995. Dr Asha-Rose Migiro held the post of Deputy UN Secretary-General from 2007 to 2012. Subsequently she was appointed the UN Secretary-General's Special Envoy for HIV/AIDS in Africa in 2012. Women's rights activist Anna Tibaijuka served as an Under-Secretary-General of the UN and Executive Director of the UN Human Settlements Programme (UN-HABITAT) from 2006 to 2010. She was the second highest ranking African woman in the UN system after Migiro at the time. Within Tanzania, feminists have a varied profile. A select few are featured below to provide a sense of their work, interests and activities, and how they also engage with broader international feminist communities.

Fatma Alloo is a founding member of TAMWA and a specialist in promoting the use of ICT in feminist advocacy around Africa. She also organises the annual Zanzibar International Film Festival – the Festival of the Dhows – that celebrates the Indian Ocean cultures where the ancient dhow sailing boats travel along the eastern part of the African continent, the Gulf states, Iran, India and the Indian Ocean islands. She uses the festival to highlight women's stories and Tanzanian heroines such as Bi Kidude, who drums and sings. She showcases women's work in the visual arts and theatre media. One year, for example, they featured the story of Princess Salma (who, in the nineteenth century, was the first woman to write a historical documentation of life in Zanzibar).

Demere Kitunga is a founding member of four activist organisations, including TGNP. She heads a non-profit called E&D Readership and Development Agency-Soma, which works with a sister organisation named E&D Vision Publishing. The agency is founded on feminist principles. Soma (which means 'to read' in Swahili) operates a book café, publishes a literary magazine and hosts reading, literary and debate clubs, book exhibitions, dialogues between genders and generations, as well as author profiling and talent shows.

Leila Sheikh is a founding member of TAMWA. She owns a consultancy firm, Studio Calabash Ltd, that designs lobbying strategies and public education programmes. She produces TV and radio programmes and helps write scripts for radio, television, community theatre and billboards.

Marjorie Mbilinyi is a founder of several feminist organisations and networks in Tanzania and an active member of several feminist and human rights organisations and networks in Tanzania and Africa, including TGNP Mtandao, HakiElimu and the African Feminist Forum. She is a retired Professor of Education at the University of Dar es Salaam and has extensive experience in gender policy and budget analysis, participatory action research, and the feminist political economy of agrarian issues, education and social change. Mbilinyi is co-editor with Mary Rusimbi, Chachage S. L. Chachage and Demere Kitunga of *Activist Voices: Feminist Struggles for an Alternative World*, and co-editor with Chachage S. L. Chachage of *Against Neoliberalism: Gender, Democracy and Development* (both 2003).

Mwajuma Masaiganah is Director of Mwasama Preschool and Primary School in Bagamoyo as well as a secondary school. Her goal is to promote quality education for both boys and girls. She also chairs the Bagamoyo Women Development Network (BAWODENE), the

Training and Research Support Centre (TARSC) and the Bagamoyo District NGO Network. She is a participatory rural appraisal trainer and is especially interested in women's role in the care economy and why the care and social economy should be supported as an alternative economic model that can sustain women's and communities' livelihoods.

Salma Maoulidi is the Executive Director of the Sahiba Sisters Foundation, a women's development and advocacy network with members in thirteen regions of Tanzania that is concerned with the impact of cultural and religious discourses on women. She has published widely on legal and development issues from an African woman's feminist activist perspective. Her current research interest is documenting the history of women in Zanzibar, with a focus on women's legal, educational and political status over time.

Usu Mallya is an activist and coach who works with FemAct at the national level, the Intermediary Gender Network at local levels, the Gender and Development Seminar Series and the Gender Festival. She is the former Executive Director of TGNP.

Elsie Eyakuze is a columnist for *The East African* newspaper and a blogger who publishes *The Mikocheni Report*. With an undergraduate degree from Bryn Mawr College in the US and having conducted postgraduate studies at the University of Sussex, she started out working with NGOs such as CARE. The mission of her blog, she says:

> is to spread the gospel of feminism. In truth, it would be nice to write about politics from another ideological perspective. But [sic]. There are some rather serious challenges that come with being a woman in our society, and they get in the way of my pursuit of happiness, which makes me cranky. I am compelled to defend my freedoms and engage with politics as a female citizen, and kick some patriarchal behind as often as I can manage it.

Conclusions

These, then, are some of the people and issues that have animated the women's movement in Tanzania. As this chapter has shown, Tanzania has been a leader in women's rights globally, particularly in advancing women in politics early on but also in such practices as analysing the gendered impacts of national budgets.

This chapter has shown how the contemporary women's movement in Tanzania was influenced by the women who participated in the independence movement, by the egalitarian and socialist ideology of the country's first president, Julius Nyerere, and by the early efforts made by the UWT to pass key legislation to advance the status of women. It was also influenced by changes in international norms regarding women's rights that were evident in the UN conferences on women in Nairobi (1985) and Beijing (1995). The chapter shows how these events helped shape and energise women's rights mobilisation and networking within Tanzania, in the East African region, across Africa, and ultimately within the international arena. Tanzania has had its share of women's rights activists who have participated in continental and international forums, sometimes at very high levels, as in the case of Gertrude Mongella, Dr Asha-Rose Migiro and Anna Tibaijuka.

The women's movement was characterised from the outset as one that sought unity across religion, ethnicity and other differences. The national character of the independence movement was what appealed to women activists at the time, and their desire to work across difference was notable. This spirit of working across differences is something that has continued to this day. For those sceptics not familiar with African women's mobilisation, it is also interesting to note that Muslim and Christian women have been equally engaged during and since the independence movement. At many key junctures, it was Muslim women who took the lead in women's rights mobilisation in a country that is evenly divided between Christian and Muslim populations. It should be noted that Christian churches had played a role early on in educating girls: in 1927 there were 60 government schools and 2,200 mission-run schools, where girls made up 41 percent of those enrolled. In some regions like Kilimanjaro girls even exceeded boys in Church-run primary schools as far back as 1931 (Swantz 1985). This had implications later for female employment for membership in such women's organisations as the Young Women's Christian Association, which played an important role in advancing women's status in Tanzania. Tanzanian sensibilities and the strong ideology of ethnic unity often do not allow for such a discourse of difference, but it is nevertheless important to recognise the strength that this unity of differences brings. It is also an important aspect of the way in which Tanzanian women have shown leadership globally, living in a culturally pluralistic society.

The women's movement has faced numerous challenges over the years, having to assert independence from the state and ruling party and needing to fight to be able to engage in advocacy without being regarded as anti-government. These issues have largely gone by the wayside as the government and women's NGOs work fairly closely these days. The issues have shifted to more substantive ones: how to best make use of the laws that exist; how to pass laws in areas where the legislation has not been reconciled with international treaties; and how to improve existing legislation.

References

Akyeampong, E. K. and Gates, H. L. (eds) (2012) *Dictionary of African Biography*. New York: Oxford University Press.

CEDAW Task Force (n.d.) 'Thematic Issues for Tanzania CEDAW Shadow Reporting'. Dar es Salaam: CEDAW Task Force – WLAC, WiLDAF, TAWLA, TAMWA, CWCA, TWCWC, LHRC and Envirocare.

Chachage, C. and Cassam, A. (2010) *Africa's Liberation: The Legacy of Nyerere*. Nairobi and Kampala: Pambazuka Press and Fountain Publishers.

Elson, D. and Sharp, R. (2010) 'Gender-responsive Budgeting and Women's Poverty' in Chant, S. (ed.) *The International Handbook of Gender and Poverty: Concepts, Research and Policy*. Cheltenham: Edward Elgar, pp. 522–7.

Geiger, S. (1987) 'Women in Nationalist Struggle: TANU Activists in Dar es Salaam'. *International Journal of African Historical Studies*, 20(1), 1–26.

Geiger, S. (1997) *TANU Women: Gender and Culture in the Making of Tanganyikan Nationalism, 1955–1965*. Social History of Africa series. Portsmouth NH, Oxford, Nairobi and Dar es Salaam: Heinemann,

James Currey, EAEP and Mkuki Na Nyota.

Hughes, M. and Tripp, A. M. (2015) 'Civil War and Trajectories of Change in Women's Political Representation in Africa, 1985–2010'. *Social Forces*, 93(4), 1513–40.

IPU (1997) *Men and Women in Politics: Democracy Still in the Making*. Study No. 28. Geneva: Inter-Parliamentary Union (IPU).

Kitunga, D. and Mbilinyi, M. (2009) 'Rooting Transformative Feminist Struggles in Tanzania at Grassroots'. *Review of African Political Economy*, 121, 435–42.

Kivamwo, S. (1997) 'Keep Off Politics, Kigoda Advises Women Miners'. *Daily News*, 30 December.

Kovsted, J. (2008) *Gender Responsive Budget in Tanzania*. Dar es Salaam: Centre for Economic and Business Research.

Maoulidi, S. (2010) 'Strides in Gender Parity in Peril: Tanzania's General Elections 2010'. *Pambazuka News*, 28 October. Available at http://www.pambazuka.org/gender-minorities/strides-gender-parity-peril.

Mbilinyi, M. (2015) 'Transformative Feminism in Tanzania: Animation and Grassroots Women's Struggles for Land and Livelihoods' in Baksh, R. and Harcourt, W. (eds) *Oxford Handbook of Transnational Feminist Movements: Knowledge, Power and Social Change.* New York: Oxford University Press.

Mbilinyi, M., Rusimbi, M., Chachage, C. S. L. and Kitunga, D. (eds) (2003) *Activist Voices: Feminist Struggles for an Alternative World.* Dar es Salaam: Tanzania Gender Networking Programme.

Meena, R. (2003) 'A Conversation with Bibi Titi: A Political Veteran' in Mbilinyi, M. and Rusimbi, M. (eds) *Activist Voices Feminist and Feminist Struggles for an Alternative World.* Dar es Salaam: TGNP and E&D.

Meena, R. and Mbilinyi, M. (1991) 'Women's Research and Documentation Project (Tanzania)'. *Signs: Special Issue on Women, Family, State, and Economy in Africa,* 16(4), 852–9.

Mushi, V. A. and Edward, M. C. (2010) 'Challenges and Success of Gender Budgeting Initiatives: A Case of Tanzania'. *Accountancy and Business Review Journal,* 7(2), 19–24.

Mwambulukutu, U. (2013) 'The Passing of a Leading Nationalist'. *The Citizen,* 17 November. Available at http://www.thecitizen.co.tz/News/national/The-passing-of-a-leading-activist/1840392-2076260-957q2ez/index.html.

Myamba, F. P. (2009) 'Domestic Violence Rights Movement in Tanzania: An Exploration'. PhD thesis, Department of Sociology, Western Michigan University.

Omale-Atemi, J. (2007) 'Profile: Fatma Alloo'. Africa Woman and Child Feature Service, 23 April. Available at http://www.awcfs.org/index.php/content-development/features/women-who-make-a-difference/item/231-profile-fatma-alloo.

Peter, C. M. (1999) 'The State and Independent Civil Organisations: The Case of Tanzania Women's Council (BAWATA)'. Case study prepared for the Civil Society and Governance in East Africa Project. Dar es Salaam: Department of International Law, University of Dar es Salaam.

Rusimbi, M.(2002) 'Mainstreaming Gender into Policy, Planning and Budgeting in Tanzania' in Judd, K. (ed.) *Gender Budget Initiatives: Strategies, Concepts and Experience.* New York: United Nations Development Fund for Women (UNIFEM).

Shechambo, G. and Mbilinyi, M. (2015) 'Experiences in Transformative Feminist Movement Building at the Grassroots Level in Tanzania' in Ampofo, A. A., Rodriguez, C. R. and Tsikata, D. (eds) *Transatlantic Feminisms: Women and Gender Studies in Africa and the African Diaspora.* Lanham MD: Lexington Books.

SIGI Index (n.d.) 'Social Institutions and Gender *Index (SIGI)*'. Paris: OECD Development Centre. Available at http://www.genderindex.org/ (accessed 24 October 2016).

Swantz, M. L. (1985) *Women in Development: A Creative Role Denied? The Case of Tanzania.* London and New York: C. Hurst & Company and St. Martin's Press.

Tenga, N. and Peter, C. M. (1996) 'The Right to Organise as Mother of All Rights: The Experience of Women in Tanzania'. *Journal of Modern African Studies,* 34(1), 143–62.

TGNP (1993) *Gender Profile of Tanzania.* Dar es Salaam: Tanzania Gender Networking Programme.

TGNP (1999) *Budgeting with a Gender Focus.* Dar es Salaam: Tanzania Gender Networking Programme.

Tibaijuka, A. (2016) 'My Encounter with Mwalimu on Womens Rights and the Formation of BAWATA by Prof. Anna Kajumulo Tibaijuka, Member of Parliament for Muleba South and Founding Chairperson of BAWATA'. Available at http://www.annatibaijuka.org/?p=2715.

Tripp, A. M. (1997) *Changing the Rules: The Politics of Liberalisation and the Urban Informal Economy in Tanzania*. Berkeley and Los Angeles: University of California Press.

Tripp, A. M. (2000) 'Political Reform in Tanzania: The Struggle for Associational Autonomy'. *Comparative Politics*, 32(2), 191–214.

Tripp, A. M., Casimiro, I., Kwesiga, J. and Mungwa, A. (2009) *African Women's Movements: Transforming Political Landscapes*. New York: Cambridge University Press.

UWT (1962) *Constitution of the Umoja wa Wanawake wa Tanganyika*. Dar es Salaam: Umoja wa Wanawake wa Tanganyika.

von Freyhold, M. (1979) 'Kitumbi-Chanika and Kitumbi-Tibili: Two Ujamaa Villages that Refused to Become One' in Coulson, A. (ed.) *African Socialism in Practice: The Tanzanian Experience*. Nottingham: Spokesman.

Yoon, M. Y. (2008) 'Special Seats for Women in the National Legislature: The Case of Tanzania'. *Africa Today*, 55(1), 60–86.

8 | THE WOMEN'S MOVEMENT IN KENYA

Regina G. Mwatha

The evolution of the women's movement in Kenya is synonymous with the emergence of women's groups. These can be understood from a three-pronged perspective: The women's group movement, largely rural and grassroots in nature, formal women's organisations, and the actions of individual women. These three levels of women players are influenced or juxtaposed with the dominant role played by patriarchy and socio-cultural and economic factors. Further, the women at different times relate differently to the state, either forming a strong relationship or pushing the state to deliver on different needs and expectations. This chapter brings these scenarios together to showcase how the characteristics of the women's movement shaped the positioning of women and the gender agenda in Kenya over time. The chapter also discusses the relationship of the state and the impact of its different relationships with the women's movement at different times in Kenyan history.

The women's movement in Kenya is viewed as one that, in general, emphasises common objectives, continuity, unity and coordination. Women in Africa have traditionally formed groups to assist each other in several ways, such as through labour-saving activities. They also formed groups that were political in intention. Similarly, the women's movement in Kenya can be traced to the traditional communities where women assisted each other on different economic, social-cultural and political matters, as shall be seen later in this chapter. Later, the same networks became powerful tools in the fight against colonial domination. After that, they strongly advocated for women's voice and presence in decision making at the highest levels, and they have fought against discrimination and for women's rights.

Maendeleo ya Wanawake Organisation had been formed in 1952 by the Department of Community Development and Rehabilitation within the colonial government. It was seen initially as a tool for keeping women from joining the Mau Mau freedom fight for independence but, after independence, it was taken over by African women and was made up of grassroots organisations of rural women throughout the country. Today it boasts a membership of 4 million and 25,000 chapters. It served as a strong instrument of unity among women in the early post-independence years.

After independence, women also formed different women's groups to assist each other in various socio-economic activities. At this time, unfortunately, women were not seen from a political participation perspective, and women's representation in key positions of leadership and decision making was not felt. However, women began to struggle not only for their rights but also for democracy, multipartyism and a better constitution. The onset of the multiparty system in the early 1990s did not bring equality for women, and thus the push for a constitution became further intertwined with the push for women's rights.

The chapter concludes by arguing that the women's movement in Kenya has a traditional origin and that it has metamorphosed through space and time to deal with challenges and issues affecting women and gender relations in the country at the level of the community and at the level of individuals in an attempt to improve the status of women. Some of the moves have been very strategic and others were counterproductive vis-à-vis the forces of the state. It also concludes that patriarchy and socio-cultural factors, as well as politics and tribal conflicts, have affected the women's movement at different times.

Introduction

The women's movement in this chapter is viewed as one that emphasises a common objective, continuity, unity and coordination. Women in Africa have traditionally formed groups to assist each other in several ways, such as through labour-saving activities. They formed groups that sought economic improvement of their families' livelihoods. They also took positions that were political in nature, sometimes conflicting with the state and at other times partnering with government. At some points, they sought democratic space and inclusivity as well as struggling for the constitution, which became law in 2010. Each of these moves had consequences for the women's movement. This chapter discusses all these elements, bringing to the fore the character of the women's movement in Kenya.

The precolonial and colonial setting The women's movement in Kenya has its origins in the precolonial period, when women formed self-help groups and work parties to assist one another in times of economic stress. The Gikuyu women, for instance, had a *ngwatio* system, in which women assisted each other in labour provision in their farming, as well as in other activities. Among the Gusii, the groups were known as *risaga* and among the Luo they were called *saga*. Among the Kamba, Mutiso (1975) identified three types of groups. The first was *mwilaso*, a small group of friends and neighbours, traditionally boys or girls who worked on each other's farms on a strictly rotational basis. The second was *mwethya*, where an individual with a specific short-term task asked women friends, relatives and neighbours to assist. This was a village organisation. It was expected that such help would be provided to a neighbour when need arose. The third was *vuli*, where the task was too large to be handled by the village and elders and friends from different villages came to help. The purpose of *vuli* was to create a new capital asset, and it was largely used by the wealthy.

During the colonial period, the form and substance of women's organisations changed considerably. These changes were catalysed by colonial policies and the labour laws designed to meet the demand of the market economy, which disrupted traditional social structures and shifted responsibilities that were gendered in nature. The colonial period saw the strengthening of the women's movement. This was typified by two parallel movements that were formed almost simultaneously, and both drew their roots from the traditional support networks and self-help groups discussed above. The first movement was composed of militant but informal associations of women, which mobilised existing women's groups to rebel against the colonial policies that they deemed to be destroying their local culture and economy and institutionalising colonial structures and ideology. The colonial government imposed a series of laws and legislation that drew Kenya into the exploitative colonial global market economy. In 1902, for instance, an ordinance was enacted empowering traditional village headmen to enforce forced labour policies. Between 1912 and 1922, the Native Authority Ordinance reinforced this policy by legalising forced labour on European farms with minimal pay.

The 1926 Native Ordinance and the hut and poll tax further ensured the availability of labour on European farms by necessitating cash income to meet tax obligations. This resulted in massive out-migration in search of wage employment, disrupting the traditional family and social networks. As a direct consequence of these policies, many women became heads of households; they continued to shoulder all their traditional responsibilities while taking up those previously carried out by men. Women relied heavily on their traditional workgroups to help meet these responsibilities. Furthermore, in areas where cash crops were predominant, women performed all the manual tasks such as picking tea and coffee, while men dominated the mechanised agricultural work.

The Swynerton Plan of 1955, which was the colonial agricultural policy aimed at expanding cash crop production to increase overall agricultural production, led to the privatisation of land and the consolidation and registration of land holdings and title deeds granted to individual African male household heads. Kenyans were encouraged to produce cash-value crops for export, which further marginalised the labour of women in food production. The plan set a precedent for African male domination of income-producing agriculture and transformed land from a source of family food to a commercial asset, from an abundant resource valued for its ability to provide food to a scarce commodity with cash value (Nasimiyu 1985).

The colonial administration encouraged the formation of farming groups that existed parallel to these traditional groups. The traditional groups are said to have disintegrated during the emergency period from 1952 to 1954. Furthermore, the introduction of Christianity made the social and cultural practices that led to the existence of these groups redundant. Stamp (1986) attributes the disintegration of the traditional groups, especially among the Gikuyu women, to the rapid social change taking place at that time. Organised group meetings were prohibited at this time, especially among the Gikuyu. Bahemuka and Tiffen (1992) also attribute the disintegration of the traditional Akamba groups to social changes in the community.

While these changes took place among the African communities, the wives of colonial administrators formed groups modelled on the women's institutes of Canada. Wipper (1975) shows that the groundwork for women's clubs was laid by the wives of colonial administrators in the 1940s. The movement was originally a type of self-help group. The wives of colonial administrators wanted to involve African women in groups where they would be taught sewing, handicrafts, health, nutrition, literacy and income-generating activities. These clubs emphasised domestic crafts such as embroidery and the improvement of the family diet, especially for children. Although this organisation started in the 1940s, European women received no assistance from the colonial administration, despite several attempts to seek government support. However, in the 1950s, the movement did receive assistance from the colonial government to carry out its activities. Wipper (1975–76) notes that the reason for this shift was twofold. The African veterans of World War II returned home, and classes to teach them some skills or a trade were held at the Jeans School, which was organised to provide training in leadership, social work and technical specialties. Veterans were accompanied by their wives, who also attended leadership classes. These women wanted to keep in touch with each other when they returned to their rural homes, so they formed clubs, assisted by the settlers and administrators' wives, who had taught them sewing and other Western home-craft skills. Second, in 1946, the Colonial Secretary in London issued a circular calling for popular participation in planning. This had only a limited effect on entrenched, top-down planning mechanisms. It was followed in 1948 by a dispatch on community development.

In Kenya, what was known as the Department of Community Development or mass education department was established; it later became the Ministry for Culture and Social Services. The Jeans School later became the Institute for Administration, established to train workers and leaders. The existence of women's institutes and other groups in the Reserves and the White Highlands created a sound base that the colonial administration could use to develop Maendeleo ya Wanawake Organisation (MYWO), which translates as women's progress clubs, at the end of 1951. The Department of Community Development, through the Jeans School, trained African women who would go out to the districts and foster the formation of the clubs. Bahemuka and Tiffen (1992) argue that the Maendeleo clubs encouraged better use of land and the growing and cooking of nutritious foods, as well as the improvement of livestock. They also emphasised the importance of women's reproductive roles through activities focused on motherhood, childcare and housekeeping. Wipper (1975), however, noted that at this time

Nancy Shepherd, the assistant commissioner for community development and rehabilitation, began to organise women's clubs with the aid of volunteers. Professional leadership was supplied by the community development personnel, but the main motivating force came from volunteers at the local level. The process of Africanising the staff also began early. By 1955, for instance, the executive in Nyanza was an African.

Wipper (1975–76) concluded that the mere coincidence in timing of Maendeleo organisations and the outbreak of conflict might lead one to conclude that MYWO was a response on the part of the government to the Mau Mau uprising against colonial rule. It is the contention of this chapter that the colonial administration did use these clubs when needed to suppress the spread of Mau Mau. The Maendeleo organisations appeared at the right time and within the required space. Indeed, they were used to curb the growth and spread of Mau Mau among the Kamba, who border the Kikuyu. Kabira argues that, in return for this support, the colonial government awarded the Maendeleo ya Wanawake an annual grant for capital development and equipment and its members were exempted from forced labour by the colonialists. In Central Province (today's Kiambu, Nyeri, Muranga and Nyandarua counties), this created tension between the Mau Mau activists and those women's groups that supported Mau Mau, on the one hand, and the members of Maendeleo ya Wanawake on the other. Wipper (1975–76) notes that registration of the Maendeleo ya Wanawake women's groups was highest among the Akamba, as well as being common in other ethnic groups, but that among the Kikuyu it was unpopular, being seen as a loyalist creation to support the colonial government and as a tactic to suppress the Mau Mau uprising. Holmquist (1984) takes an even more radical view. He argues that the support provided by the government to women's groups and other self-help groups was a thoroughly pro-state measure and part of a state counter-insurgency effort built around community development as an attempt to stop the Mau Mau. Different lines of thought are presented in literature by Monsted (1978) and Wamalwa (1987), who argue that the Maendeleo ya Wanawake Organisation was built on the foundation of traditional groups.

Thus, there are different scholarly assessments regarding the success of MYWO in promoting the welfare of women. Scholars such as Nasimiyu (1993) argue that the MYWO had about 508 groups with a membership of 36,970 in 1954. They further assert that Maendeleo ya Wanawake is the only women's organisation that has provided a sense of continuity for the women's movement over the last three decades.

The key feature of these two sets of women's movements – one led by the colonial administrators and the other made up of traditional groups – was the fact that they were coordinated and cohesive. However, as shall be seen, immediately after independence, the women's movement lost this sense of coordination, although several groups existed and were cohesive. Maria Nzomo (1989) also notes that the MYWO was co-opted by the ruling party. In 1990, the ruling Kenya African National Union (KANU) party incorporated the Maendeleo ya Wanawake Organisation. This happened at the leadership level and as a result women at the grassroots broke away and formed their own groups outside the umbrella of Maendeleo ya Wanawake. The state at this particular time dealt with the leadership and did not partner with the grassroots women. At the state and women's leadership level, the movement was possibly coordinated, but it was not cohesive, especially at the grassroots.

The character of the women's movement in the postcolonial era

The efforts of the women's movement in Kenya after independence can be classified in three broad categories. The first category included a movement of women's groups, which was concentrated in rural areas and has slowly crept into the urban areas since 2000. The second category was made up of the formalised women's movement, based on large umbrella organisations, which purported to have a national outlook because the membership is drawn from a nationwide level. The third category was constituted through the efforts of individual women.

The women's movement at the national level

Maendeleo ya Wanawake The first and possibly oldest such movement is the Maendeleo ya Wanawake Organisation, which was discussed earlier as having its origins in the colonial era. After independence, the government and ruling party decided to strengthen its links with the MYWO. Wipper (1975) shows that MYWO was unable to reach to the grassroots level, as the leaders became highly elitist. Wipper (1975) also notes that, at this time, Maendeleo ya Wanawake clubs changed, since the leadership became highly politicised and lost touch with the grassroots level. During this time, the political struggles of the young state were inculcated into the women's movement so that the politics of the day also affected MYWO's internal organisations. Partly this can be explained by the fact that women were and still are an integral part of the electoral process. They are important in participating in the vote, and their vote is very important to winning elections from the lowest elected position to the highest. In 1990, the Maendeleo ya Wanawake Organisation was incorporated into the ruling party, KANU. Critically, this related to a form of one-party rule that was not democratic. Kiragu (2006: 18) notes 'MYWO at its inception did not challenge patriarchy; rather it sought to find ways and means through which women would weave around the imbalance of power to improve the quality of their lives and that of their households'.

Over the years, the Maendeleo ya Wanawake Organisation changed from being just a welfare organisation and became almost the women's wing of KANU. This status was consolidated during the twenty-four years of KANU rule. This created a great disconnect between the Maendeleo ya Wanawake Organisation membership and its leadership.

National Council for Women in Kenya The National Council of Women of Kenya (NCWK) was founded in 1964 as an umbrella organisation to coordinate the activities of Kenyan women, and it was formed as the Kenyan chapter of the International Council of Women. There are now more than 150 women's organisations affiliated to the NCWK. It is registered in Kenya as a non-governmental organisation (NGO) – non-profit and non-political. The NCWK concentrates on women's issues, education and the environment. It holds workshops and seminars in Kenya on gender, health issues and human rights.

In 1980, Wangari Maathai was elected as chair of the NCWK. Unfortunately, government pressure led to funding being diverted to similar organisations that were friendly to KANU, the ruling party. The NCWK ended up nearly bankrupt and survived only by concentrating on environmental issues. Maathai remained chair until she was forced to retire in 1987 through governmental intervention. The divisive strategy of the government to designate the MYWO as pro-state and NCWK as anti-state has affected NCWK for many years, leading to internal wrangles over leadership that have made it quite ineffective. In 2009, for instance, the organisation had two women claiming to be the chair, and some time later it was still not clear who exactly the chair was.

The Green Belt Movement The women's movement in Kenya has also included small groups of women affiliated to the umbrella organisation the Green Belt Movement (GBM). In this movement, women in rural settings use the greening concept to combat poverty, protect their environment, and improve their livelihoods and those of their families. The GBM was established by Professor Wangari Maathai under the auspices of the NCWK in 1977. It is an indigenous, grassroots NGO that takes a holistic approach to development by focusing on environmental conservation, community development and capacity building. The GBM organised women in rural Kenya to plant trees, combat deforestation, restore their main source of fuel for cooking, generate income, and stop soil erosion. The GBM, through the leadership of Professor Maathai, incorporated advocacy and empowerment for women, eco-tourism and just economic development.

The movement currently takes responsibility for having planted 51 million trees. Over 30,000 women have been trained in forestry, food processing, beekeeping and other trades that help them earn income while preserving their lands and resources. Communities in Kenya (both men and women) have been motivated and organised to both prevent further environmental destruction and restore that which has been damaged. The movement also underwent adaptations, including at the global level, even when policies were deemed anti-state. In 1972, the environmental movement revolutionised advocacy and policies surrounding environmental issues such as those in the United Nations Environment Programme (UNEP). UNEP was established in Nairobi as a result of the United Nations Conference on Human Environment held in Stockholm in the same year. This development helped arouse interest in the environment in Africa, regardless of the fact that many governments in the region held hostile sentiments towards the policies adopted in Stockholm to limit environmental degradation. Soon after, Maathai served as chairwoman of UNEP's Environment Liaison Centre board, which today is called the Environment Liaison Centre International.

In 1974, Maathai's focus became forestation and reforestation issues. She introduced a tree-planting programme and opened the first tree nursery, from which she formed Enviro-care Ltd. Although this programme experienced many setbacks because of a lack of funding and support, it facilitated Maathai's involvement with the NCWK as a member of the executive committee in 1977. Her determination to inexpensively provide rural women of the NCWK with sufficient wood for fuel and building and soil conservation measures inspired the Save the Land Harambee tree-planting initiative. This soon began a widespread tree-planting strategy in which over 1,000 seedlings were planted in long rows to form green belts of trees, which thus marked the very beginning of the GBM. These 'belts' had the advantages of providing shade and windbreaks, facilitating soil conservation, improving the aesthetic beauty of the landscape, and providing habitats for birds and small animals. During these local tree-planting ceremonies, community members usually turned out in large numbers. To conceptualise this fast-paced activity of creating belts of trees to adorn the naked land, the name 'Green Belt Movement' was used.

Two different schools of thought exist with regard to the activities of the GBM. The first argues that, from 1977 to 1988, the movement steered clear of traditional political arenas, seeking to transform the social ground through reforestation and education. It postulates that political agitation against the construction of Uhuru Park's multistorey complex was an individual agenda of the organisation's leader, Professor Wangari Maathai. In contrast, and in line with the second school of thought, this chapter argues that the conflicts between the state and the GBM leader were at the heart of the interests of the movement and that they cannot be separated from the goals of the organisation. The struggles between the state and the GBM for a safe and green environment in fact led to a separation between the NCWK and the Maendeleo ya Wanawake Organisation in 1980.

In 1985, the state pushed the NCWK to separate from the GBM in anticipation that the movement would fail. In 1991, the GBM launched a protest that saved Jeevanjee Gardens from the fate of being turned into a multistorey parking lot. In 1998, the movement led a crusade against the illegal allocation of parts of the 2,000 acre (8 square kilometre) Karura Forest, a vital water catchment area on the outskirts of Nairobi. The struggle was finally won in 2003, when leaders of the newly elected NARC government affirmed their commitment to the forest by planting trees in the area.

This activism came at a high cost to both Maathai personally and to the movement. The Kenyan government closed the GBM offices, jailed Maathai twice, and subjected her in 1992 to a severe beating by police when she led a peaceful protest against the imprisonment of several environmental and political activists. While these actions have served as impediments to the GBM, they have not stifled it, and it continues as a world-renowned and respected movement. In 2007, the GBM endorsed the Forests Now declaration, calling for new market-based mechanisms to protect tropical forests. Maathai herself won the Nobel Peace Prize in 2004 in recognition of her efforts in advancing sustainable development, democracy and peace. This made her the first African woman to win this prize.

In the early twenty-first century, the movement is now vibrant and has succeeded in achieving many of the goals it set for itself at its inception. Environmental protection has been achieved through tree planting, including soil conservation, sustainable management of the local environment and economy, and the protection and boosting of local livelihoods. In addition to helping local women generate their own incomes through such ventures as seed sales, the movement has succeeded in educating thousands of low-income women about forestry and has created about 3,000 part-time jobs.

Women's formal and informal mobilisation at the grassroots level

As mentioned earlier in this chapter, traditional women formed groups to assist themselves in different ways. These groups had their activities minimised during the struggle for independence but were revived at the onset of independence from the colonial administration. The women who really took up these activities were rural women whose intentions were to economically improve their family livelihoods. Wipper (1975) notes that women formed the Mabati and Nyakinyua self-help groups in line with the Harambee motto for development as articulated by the first President, Jomo Kenyatta. The motivating factor was purely economic.

The first category comprised large groups of up to 200 members covering large geographical areas. They formed cooperatives because they wanted to buy land or business premises and registered the properties in the group name for the purpose of protecting their interests (Monsted 1978; Bahemuka and Tiffen 1992; Mwatha Karega 1995). Others, such as the Nyakinyua (mature women past the reproductive age) and Kangei (younger women in the repro- ductive age bracket), opted to buy large commercial buildings. Joining together served as a measure for protecting their economic ventures from patriarchal interests, since men are traditionally not supposed to show an interest in women's properties. At the same time, women would not have had the financial or social leeway to enable them to own property on their own. The group provided a means for women to own property in a context of patriarchal norms where capital and assets were synonymous with masculinity.

Mwaniki (1986), Mackenzie (1990) and Stamp (1975–76) identi- fied another type of group, composed of roughly fifteen to twenty- five women who borrowed from traditional settings but incorporated modernity. These women carried out activities such as beekeeping, brick making and farming. Mwatha Karega (1996) identified these groups and went further to illustrate that they were entrepreneurial.

The efforts of individual women

Some of the pre-independence political women figures in Kenya include Mekatilili wa Menza, a freedom fighter from the coast; Wangu wa Makeri, a freedom fighter from the central area; Mang'ana Ogonje Nyar Ugu, the first African female colonial chief in Western Kenya; Moraa Moka Ngiti, a female freedom fighter from Nyanza (Kisii); Field Marshal Muthoni, a freedom fighter from Central Kenya; Eiokalaine O-M'barugu, an assistant chief in pre-independ- ence Kenya in the eastern area; Jemima Gecaga, the first woman to be nominated to the legislative council (LegCo); and Priscilla Ingasiani Abwao, the woman who attended the LegCo in Lancaster House, among others. The women's movement in Kenya has also taken the form of individual women pushing agendas for women, as well as for both men and women. The independent state in Kenya emerged from a nationalist movement that involved women in heroic roles.

Most of these women led struggles against colonial domination, protested against colonial oppression, fed and protected veterans during the fight for Uhuru, led segments of the resistance armies against colonialism, and effectively participated in the political negotiations leading to independence. However, the colonial structure was never dismantled, and its forms of class and gender discrimination and oppression persisted. At independence, Mzee Jomo Kenyatta deracialised the structures of the emerging state, but these structures were never de-gendered. On the contrary, the state was further masculinised and ethnicised. The incoming leadership was largely male and there were no women in the first cabinet that Kenyatta cobbled together.

There have also been a number of women political actors in post-independence Kenya who have played a significant role in shaping the landscape of women's political leadership in the country. The women included here are those who either became members of parliament and made a mark in politics, served as parliamentarians for more than one term, or remained active in national politics even after their term in parliament. They include Phoebe Asiyo, Grace Ogot, Professor Wangari Maathai, Charity Ngilu and Martha Karua.

The 2004 Nobel Peace Prize laureate, Professor Wangari Maathai, was the founder of the GBM, a women-driven grassroots reforestation and sustainable development movement that has planted more than 40 million trees. Some 60,000 women and 1,500 men manage the GBM's over 3,000 tree nurseries. Professor Wangari Maathai was mentioned in steering both the NCWK and later the GBM. Her relentless pursuit of the greening of the country as an economic venture cost her dearly, leading to imprisonment and threats from the state.

Maathai ran for the presidency in 1997 but lost. She also failed to capture the Tetu parliamentary seat. Later, in 2002, she was elected as a member of parliament for Tetu's constituency and served as Assistant Minister for Environment and Natural Resources in the government of President Mwai Kibaki from 2003 to 2005. A biologist, Wangari Maathai was the first Kenyan woman to earn a PhD and to teach and chair a department at the University of Nairobi. An environmental and socio-political activist, her numerous awards include the Goldman Environmental Prize, the Africa Prize for

Leadership and the UNEP/Eyes on the Environment Award. Maathai was a co-founder of the Nobel Women's Initiative, whose goal is to support women's rights around the world. Her autobiography, *Unbowed: A Memoir*, was released in 2006. She played a pivotal role in Kenya's politics and was without doubt a role model and mentor for many Kenyan women aspiring for leadership up until her death in 2011.

Martha Wangari Karua was born in Kirinyaga District, Central Province. She was first elected as a member of parliament for Gichugu constituency in the 1992 multiparty general election on the Democratic Party (DP) ticket. Between 1981 and 1987, she worked as a magistrate; she was in charge of the Makadara law courts from 1984 to 1985 and the Kibera law courts from 1986 to 1987, when she left to start her own law firm, which she operated until 1992. While in practice, Karua represented many pro bono cases, notable among them the treason trial of Koigi wa Wamwere and the late Mirugi Kariuki. She contributed immensely to the development of family law, particularly the law regarding the distribution of matrimonial property, as well as constitutional and administrative law. Martha Karua was a member of the opposition political movement that successfully agitated for the reintroduction of multiparty democracy in Kenya in the early 1990s. She joined Kenneth Matiba's FORD-Asili party, but lost the party nomination ticket to the wealthy and influential former Head of Public Service Geoffrey Kareithi. She was then offered a ticket and support by DP elders who wanted a clean break from the Kareithi–Nahashon Njuno rivalry in Gichugu constituency. Karua won the 1992 general election to become the MP for Gichugu constituency and was the first woman lawyer to be popularly elected to parliament. She was also appointed the party's legal affairs secretary between 1992 and 1997.

Martha Karua has remained a prominent national politician for almost two decades. Between 2003 and 2005, she served as Minister for Water and Resources Management and Development and was behind the implementation of the Water Act 2002, which accelerated the pace of water reforms and service provision. From 2005 to 2009, she served as the Minister for Justice, National Cohesion and Constitutional Affairs, a post from which she resigned on 6 April 2009 citing frustrations in discharging her duties.

In early 2008, Martha Karua headed the government's team in negotiations with the Orange Democratic Movement (ODM) regarding a political dispute that resulted from the 2007 election. She was later endorsed as the national chair of the NARC-Kenya political party on 15 November 2008. After her endorsement, she immediately declared that she would be running for the presidency in the 2012 elections. Her work as a human rights advocate has been recognised through several awards. In 1991, she was recognised by Human Rights Watch as a human rights monitor. In December 1995, she received an award from the Federation of Kenya Women Lawyers (FIDA) for advancing the cause of women. In 1999, the Kenya Section of the International Commission of Jurists awarded her the 1999 Kenya Jurist of the Year Award, and, in the same year, the Law Society of Kenya (LSK) awarded her the Legal Practitioners Due Diligence Award. In 2013, she ran for president through her own political party, NARC, but lost. She has come out as a strong defender of constitutionalism and devolution.

Many other women not profiled here also played an equally significant role in shaping the women's movement and society. Individual women have also stood their ground to fight backward cultural practices. Oduol and Kabira (1995) highlight the efforts of Wambui Otieno, who was the first woman to challenge backward cultural patriarchal practices in the burial of her husband, a case in which the state became involved from a political perspective to support cultural practices in disinheriting the widow from burying her husband. Wambui was denied the opportunity to bury her husband, who was from a different ethnic group. She rose up and fought the judicial system and patriarchal cultural practices, combined with an unfavourable political climate, for her right to bury her husband. Many women today still suffer the fate of Wambui Otieno in many ways, including disinheritance.

The lack of a critical mass of women in political institutions is a major constraint for women politicians, limiting their ability to effect significant and positive change in transforming the male-dominated culture of politics, public policy and resource allocation in a gender equitable manner. However, even in their small numbers, women have made an immense contribution while in parliament, both on the floor and through the Kenya Women Parliamentary Association.

The efforts of women parliamentarians through KEWOPA

The Kenya Women Parliamentary Association (KEWOPA) is a membership association of all the women parliamentarians across political parties, both elected and nominated, in the Senate and in the National Assembly. Its overall goal is to work towards ensuring that women and men are equitably represented in parliament and decision making in the public and private spheres in order to promote sustainable development. It works under the leadership of an executive committee headed by a chair and supported by a fully fledged secretariat that provides technical and administrative support in realising its vision. KEWOPA was established in 2001 by eight women parliamentarians, with its primary objective being to address the issues of women parliamentarians, building their capacities as legislators and representatives of their constituents, and lobbying for women-centred policies and laws.

As a result, KEWOPA increased the visibility and effectiveness of women leaders in influencing key political parties to support the entry of more women into parliament through direct elections and nomination to special seats reserved for parties. The number of women in parliament increased from eight to eighteen, and KEWOPA became an officially registered organisation in 2004.

KEWOPA successfully lobbied for the establishment of the Parliamentary Committee on Equal Opportunity in 2008. Until 2012, it worked to gender mainstream the standing orders of parliament, which originally barred handbags and trousers worn by women in parliament. It also successfully developed a gender-responsive budgeting guideline for the Kenyan parliament, and influenced greatly the passing of useful legislation such as the Sexual Offences Act (2006) and the Anti-FGM Act (2009), and the formation of the implementing board.

Constitutional and legislative reform in women's rights

The struggle for a new constitution in Kenya lasted about twenty years. As mentioned earlier, the women's movement as well as civil society and individual women were centre stage in this struggle. Women activists sought through constitutional reforms to tackle, among other things, the dismal performance of the state in the involvement of women in the legislature and other decision-making bodies (Table 8.1).

TABLE 8.1 Women's representation and participation in Kenya's parliament (1963–2012)

Parliament	Constituencies	Women elected % (no.)	Available slots for nomination	Women nominated % (no.)	Total percentage of women
1st parliament 1963–69	158	0 (0)	12	0 (0)	0
2nd parliament 1969–74	158	0 (0)	12	0.6 (1)	0.6
3rd parliament 1974–79	158	2.5 (4)	12	1.3 (2)	3.8
4th parliament 1979–83	158	3.2 (5)	12	0.6 (1)	3.8
5th parliament 1983–88	158	1.3 (2)	12	0.6 (1)	1.9
6th parliament 1988–92	188	1.1 (2)	12	1.1 (2)	2.2
7th parliament 1992–97	188	3.2 (6)	12	0.5 (1)	3.7
8th parliament 1997–2002	210	1.9 (4)	12	2.3 (5)	4.2
9th parliament 2002–07	210	4.8 (10)	12	3.8 (8)	8.6
10th parliament 2008–12	210	7.6 (16)	12	2.8 (6)	10.4

Due to the various ways in which women juxtaposed their marginality with the lack of a good constitution, they kept a watchful eye on parliament and networked with MPs to ensure that women's gains in the constitution were protected throughout all the debates that led to the negotiations. Although some battles were lost, the

2010 constitution resulted in revolutionary laws on affirmative action, delivering its promise on gender equality in various articles.

They first focused on equality and non-discrimination. Article 27 of the constitution demands the participation, inclusiveness and protection of minorities and marginalised groups and demands that legislative and policy measures be taken to facilitate the implementation of the constitution. Article 27(3) states that women and men have the right to equal treatment, including the right to equal opportunities in political, economic, cultural and social spheres. Equality is defined as similarity of treatment as it is legally, constitutionally and divinely given. It is a fundamental right. These provisions provide important additional protections that go beyond the protection from discrimination provided for in Article 27(4) of the constitution, which prohibits discrimination on grounds of disability and age. Article 27(6) recognises the principle of affirmative action, a concept that requires the state to take legislative and other measures designed to redress any disadvantage suffered by individuals or groups as a result of past discrimination. Article 27(8) requires the state to take measures that ensure that no more than two-thirds of the members of elective or appointed bodies are of the same gender. Separate provisions create reserved positions for women in the National Assembly, Senate and county assemblies. These provisions have had a significant positive effect on women's representation and have enhanced women's role in the decision-making process at all levels of government.

Article 21(3) of the constitution imposes an obligation on state actors to address the needs of all vulnerable groups in society, including women. It demands recognition of human rights as one of the ground rules for national development and the actualisation of fundamental rights and responsibilities for both men and women. To fully realise this gain, there is a need to integrate the promotion and protection of human rights into national policies and to support the inclusion of human rights provisions through subsequent legislation.

Unfortunately, despite these very progressive gains, the experiences and performance of women during the 2013 elections were not altered as significantly as expected. This outcome is largely due to explicit violation or half-hearted implementation of the constitution. For example, no female governors or senators were elected.

Implementing affirmative action for women in parliament The Kenyan parliament is currently made up of the National Assembly and the Senate. The National Assembly consists of 290 directly elected members from the 290 constituencies, forty-seven women members elected to represent women from each individual county, and twelve members nominated by political parties. Sixteen women were directly elected from the single-member constituencies, accounting for only 6 per cent of the directly elected members of the National Assembly, which compares with the previous 8 per cent (sixteen women out of the 210 constituencies). Of the twelve members to be nominated by political parties, five women were nominated. Considering that the tenth parliament had six nominated women, the current number has fallen. Women's representation at the county level was realised through the direct election of forty-seven women to the National Assembly. Overall, the current National Assembly has sixty-eight women, which translates to 19.4 per cent of the total membership of the Assembly.

On the other hand, the Senate consists of forty-seven directly elected members from the forty-seven counties; Kenyans did not place a single woman in a Senate seat. Thus, sixteen women members were nominated from party lists in proportion to the number of seats won by each political party; and four members were nominated by political parties – two representing people with disabilities, and two representing the youth. The total number of women in the Senate is eighteen, representing 27 per cent of the Senate membership.

In one election cycle, the constitution enabled a critical number of eighty-six women out of 418 members. These greatly increased figures, however, do not even meet the constitutional threshold of two-thirds of either gender. Five years down the line, there is no concrete, agreed-upon formula on the table that will enable the two-thirds principle to be fulfilled in the National Assembly. In a recent debate in parliament, it was proposed by the legal committee that the court should rule that the two-thirds principle is progressive, meaning that it should be achieved incrementally. However, no benchmarks were put in place; no timelines were drawn up, making it indefinitely progressive. This is against the spirit of the constitution and is retrogressive, given that affirmative action works through timelines. It also underscores a lack of political will.

Meanwhile, forty-seven county assemblies was created. In spite of the constitution being very clear on the two-thirds principle, and on the formula for counties, some counties have not met the two-thirds threshold. There are also no clear penalties for counties that do not meet the requirement, and they receive nothing in terms of punishment.

Further, the constitutional requirement is that all appointed positions must also be representative of the maximum two-thirds of either gender. There are nineteen ministries, and women's representation within cabinet positions, as well as in permanent secretary posts, although much better than ever before, merely beats the bare minimum requirement, with a current figure of 31.1 per cent.

Conclusions

This chapter has presented the character of the women's movement from the precolonial period to the postcolonial era. It has shown the struggles of women with forces such as the patriarchal nature of the state, the cultural and traditional practices of society, as well as masculinities that occupy their space. The involvement of women by the state when required and the fact that they were left out by the state when there was a need to do so are also discussed. The chapter has displayed the struggles of women united, women in civil society, and women within the intellectual community, as well as grassroots movements. Even with the highest law of the land being put in place and positioning women within a protected quota system, the state and the legislature have been overtaken by the patriarchy, defeating the spirit of equality and administering injustice and discrimination.

References

Bahemuka, J. M. and Tiffen, M. (1992) *Environmental Change and Dryland Management in Machakos District, Kenya 1930–1990, Institutional Profile: Akamba Institutions and Development 1930–1990*. Nairobi: ODI/University of Nairobi.

Holmquist, F. (1984) 'Self-help: The State and the Peasant Leverage in Kenya'. *Africana*, 54, 72–91.

Kiragu, J. (2006) 'Is There a Women's Movement?' in Muteshi, J. (ed.) *Mapping Best Practices: Promoting Gender Equality and the Advancement of Kenyan Women*. Nairobi: Heinrich Böll Foundation.

Maathai, W. (2006) *Unbowed: A Memoir*. New York: Alfred A. Knopf.

Mackenzie, F. (1990) 'Gender and Land Rights in Muranga District, Kenya'. *Journal of Peasant Studies*, 17, 609–43.

Monsted, M. (1978) *Women's Groups in Rural Kenya and their Role in Development.* CDR Paper A.78.2. Copenhagen: Centre for Development Research (CDR).

Mutiso, C. G. (1975) *Kenya: Politics, Policy and Society.* Kampala and Nairobi: East African Literature Bureau.

Mwaniki, N. (1986) 'Against Many Odds: The Dilemma of Self-help Groups in Mbeere, Kenya'. *Africa,* 56, 210–28.

Mwatha Karega, R. G. (1996) 'Women's Groups: From Welfare to Small-scale Business in Kenya'. *Small Enterprise Development,* 7(1), 31–41.

Mwatha Karega, R. G. (1995) 'Rural Women in Small Business: Entrepreneurial Group Activities in Kitui District, Kenya'. PhD thesis, University of Reading.

Nasimiyu, R. (1985) 'Women in the Colonial Economy of Bungoma: Role of Women in Agriculture, 1902–1960' in Were, G. S. (ed.) *Women and Development in Africa.* Nairobi: Gideon Were Press, pp. 56–73.

Nasimuyu, R. (1993) 'The History of Maendeleo ya Wanawake Movement in Kenya, 1952–1975' in Khasiani, S. A. and Njiro, E. I. (eds) *The Women's Movement in Kenya.* Nairobi: Association of African Women for Research and Development.

Nzomo, M. (1989) 'The Impact of the Women's Decade on Policies, Programs and Empowerment of Women in Kenya'. Unpublished paper.

Oduol, W. and Kabira, W. (1995) 'The Mother of Warriors and her Daughters: The Women's Movement in Kenya' in Basu, A. (ed.) *The Challenges of Local Feminism: Women's Movements in a Global Perspective.* Boulder CO: Westview Press, pp. 187–208.

Stamp, P. (1975–76) 'Perceptions of Change and Economic Strategy among Kikuyu Women of Mitero, Kenya'. *Rural Africana* 29, 9–44.

Stamp, P. (1986) 'Kikuyu Women's Self-help Groups' in Robertson, C. and Berger, I. (eds) *Women and Class and Africa.* New York: Holmes and Meier.

Wamalwa, B. N. (1987) 'Are Women's Groups Exploiting Women?' Discussion paper for Women's Networking Group meeting, Nairobi, April.

Wipper, A. (1975) 'The Maendeleo ya Wanawake Organization: The Co-optation of Leadership'. *African Studies Review,* 18(3), 99–120.

Wipper, A. (1975–76) 'The Maendeleo ya Wanawake Movement in the Colonial Period: The Canadian Connection, Mau Mau, Embroidery and Agriculture'. *Rural Africana,* 29, 195–8.

9 | WOMEN ORGANISING FOR LIBERATION IN SOUTH AFRICA

Sheila Meintjes

Introduction

For women's organisations, the end of apartheid and the rise of democratic government meant a shift from confrontation with the state to engaging with it, as women's associations sought to influence the political and constitution-making process. Women's activism took diverse forms, but in the transition it focused on ensuring that gender equality became integrated into the constitution. This enabled the formation of the Women's National Coalition, and a broad consensus developed around promoting women's rights, needs and interests. This chapter starts with a brief discussion of disputes within and about 'feminism' in the South African context, and then turns to a discussion of the nature of women's political demands that formed the basis of alliances between diverse women's ideological and class interests. But engaging the state meant professionalising activities and tended to exclude women from community-based organisations. The chapter uses the example of the movement combatting violence against women to show how this occurred. The NGOisation of civil society meant that women's engagement became depoliticised and the women's movement demobilised. The consequences have been that a political and professional elite now dominates the policy terrain to the exclusion and the frustration of community-based activism. While the principles of gender equality and gender mainstreaming in government are in place, this has not led to significant changes in the androcentrism embedded in society's gender politics.

The shift from anti-apartheid movement politics to democracy and social integration after long years of segregation changed both the nature of politics and the nature of organisation in South Africa. Opposing the state was replaced with engaging the state in the first decade or more following the first democratic elections in 1994. This entailed a change in both the form and content of social and political organisation in every sector of civil society. As evidenced in other parts of the world where transitions from authoritarianism to democracy occurred, transition meant a shift from 'movement activism' to more 'issue-specific interventions and pragmatic strategies' (Lang 2013). In Germany after unification, for instance, Sabine Lang identified what she called 'the NGOisation of feminism'. Voluntary rape crisis intervention and support groups, legal aid groups as well as environmental groups, among others, established more formal organisations and began to employ professionally qualified personnel. Professionals replaced unqualified, voluntary staff. This trend can also be seen in feminist and women's groups in South Africa, particularly in the arena of organising against violence against women. The purpose of this chapter is to critically examine the evolving forms that women's organisations in the arena of violence against women took in the context of a developing relationship between the state and civil society in South Africa.

It begins with a brief discussion of the significance of the notion of 'feminism' in the South African context. It then turns to an evaluation of the nature of women's political organisation in the past and the issues and demands that formed the basis of women's political involvement. This provides a context within which to understand the developments that occurred in the very different political conditions of democratic change in a post-1995 South Africa. The final part of the chapter provides a brief case study of the arena of violence against women and traces the effects of changing state–society relations on organisations.

Feminism and South Africa

The term 'feminist', as most of us have come to understand it, has its origins in the struggles of women in Europe and North America, and of white women in colonial situations, for equal rights and equal status with men. During the second wave of feminism that emerged in the late 1960s, this view was challenged in the West, where winning formal equality did not alter the exclusion of women from decision making in public life and even in the economy. Women began to organise in loose consciousness-raising groups to explore the structural and political underpinnings of this exclusion. There was an outpouring of literature – popular and academic – which sought to understand why women remained secondary subjects and could not enjoy full equality. This brought to the surface the more systemic relations of subordination and oppression of women. Initially, the discussion presupposed a somewhat essentialist notion of womanhood and placed in the foreground factors that identified a universal subordination of women. The outcome was an intellectual challenge to the dominance of a male-centric theoretical, political and social world.

The different strands of feminism – liberal, socialist and radical– suggested quite different political strategies to achieve liberation. There were those who saw liberation in the achievement of a more substantive equality with men, which required recognition of the role that the private/public dichotomy played in subordinating and oppressing women. Corrective measures were conceived as more childcare facilities and greater sharing of tasks in the home. Others argued that the whole economic system needed to be overthrown if women were to achieve liberation. Others still argued that it was patriarchy – the dominance of men – that needed to be overthrown.

The terms 'women's liberation' and 'women's movement' were coined to describe the political activities of different feminists. This ferment did not leave women in the developing world out of the discussion entirely. There were those who debated issues of subordination in less developed regions – but it was more of a debate *about* than a debate *with* women of those regions. In the United States, African-American women were the first to challenge the Euro-centrism of the concerns and debates of feminists, pointing out that the notion of the private sphere as the *central* locus of oppression ignored the nature of systemic oppression along different axes – of both class and, more significantly, race – found in wider society. Moreover, the suggestion by socialist feminists that *class* formed the key nexus of gender oppression obscured the way in which *race* operated to structure the oppression of black people in general, and black women in particular. This was the origin of the debate on difference that has completely transformed the politics and discourse of feminism during the previous thirty years. Since the late 1980s, indeed, the theorising of difference and of the intersection of different forms of oppression and systemic blockages to full equality has spawned a remarkably rich theoretical debate, starting with Kimberlé Crenshaw's seminal article in 1989 (Crenshaw 1989).

In South Africa, robust debates among women political activists characterised their involvement in the political struggle for liberation. There was not always agreement about how to position themselves in relation to feminism. Some eschewed any association with the concept of 'feminism', claiming that it was Western in origin and that in the context of the South African struggle it had divisive effects. It divided women from each other, for there were many women who could not identify with the idea of feminism and women's liberation. It also divided men and women from each other. Others embraced the term, and attempted to give it a meaning germane to the national struggle in which South Africans were engaged. Thus, women in the African National Congress Women's Section (ANCWS) during the 1980s fought for the recognition of a simultaneous struggle against apartheid oppression and gender oppression. Some of the progressive leaders in the organisation took up the refrain that this was the only way for true national liberation to be achieved.

The dramatic release in 1989 and 1990 of political prisoners serving life sentences for their participation in actions aimed at bringing down the apartheid regime accelerated the process of negotiating South Africa's transition to a democracy. In this new political milieu, exiled movements were unbanned and exiles returned home. For women political activists, this meant ensuring that the emancipation of women from gender discrimination or gender subordination was put on the national agenda. The ANCWS and internal women's organisations met in Amsterdam in January 1990 to debate these issues. It was agreed at this conference that 'the point of departure is to start with women's needs and their level of understanding of their reality and to move at their pace' (Malibongwe Conference Papers 1990). This perspective had permeated progressive women's organisations in South Africa and was one with which all women could identify. There were a number of women who defined themselves as feminists and who felt that this blocked the possibility of a more transformative politics, but this aspect of the debate was muted. Kemp et al. suggest that this is one of the reasons why, earlier, some Rape Crisis members resigned from the organisation when it joined the United Democratic Front (UDF) in Cape Town in 1983 (Kemp et al. 1995: 140).

Less than a year later, however, in a changed political environment, transformation was seen in much more pragmatic terms. The African National Congress Women's League (ANCWL), relaunched in

South Africa in August 1990, envisaged a much broader coalition of interests to create a 'Woman's Agenda' to place on the national negotiating table. This vision led to the creation of a Women's National Coalition (WNC) in April 1992, comprised initially of four regional coalitions and approximately sixty national organisations. Its specific objective was to ensure equality for women in the new constitutional dispensation (Meintjes 1998). The WNC played a pivotal role in promoting a nationwide debate on gender equality and its meaning in society and in a constitutional dispensation.

In September 1991, the ANCWL called together women's organisations across the political and ideological spectrum to raise awareness of the neglect of women's issues among the country's leaders. There was a need to establish a position that reflected the broad objectives of all women across social, political and ideological divides to ensure that this neglect was not entrenched in a new political dispensation. In particular, the new constitution should reflect a commitment to full and substantive equality between men and women. The meeting, attended by representatives from political parties and a wide range of women's organisations, not all of them progressive in a liberal sense, established a broad principled agreement on this objective. A fascinating consensus also emerged on the question of the status of women in society: all accepted the idea that women experienced subordination in society that should be combatted. They agreed that a coalition, rather than a new organisation, was the best means of achieving this end.

The launch of the WNC in April 1992, after widespread consultations and preparations, was a historic moment. It saw women from different class backgrounds, racial groups and political parties, as well as from different kinds of women's organisations, including religious, welfare and the health sectors, rub shoulders with one another. They found much to agree upon in the search for common goals, although these agreements were based on recognition of their differences as well. They would not always agree on the details of what gender rights and gender justice might mean.

Women in the transition: women's response to political change in the 1990s

During the 1980s, women had mobilised across the social spectrum in political, civic and independent organisations. These organisations laid the basis for the emergence of a strong women's leadership network, which demonstrated its capacity to intervene strategically in the interests of women in the ensuing decade. A question for this leadership was whether women's organisations should remain autonomous or join the ANC, the new 'government in waiting'. One of the lessons learned from Mozambique and Zimbabwe had been how the incorporation of women's organisations into the state had demobilised women's initiatives. Would dissolving into the ANCWL fetter independence? The reappearance of the ANCWL as an autonomous organisation aligned with the ANC seemed to put these concerns to rest and the regional organisations did in fact dissolve and join the League. This was to prove a contentious and somewhat demobilising decision once the constitutional objectives of gender rights had been achieved. Still, in the early 1990s, the euphoria of freedom and democracy blinded even the most astute political critics to this possibility.

For the ANCWL, a major issue was that of translating the commitment of the ANC to women's emancipation into a reality reflected in leadership positions and the treatment of women as equals. Frene Ginwala suggested that there was a growing understanding within the ANC of 'gender oppression' as a structural condition. Ginwala had been a senior member of the ANC in exile. As deputy head of the ANC Emancipation Commission and head of the ANC Research Department before she was elected to parliament in 1994 and made speaker of the House of Assembly, Ginwala had proclaimed her identity as a feminist. For Ginwala, radical change was required to eliminate gender oppression (Beall 1990). Ginwala may well have drafted the 2 May National Executive Committee (NEC) statement on the 'Emancipation of Women in South Africa'. This took the movement's commitment beyond its previous position of simply mobilising women for the struggle against apartheid. The 1990 statement committed the ANC to including women's oppression as an integral part of the struggle for liberation. That a fundamental restructuring was in order was reflected in the commitment to tackling 'the material base, the legal system, the political and other institutions and the ideological and cultural underpinning of gender oppression now and in the future'. It acknowledged that affirmative action would have to rectify 'patterns of discrimination'.

There was little discussion of the meaning of gender oppression in the newly established branches of the movement. It was hardly surprising that, at the ANC July 1991 conference, when the ANCWL pushed for a quota system in the NEC, it was baldly rejected. Although the majority of the 2,000 delegates did not support the proposal, the debate was conducted at length and with intensity. Not a single member of the NEC spoke in favour. The ANCWL had underestimated the conservatism of the broad membership of the ANC, including that of many women who also voted against the quota (Horn 1991: 37). This was a salutary lesson about the need for political and social education about human rights and democracy.

The defeat led the ANCWL and the ANC Emancipation Commission to debate the value of a broader consensus about gender equality, and the need to revisit the idea of a new women's charter or similar document that would reflect the current demands of women from all walks of life in South Africa. 'It is an issue for all South African women, not just ANC women, although the League will have to spearhead the campaign,' said Baleka Kgositsile Mbete, Secretary-General of the ANCWL. In September 1991, the ANCWL thus called the first meeting of organisations outside the movement to propose an alliance of women's organisations to launch a 'Charter Campaign'.

The Women's National Coalition and the Charter campaign

On 27 September 1991, the first of a great number of conferences, workshops, seminars and consultations was held with thirty women's organisations to discuss the aim of drawing up a women's charter for equality. At this meeting, the delegates found common interests and concerns in a number of key areas. They agreed on the fact of gender oppression and that in diverse ways it affected all women in South Africa. They agreed, too, that fundamental changes must eliminate not only racism but sexism as well. Frene Ginwala's opening address at the official launch in April 1992 pinpointed the objectives of the coalition: 'Women will have to make sure that the constitution goes beyond a ritualistic commitment to equality and actually lays the basis for effective gender equality.' The launch of the WNC comprised sixty national organisations and four regional coalitions affiliated to it. By February 1994, when it presented the outcome of its campaign, the 'Women's Charter for Effective Equality', to the final WNC national convention, ninety national organisations and fourteen regional coalitions were members. The campaign had reached more than 2 million women.

The WNC recognised that women across the diversity of race and class shared the experience of subordination and oppression although their everyday lives differed according to material circumstances. Recognition of difference made possible the coalition of women across a broad ideological and political range. It moved away from the essentialism that had dogged feminist initiatives elsewhere in the world. Nonetheless, there were problems in reaching an agreement about the structure of the coalition and its relationship to member organisations. Fears were expressed that the WNC might impinge on the autonomy of organisations, while a number of women feared the dominance of political parties. The number of voting delegates to the conference also created tensions, with smaller organisations resisting the possibility of being swamped by more numerous, politically aligned groups. Once these problems were resolved, the WNC was mandated to organise a campaign to consult with women throughout South Africa about their problems, needs, hopes and dreams for the future.

The WNC set up a Negotiations Monitoring Team to keep tabs on the constitutional talks then taking place in South Africa. It provided reports and information to the WNC member organisations (Albertyn 1994). Its work made possible the most significant intervention of the WNC in the constitutional process. This was over the question of the equality provisions in the bill of rights, to which traditional leaders objected. Chief Nonkonyana, a member of a supposedly 'progressive' organisation of traditional leaders, CONTRALESA (Congress of Traditional Leaders of South Africa), himself a young lawyer at the time, led the assault on equality for women by seeking the exclusion of customary law from the purview of the bill of rights. This would have meant that women living under customary law would forever be treated as minors. He also sought recognition of the powers and status of chiefs. The ANC was sympathetic to these perspectives. The WNC reacted instantly, condemning this attempt to exclude a large proportion of women from enjoying the fruits of democracy. The ANCWL was particularly offended at the views of its own party, which seemed prepared to compromise women's rights to equal citizenship and full equality. The debate was aired on radio and television, which gave the WNC much needed publicity. The WNC, led by the ANCWL, held protests outside the venue where the constitutional talks were being held. The final outcome was the removal of the offending compromise clause from the draft constitution.

The WNC campaign had three objectives: to educate women about human rights and equality, to elicit women's demands for the charter, and to engage in a nationwide participatory research project. The findings of the research formed the basis of the 'Women's Charter for Effective Equality' (Meintjes 1998). It was envisaged that the charter would perform a dual function. It would reflect the diversity of demands of South African women, and it would also become a political document around which women's organisations could mobilise and act in their own chosen ways. Some hoped that the charter would also become the focus for the mobilisation and organisation of a strong and effective women's movement in South Africa. Since the release of the charter in 1994, this hope has never been realised. Part of the reason for this failure lies in the very diversity of interests involved in the WNC: there had been little to hold a sustained movement together, apart from the desire for effective equality in the constitution. Recognition of diversity would not be enough. The notion of developing and building a women's movement was instead replaced by the less encompassing objective of developing a charter that could become the basis for policy.

The experience of South Africa's WNC confirms the experience of women's movements elsewhere: that the capacity for a diversity of organisations with differing ideological interests to work together depends upon mobilising around a unifying issue. Once this is achieved or off the agenda, the raison d'être for unity falls away. Since 1994, there have been significant issues around which women have mobilised, but the nature of women's organisations in South Africa has tended to block the evolution of what Lang has called a politicised and mobilised 'feminist public'. Instead, many of the initiatives taken around particular issues have been spearheaded by issue-based organisations, such as those concerned with violence against women. These have been quasi-professional civil society organisations offering counselling services or advocacy around policy and legislation, and therefore should not be seen as a feminist movement per se.

Once the charter was ratified in June 1994, the WNC elected to continue its existence in order to popularise and take forward the aims expressed in the charter. However, it faced leadership challenges as well as lack of funding to sustain itself. Capable leadership that would have balanced the diverse interests of women at a national level went into parliament, where their energies turned to national politics and the tasks of the moment, rather than to fighting the gender struggle. However, a women's caucus in parliament made significant gains for women. In 1996, for example, it launched a 'Women's Budget' initiative that drew its inspiration from the Australian gender mainstreaming of that time and focused on the areas in which policy needed to address the specific needs of women, particularly among the urban poor and in rural areas. It also developed a legislative agenda in 1998 that introduced progressive improvement in customary marriage laws, in reproductive health, and in domestic violence. The process was spearheaded by Pregs Govender, who had been the campaign manager of the WNC until the 1994 democratic elections and who became chair of the Joint Parliamentary Committee on the Quality of Life and Status of Women. Another key area where the lobbying of parliamentarians made significant advances for women's concerns was in the establishment of the Office on the Status of Women (OSW), which was attached to the then Vice President's office. Since Mbeki, Mandela's Vice President, effectively managed the governance of the country, this was significant. Within government departments, gender desks were established to monitor the progress of gender equity inside the state.

During the first three democratic governments under Mandela and Mbeki, gender mainstreaming resulted in a greater presence of women in governance, although not always in great numbers. The OSW and the Commission for Gender Equality (CGE) monitored the progress of mainstreaming gender policy and gender equity. Under the leadership and presidency of Jacob Zuma since 2007, the ANC has taken a more conservative and tradition-oriented turn. However, women continued to be appointed to high office in the cabinet. In the last decade, indeed, the principle of fifty–fifty has been adopted by the ANC in its vision for gender equity. The principle of establishing a national CGE to promote and monitor the progress of gender justice and gender equality in state and society was established in the interim constitution. Although it took some years for the law to be passed, the CGE was set up in December 1996, when the appointment of its first eleven gender commissioners was made.

How effective were these organisational realignments for women's interests? The WNC dramatically altered the visibility of women during the height of its campaign to promote gender equality from June 1993 to February 1994. This had significant influence on the negotiations for a new constitution, particularly with respect to ensuring the protection of gender and sexual rights in the bill of rights. It also heightened the visibility of women as political actors, and women's representation in parliament was never questioned. The WNC campaign was significant too in raising public awareness in the media, while its education workshops around the country on the themes of women's legal status, access to rural and urban land and resources, violence against women, and health and work left a legacy of gender rights that people have called upon in their campaigns for social rights. The campaign transformed the profile and discourse around women and gender relations. It gave substance to the shadowy notion of 'non-sexism' and asserted the importance of women's particular disabilities in the debate about human rights in South Africa at the time. The WNC campaign engaged the whole of South African society in questioning its norms about women's status and women's citizenship. Yet the organisation could not sustain itself, and within a short number of years it was limping along, with no organisational membership. Today, it exists in nothing but name.

More important and long-lasting were the state institutions set up to promote the rights, needs and interests of women, even for those living under customary law. Changes to the law subsequently outlawed rape in marriage, offered protection from domestic violence for women, and made discrimination against women illegal. The reform of customary marriage laws in particular recognised customary unions and gave women equal proprietary, contractual and judicial status with men. These changes signalled the success and influence of women's campaigns for their rights, even in the private sphere. The CGE promotes the implementation of gender equality in state and society. It monitors new legislation for its implications for gender equity and reports annually to parliament on its activities. It identifies gaps and offers suggestions for policy and legislation. It has been particularly critical of the way in which traditional authority and customary practices have been promoted by the ANC government because of the way this undermines some of the gains made by women living under customary law. A significant aspect of its work is that it cooperates and engages with civil society organisations with the same aims and objectives. It is also proactive in evaluating the ways in which political parties promote gender equality – particularly during election periods.

Women's organisations and feminism: post-1994 elections

The fact that women's organisations in South African managed to achieve so much in terms of a constitutional dispensation that reflects substantive equality and spells out the objective of 'non-sexism' was remarkable. In no other constitution in the world have such progressive ideas been articulated. The problem, though, is that effective equality can be achieved only if everyone – women, men and children – are able to claim and access their rights. In a society that remains strongly tied to patriarchal notions of authority and power, women's autonomy is not guaranteed. South Africa remains a society that has not reconstructed its gender power relations – despite the struggles of the WNC and the later gender violence movement – and men and women are not easily going to give up the benefits of the current gender order.

Significant during the 1990s was the manner in which the strategies of women's organisations adapted to the new democratic order. We have seen how the WNC placed pressure on the negotiation process and influenced the outcome, shaping aspects of the new constitution. However, after the 1994 elections, the WNC came adrift. As a coalition of a wide spectrum of women's organisations, it was well positioned to take up the agenda defined by the Charter for Effective Equality. Yet it failed to do so, partly because of a failure of leadership. Those who could have defined a programme of action had gone to parliament, while the constituent parts of the coalition that might have developed into a more broad-based movement were either averse to politics or too closely aligned to political parties. At the same time, there was general recognition among feminists that without a women's movement in civil society to press for transformation, the driving force that would lead to change would evaporate.

The ANCWL lost the non-partisan leadership role it had played in the early 1990s and reverted to its role as a mobilising agent for the ANC, which made membership both desirable and competitive for women who wanted to enter politics. During the first twenty years of democracy, its fortunes ebbed and flowed. It faced leadership and financial problems. Its membership, however, is very diverse, including both the middle class and the urban and rural poor in its rank and file. Thus, it was important for political leaders to ensure that the ANCWL retained some legitimacy through its links with 'the people'. In high-profile cases involving either rape or the murder of women, the ANCWL has a significant presence, monitoring the outcome and making statements to the media. In the Oscar Pistorius trial in June 2016, the ANCWL was vocal in its condemnation of the light sentence accorded to the famous 'blade-runner' for the murder of his girlfriend. However, despite its strong stance on gender violence, the leadership of the ANCWL has taken increasingly conservative positions on issues such as virginity testing and criticism of free artistic expression of sexuality, or towards Jacob Zuma, who has made both homophobic and sexist comments from time to time. Thus, the earlier leading role of the ANCWL in driving progressive and feminist issues has declined in the decade since the Zuma rape trial of 2006.

While the ANCWL may not have pursued a feminist trans-formative agenda, the legacy of the WNC in the arena of gender violence has been taken up by campaigns of broad-based, visible and effective non-governmental organisation (NGOs) working with community-based organisations. These campaigns cut across the boundaries of difference and forge new kinds of alliances to end violence against women. During the transition in the 1990s, the issue gained considerable prominence thanks to the campaigns first conducted by the WNC and followed by the establishment of a network of organisations linked together by a shared concern about the prevalence of violence against women. This network coordinated annual national campaigns around the issue of vio-lence against women in collaboration with the government minis-try in charge of promoting gender equality. The month of August has become known as 'women's month' and celebrates the role of women in the struggle for gender equality. It is possible that this network may yet form the nucleus of a transformative South African feminism. What follows is an example of how engaging the state has required considerable expertise and has transformed the nature of organisations themselves.

Engaging the state: violence against women

Violence against women is endemic. In the past, the issue was neglected and there was a silence around its existence and its horrendous effects, but the transition to democracy changed this. As the political struggle against apartheid waned, social issues became more clearly articulated by different lobby groups. Rape crisis organisations had emerged in the late 1970s to provide support for survivors of violence against women. However, during the apartheid period, the focus on this issue was seen as divisive and peripheral to the anti-apartheid struggle. Thus, rape crisis groups and organisations were seen as aligned with the concerns of Western feminists who had no understanding of the African context. That there was any connection between patriarchy and apartheid was simply ignored or denied. During the 1970s and 1980s, anti-violence activists and professional psychologists focused on support during court cases, counselling victims of abuse, and on providing information that would enable victims to survive. Little was known about the extent of violence against women. The reasons for this silence are complex, but it seems to relate to the prevalent myth that women invite rape. There was almost no discussion of violence and abuse against women in the liberation and anti-apartheid movement. At the opposite end of the spectrum, until 1979, the issue of abuse and rape was not addressed by the apartheid state either. Any relationship between rape crisis organisations and the state would wait nearly two decades, until the 1990s and the transition to democracy.

However, in 1982–83, the South African Law Commission set up a project committee on the subject of sexual offences. Its brief was to explore the limits of the common law in dealing with domestic violence. This was the context within which the state began to interact with anti-gender violence organisations. In the course of the 1980s, as South Africa moved more clearly into what one might call a 'civil war', the context of violence changed. State strategies to deal with growing popular opposition turned all critics of the government into potential 'terrorists', and terror tactics were used against them. Women political activists in detention faced both threats of sexual violence and egregious sexual abuse (Russell 1989; Goldblatt and Meintjes 1998).

While the commitment to end violence against women was at first seen as 'irrelevant' to the mainstream struggle against apartheid, this view began to change during the mid-1980s. Rape crisis activists became increasingly drawn into the mainstream struggle in their provision of psychological counselling for detainees in the 1980s. This created a more sympathetic milieu for women's organisations dealing with gender violence to emerge in the townships and suburbs. In Lenasia, an Indian Group Area built some 40 kilometres outside Johannesburg, Women Against Violence and for Emancipation (WAVE) was formed in 1988 to support abused Muslim and Indian women. The organisation changed its name later to the Nisaa Institute for Women's Development. In Eldorado Park, a coloured township of Johannesburg, a women's crisis centre known as Women Against Woman Abuse (WAWA) was established in 1989. In Alexandra township on the north-eastern periphery of Johannesburg, the Alexandra Health Clinic began to provide counselling support to abused women during the late 1980s. This grew in the 1990s into Agisanang Domestic Abuse Prevention and Training (ADAPT).

While the silence surrounding abuse was not broken, support in communities where its incidence had been denied broadened the base of the anti-violence against women movement. At the same time, in the late 1980s, more attention began to be paid to the reasons for the abuse of women. As more and more organisations began to realise the extent of violence experienced by women in South Africa, so some feminists began to theorise that the nature of the rape experience was tied to the ways in which masculinities were constructed in society. Others began to identify a condition of 'endemic violence' for a large proportion of women in personal relationships. This crossed the boundaries of race, class and culture. Increasingly, too, awareness of the widespread incidence of public, arbitrary, yet collective gang rapes became the subject of debate and concern for feminist activists and academics (Meintjes 2003). The organisation of rape crisis centres and interventions during the 1990s made the issue of the abuse of women much more widely acknowledged, if not completely understood.

Rape crisis activists, despite their reluctance to deal with the state, did make proposals to the South African Law Commission for changes to the policing and legal framework for rape and other sexual offences in the 1980s. This engagement with the state required considerable understanding of the principles and nature of legal discourse. This paved the way for a change in the nature and scope of organisations working for the eradication of violence. The focus on support and counselling for survivors provided by volunteers faced new demands for professional psychological and legal expertise. The effect of this engendered tension between a new cohort of professionals and a whole generation of experienced voluntary workers. As organisations sought new and greater funding, so expertise in budgeting and finance was required. The voluntary organisations were gradually replaced by professional NGOs, confirming the argument made by Sabine Lang.

These new organisations stepped into a new space, where they were able to influence government policy. Criminologists, lawyers and researchers – albeit feminists – provided direction and leadership in this process. The 'window of opportunity' opened up by the democratic space of the new South Africa was perceived as one that might be short-lived, as experience elsewhere had indicated. This meant that volunteers were sidelined, not having the necessary skills to engage the state. Thus the democratic space was dominated by professionals able to access comparative experience elsewhere and to develop strong evidence-based policy arguments. Desiree Hansson, a criminologist from the University of Cape Town and a rape crisis activist, was influential in the thinking that went into addressing the problems of rape crisis from a strategic policy point of view. She argued that in order for change to be effected in society, it was necessary for government structures to be set up with the objective of serving women's interests. Moreover, such structures needed adequate budgetary allocations (Hansson 1991). Her arguments were taken up within the WNC, which in 1993 held an international conference to discuss the kinds of institutional mechanisms needed in state and society to end violence against women. Hansson had envisaged a violence prevention committee to deal with the context of violence against women. In Australia, such a committee coordinated taskforces in three areas relevant to dealing with the problems of violence: housing equity and access, professional education, and community education. But the new mechanisms instituted by the democratic state did not go so far.

Because of the enormity of the problems faced by the new South African democratic state, which came to power virtually bankrupt, and the widespread nature of the priorities it faced in dismantling apartheid, it was thus left to the NGOs to begin the process of pushing for appropriate legislation and institutional support. In 1998, the Domestic Violence Act was enacted. It was pushed through parliament with the support of President Mbeki and driven by Pregs Govender, the indomitable chair of the Joint Parliamentary Committee on the Quality of Life and Status of Women. The act was very much the outcome of the collaborative effort of the Law Commission and a cohort of civil society lawyers working in the field of gender violence, and the Parliamentary Committee (Meintjes 2003). It was seen as a triumph of collective participatory governance. The gender violence debate was, in effect, conducted at a fairly theoretical and legalistic level that tended to silence grassroots activists. As this example shows, engaging the state in the new era shifted the structural relationship and political space in which voluntary community-based organisations operated. From a focus on the survivor of violence and a confrontational relationship with the state, which had been their experience under apartheid, organisations in the new democratic dispensation were able to engage the state, influence the shape of policy and legislation, and subsequently monitor the implementation of such policy. However, the 'volunteers' often found themselves excluded. The engagement of the NGOs with the state did not so much create a new social movement as enable a new set of professional civil society actors to be involved in the national policymaking framework. This provided significant opportunities for progressive gains for a feminist agenda within the state. The difficulty with this process was that, because of the issue-based focus of the policy process, it was not tied to a broader strategy to mobilise women. The early hopes that the openness of the state and its 'women friendly' nature might lead to a new impetus for the mobilisation of a more feminist-oriented movement were not fulfilled.

Conclusions

The transition to democracy in South Africa, as transitions from authoritarianism or post-war situations elsewhere have shown, provided a window of opportunity for women's organisations, such as the WNC, to make rights claims and have them integrated into constitution-making processes. However, while this meant gains for women's rights, it also meant that women's organisations were required to become more professional in their ability to engage the state. It required knowledge, skill and professionalism. In South Africa, the campaigns of the WNC had contributed to a debate about women's rights and to the promotion of gender equality through the establishment of new national institutions, such as the OSW and the CGE. While the process should have led to a much greater sense of women's agency, in fact many women activists found themselves silenced and their activism sidelined. A process of demobilisation of social movements, their 'NGOisation' and morphing into 'civil society', tended to depoliticise the issues that were of concern to women. While feminist perspectives had percolated into the liberation movements, in particular the ANC, there was hostility from many women activists, including professionals, to what was seen as 'Eurocentrism' and the importation of a 'foreign' ideology.

So feminist agendas of social transformation were also sidelined despite much of the rhetoric about women's rights. But in many respects, rights were conceived even by women activists in static, bounded ways, and they referred to women's right to autonomy rather than seeing this in the context of more flexible social relations, where the content of rights is negotiated, disputed and, most importantly, defended. If the Women's Charter for Effective Equality had been seen as a living document, which some members of the coalition certainly argued, then it might have become a tool for transforming gender power relations in the context of constitutional rights to full equality. Instead, the influence of the WNC lasted only as long as it took for its objectives of ensuring that gender equality was embedded in the bill of rights to be fulfilled. The WNC's decline tended to confirm international perspectives that the weakness of women's mobilisation was precisely its focus on specific issues, rather than seeing this as one among other strategies geared towards transformation. The WNC could not sustain its existence once gender equality was included in the constitution. Instead, its influence was eclipsed by the campaigns of a national network of organisations that focused on the endemic gender violence that pervaded society. In the gender violence sector, too, organisations became more professional as they participated in the Law Commission, or provided legal, research and advocacy services for less skilled community-based organisations.

In the course of these processes that saw women's interests reflected in the constitution, law and policy, ironically the voices of women in communities were virtually silenced. It is clear from the experience of the demise of the WNC and the professionalisation of NGOs, combined with a growing conservatism among the political elite, that a gap has emerged where a women's movement used to be. That this poses a threat and undermines the gains made in the first twenty years of democracy is becoming clear. But new kinds of coalitions between social activists are emerging in South Africa. In 2015, students rose up to demand that the unfinished business of apartheid needed attention. The youth comprise the largest numbers of the unemployed and students demanded a transformation in the ownership of the economy and of land, and access to education and jobs. They argued that the benefits of democracy had not reached the majority, who still languished in poverty. They demanded the 'decolonisation' of university curricula, and an end to the domination of Western ideas in a largely white-dominated academy. They demanded free tertiary education. However, none of these demands had a gender content to them nor acknowledged and recognised the gender equality deficits that exist in South Africa. The radicalism of student demands, among others, poses both an opportunity and a threat.

It is clear that a more collective approach is thus needed if society is to make any headway in dealing with patriarchal domination. There is therefore an important role for new forms of collaboration to be established between the institutional mechanisms set up to protect democracy and gender equality in particular, including the parliamentary committee devoted to monitoring and protecting the quality of life and status of women, and the professional NGOs working to promote women's needs and interests, and community-based organisations that express and reflect women's claims, needs and interests. Feminist activism presents the most hopeful means for such collaboration, because it is perhaps the most sensitive to the interdependence of relationships within the context of South Africa's extreme differences of wealth, class, race and gendered experience.

References

Albertyn, C. (1994) 'Women and the Transition to Democracy in South Africa'. *Acta Juridica*, 1, 39.

Beall, J. (1990) 'Picking up the Gauntlet: Women Discuss the ANC Statement'. *Agenda*, 8, 5–18.

Crenshaw, K. (1989) 'Demarginalizing the Intersection of Race and Sex: A Black Feminist Critique of Antidiscrimination Doctrine, Feminist Theory and Antiracist Politics'. *University of Chicago Legal Forum*, 140(1), 139–67.

Goldblatt, B. and Meintjes, S. (1998) 'South African Women Demand the Truth' in Turshen, M. and Twagiramariya, C. (eds) *What Women do in Wartime: Gender and Conflict in Africa.* London: Zed Books.

Hansson, D. (1991) 'Working against Violence against Women: Recommendations from Rape Crisis (Cape Town)' in Bazilli, S. (ed.) *Putting Women on the Agenda.* Johannesburg: Ravan Press.

Horn, P. (1991) 'Post-apartheid South Africa: What about Women's Emancipation?' *Transformation*, 15, 26–39.

Kemp, A., Madlala, N., Moodley, A. and Salo, E. (1995) 'The Dawn of a New Day: Redefining South African Feminism' in Basu, A. (ed.) *The Challenge of Local Feminisms: Women's Movements in Global Perspective.* Boulder CO: Westview Press.

Lang, S. (2013) *NGOs, Civil Society,* *and the Public Sphere.* Cambridge: Cambridge University Press.

Meintjes, S. (1998) 'Gender, Nationalism and Transformation: Difference and Commonality in South Africa's Past and Present' in Wilford, R. and Miller, R. L. (eds) *Women, Ethnicity and Nationalism: The Politics of Transition.* London: Routledge.

Meintjes, S. (2003) 'The Politics of Engagement: Women Transforming the Policy Process – Domestic Violence Legislation in South Africa' in Goetz, A.-M. and Hassim, S. (eds) *No Shortcuts to Power: African Women in Politics and Policy-making.* London: Zed Books.

Russell, D. E. H. (1989) *Lives of Courage: Women for a New South Africa.* New York: Basic Books.

Documentary sources

Malibongwe Conference Papers (1990) are held in the Library, Centre for Applied Legal Studies, University of the Witwatersrand.

10 | AFRICAN WOMEN ACTIVISTS: CONTRIBUTIONS AND CHALLENGES AHEAD

Balghis Badri

Introduction

Building on the individual chapters that have contributed to this book, this concluding chapter focuses on the challenges African women and activists face, highlighting the diversity and complexity of the struggles around their concerns. It starts with a discussion of how some of the issues discussed in the individual chapters have helped shape and influence international norms and practices regarding women's rights. It then explores the multifaceted challenges confronting activists, ranging from patriarchy to ideological constraints, challenges of building alliances, socioeconomic concerns, political constraints, fundamentalism and terrorism, lack of democratisation, challenges of realising substantive reforms, and finally the capacity of women's organisations themselves to effect change.

These challenges do not operate in isolation, but rather are interrelated, requiring comprehensive strategies to tackle them. This book has shown the ways in which African women's rights activists have responded to these challenges and have contributed significantly to global understandings of women's role in politics, in the economy, in peace-making, and in legal and constitutional reform, as evident in Chapter 1.

More than twenty-five years ago, in 1981, world leaders agreed to eliminate all forms of gender discrimination when they adopted the Convention on the Elimination of all Forms of Discrimination Against Women (CEDAW), and since then 189 countries have ratified the treaty. The historic 1995 Beijing Fourth United Nations (UN) Conference on Women's Platform of Action pledged to increase women's representation in all areas of leadership. The Millennium Development Goals of 2000 sought to promote gender equality and empower women. While some gains have been made in the areas of education, employment and political representation, many of the key women's empowerment goals remain elusive, while the gains are uneven across the globe. As Secretary-General Ban Ki-moon (2010) stated: 'Until women and girls are liberated from poverty and injustice, all our goals – peace, security, sustainable development – stand in jeopardy.'

African contributions to changing international norms and practices

In Chapter 1 we highlighted some of the key areas in which African women have been global leaders and have influenced global discourses, norms and understandings of women's rights, namely the political representation of women, accessing economic opportunities, peacebuilding, and legal and constitutional reforms that have tackled challenges from traditional and religious authorities and customary law that stood in the way of advancing women's rights. In several key areas, African women's movements have shaped outcomes in ways that have put African women in the lead globally.

The struggles for women's political visibility and the importance women place on political representation are evident throughout the book. Samia Al Nagar and Liv Tønnessen show in their chapter on Sudan how women activists mobilised for the passage of the 2008 National Election Act, which gave women 25 per cent of the seats in the national and state legislative assemblies. Similarly, Nana Pratt describes a 50/50 movement for quotas and greater political representation of women that emerged in Sierra Leone, and campaigns to increase female legislative representation were described in the chapters on South Africa, Ghana, Kenya, Morocco, Tanzania and elsewhere.

While Rwanda has the highest rate of legislative representation of women in the world, the three North African countries discussed in this book (Tunisia, Morocco and Sudan) are leaders among the Arab countries in terms of women's political representation, with Tunisian (and Algerian) women claiming 32 per cent, Sudanese women holding 31 per cent, and Moroccan women 18 per cent of the legislative seats. Moreover, all the predominantly Muslim countries with the highest rates of representation for women in legislatures can be found in Africa, with Senegal leading at 44 per cent.[1] It

1 See the Inter-Parliamentary Union website: http://www.ipu.org/wmn-e/classif. htm (accessed 19 July 2016).

is also the case that post-conflict countries have on average among the highest rates of representation of women in legislative and government positions, and African countries have had proportionately more than their share out of all countries exiting war since the 1990s and especially since 2000 (see Chapter 1). The speed with which many African countries increased female representation prompted discussions throughout the world about the utility of gender quotas and how others might emulate these strategies. Rwanda, in particular, created new global precedents when it surpassed Sweden in 2013 with the largest percentage of women in the legislature and became the only country with a majority of women represented in parliament (64 per cent) (for more on these debates, see, for example, Dudman 2015).

Women's movements in Africa have not only influenced global discussions regarding women's political representation, they have brought to international attention the constraints on women in terms of economic opportunity, such as limited access to credit, land ownership, inheritance, business skills, and other support services. Women in the informal sector face additional challenges of limited access to public services such as water and electricity and to new technologies (Quartey et al. 2014).

Today, African countries, particularly in sub-Saharan Africa, are global leaders in female labour force participation. There are as many women entrepreneurs as men in Africa, according to the Global Entrepreneurship Monitoring Survey 2010, and, in a country such as Ghana, the numbers of women exceed those of men as entrepreneurs. Many women are involved in the informal economy and, in particular, in the kinds of market-related activities discussed by Akua Britwum and Angela Akorsu in their chapter on 'Market women's associations in Ghana.' Ghanaian women's mobilisation has sought to improve the conditions of market women and give them access to credit and political influence, and this is reflected in the experiences of women throughout the continent. The informal economy expanded in Ghana and elsewhere during the years of economic crisis and structural adjustment in the 1980s, propelling women into positions of greater economic efficacy.

The percentage of women in the labour force globally has been slowly declining since 2005, when it reached a high of 40.2 per cent, dropping to 39.6 per cent by 2014. However, in Africa women's labour force participation has continued to increase, as it has in Latin America and the Middle East. The gap between male and female labour force participation is closing in Africa and has decreased from women making up 43.6 per cent of the total labour force in 1992 to 45.9 per cent in 2010, a total increase of 2.3 percentage points, according to World Bank indicators. Moreover, the overall percentage of women's labour force participation is roughly the same as that of North America, making these two regions the highest in the world in this area (Table 10.1).

TABLE 10.1 Female labour force as a percentage of total labour force participation

Region	2014
North America	46.0
Sub-Saharan Africa	45.9
Europe and Central Asia	44.8
East Asia and Pacific	43.5
Latin America and Caribbean	41.5
South Asia	26.5
Middle East and North Africa	21.3
World	39.6

Source: World Bank series, WP14911.3, http://databank.worldbank.org/ (accessed 9 October 2016).

Women's visibility in the economic sphere in Africa has implications for their capacity to mobilise, their access to resources, the nature of the kinds of demands they make in the political arena, and, ultimately, their ability to translate their concerns at the national level and even within international forums.

African women's rights activists have also been world leaders in peace-making. As Nana Pratt shows in her chapter in this book, Sierra Leone was one country where women's role in peace-making and their contributions to ending the 1991–2002 civil war were lauded both nationally and internationally. As a result of this type of activist pressure, African peace treaties mentioned women's rights in 23 per cent of the treaties compared with such references in 17 per cent of treaties globally, according to UN Peacemaker data (Tripp 2015: 148). African women also built bridges across difference in numerous conflicts and came together to demand seats at the peace talks and pressed for democratic elections that would transfer power from a military regime to an elected government.

Zainab Bangura, who is mentioned in Pratt's chapter on Sierra Leone, embodies many of the ways in which African women activists have shaped global discourses on peacebuilding. She took her experiences during the conflict in Sierra Leone into the global arena, particularly after she was appointed in 2012 as Special Representative of the UN Secretary-General (UNSG) on Sexual Violence in Conflict. This was after she served as Sierra Leone's foreign minister. In 1994, during the civil war, she founded Women Organised for a Morally Enlightened Nation (WOMEN), which was the first non-partisan women's rights group in Sierra Leone. Pratt discussed the central role the organisation WOMEN played in demanding female representation in the peace talks and in building peace. Bangura and others strongly condemned the atrocities of the Revolutionary United Front against civilians. She also helped found Campaign for Good Governance and used it to campaign for the holding of national elections that finally helped oust from power the military government of the National Provisional Ruling Council (NPRC). This paved the way for Sierra Leone to eventually democratise and hold its first democratic elections in twenty-five years.

In her position as Special Representative of the UNSG on Sexual Violence in Conflict, Bangura was able to put the spotlight on sexual violence in conflict in the international arena. As a result of her involvement in these issues, the UN Security Council voted unanimously on 24 June 2013 to adopt a resolution condemning sexual violence in conflict and impunity for such crimes. This is just one example of the ways in which women in Africa influenced global action around violence against women in conflict.

Finally, chapters on Morocco, Tunisia, Sudan, and Kenya show how central discussions of customary law, traditional and religious authorities and culture have been in efforts by African women's movements to change the legal and constitutional structures in their countries. In Sudan and elsewhere, it is generally the sphere of customary law and personal law that governs the family, and this is where resistance to reform is greatest and where the pushback from Islamists and Salafist groups, as well as from traditional authorities and clan leaders, has been most strong. Laws and constitutional reforms pertaining to the state (for example, female quota provisions and education of girls) or the market (such as maternity provisions) may be controversial, but rarely to the extent of family law provisions.

The rewriting of almost all constitutions in Africa after 1990 in the context of democratisation and post-conflict dynamics made it possible to introduce broad reforms in women's rights. Tunisia and Morocco were leaders in the Middle East and North Africa region, and more generally among predominantly Muslim countries, in reforming their personal status laws, but the chapters by Labidi and Sadiqi show just how challenging these reforms were to pass and implement.

The decline in female genital mutilation (FGM) in Africa has also been, in part, a product of lobbying by women's rights organisations supported by the health community. The legal initiatives have generally been complemented by other efforts to educate people and create incentives to abolish the practice. By 2015, twenty-three out of twenty-seven countries in Africa that practise FGM had passed legislation restricting it. Sudan was among the few countries that resisted. Liv Tønnessen and Samia Al Nagar (see Chapter 6 on Sudan; also Tønnessen and Al Nagar 2016) argue that in spite of the widespread use of Islamic arguments against FGM by women's rights activists, mobilisation by the religious conservatives succeeded in preventing legislation that would have criminalised FGM within the National Child Act. However, in other countries such as Kenya (see Chapter 8 by Mwatha), the effort to pass a law banning FGM succeeded in 2009 after many years of mobilisation for it.

Child marriage is another contested issue, which is raised by several of the authors in this collection. According to the Social Institutions and Gender Index regional report for sub-Saharan Africa (2016), only nine out of forty-six countries allow girls to be legally married under the age of eighteen and some allow girls younger than eighteen to be married with parental consent. There have been numerous efforts to pass legislation and take other measures to address the issue of early marriage. The African Union's Campaign to End Child Marriage was launched in 2014 in Addis Ababa at the Conference of Ministers of Social Development and is focusing on thirty countries.

Early marriage is seen to have a negative effect on women because it limits their chances of gaining an education; it is tied to poor health outcomes for both the girls and their children; it is associated with greater risk of domestic violence and less reproductive decision making; and with it comes a higher risk of maternal mortality. In spite of resistance to the reforms that would increase the age of marriage, 24 per cent of women aged fifteen to nineteen were married in Africa in 2014, which was a drop from 26 per cent only two years earlier. However, this rate is still almost twice the world average of 13 per cent.

As African women's movements tackle these issues of political representation, economic opportunity, peacebuilding and family law reform, they continue to make their mark on international debates and influence the ways in which international actors and leaders think about these issues. At the same time, they continue to face enormous challenges, which are summarised below based on the contributions to this volume.

The challenges of patriarchal ideology

The challenge of patriarchal ideology is a central concern of the authors in this book. Patriarchy is not unique to Africa and is found globally, but it takes on its own specificities in Africa. This point is also emphasised by Sheila Meintjes (Chapter 9, 'Women organising for liberation in South Africa') in discussing the obstacles that South Africans confront in implementing their constitution, which is one of the most progressive in the world when it comes to articulating goals of non-sexism. However, society strongly adheres to patriarchal notions of authority and power, making it difficult for women to assert their autonomy and for all family members to access their rights and claim equality. Gender power relations remain unreconstructed, while men are not easily going to give up their privilege, power and authority. Pratt (Chapter 2, 'The Evolution of the women's movement in Sierra Leone') similarly regards patriarchy as an obstacle in her chapter on the women's movement in Sierra Leone. As she explains: 'The continuing patriarchy and male dominance in Sierra Leone take the wind out of the sails of the women's movement. Men often use rural women's illiteracy and ignorance to undercut support for women leaders who understand the issues and are poised to mobilise women from all regions. Men often tell rural women that the actions to be taken will benefit only educated women.'

Finally, Lilia Labidi in Chapter 4 ('Tunisian women's literature of denunciation') discusses the patriarchal mindsets of some male authors in North Africa. According to Joseph T. Zeidan, the well-known and widely published Egyptian writer Abbas Mahmoud Al-Aqqad (who died in 1964) 'saw women as dependent and weak by nature, needing the guidance and supervision of men'. He regarded women as disobedient because of 'their resentment of the way men had been their masters throughout history and that now they had enough and wanted revenge'. She also shows how 'Taoufik al-Hakim attributed the absence of women in fields such as musical composition and architecture to their lack of capacity to think and to concentrate', thus betraying a patriarchal regard for women.

Moreover, resistance to undertaking legal reform has been attributed to the dominant patriarchal ideology, which sometimes takes the form of customary beliefs. Women's activism in many African countries still needs to address many issues to achieve both legal reform and changes in practice. There has been considerable resistance in many countries to such issues as legal reform in the areas of land and property inheritance by women, female genital cutting, child marriage, forced marriage, bride wealth, polygamy and marital rape. Legal change often precedes actual changes in practices. However, even countries that have tried to harmonise the contradictory impulses of supporting women's rights while at the same time protecting customary law adjudicated by traditional authorities have run into problems in practice.

Religious and secular ideologies

The other, related dimension of an ideological challenge is of religious beliefs and customary laws. This is predominantly witnessed in Muslim countries, but it is also linked to traditional and Christian African beliefs. The greatest challenge facing Muslim women's movements in African countries with regard to gender equality relates to family law, especially as it pertains to Islamic law. Challenges to customary law have been more challenging than many other areas of reform because attitudes are slow to change, particularly when it comes to sharia-derived family laws (Logan 2009). It has been harder to pass legislation regarding women's rights to land and inheritance. Religious leaders, chiefs, elders, clan leaders and others who adhere to older norms and cultural practices have sometimes actively resisted improving women's legal status, particularly in the area of family laws. Many of these individuals benefit politically and even economically from maintaining the status quo (Tripp 2015).

Women's movements in some Muslim countries find it challenging to reconcile international standards with Islamic sharia laws. Samia Al Nagar and Liv Tønnessen discuss this at length in the case of Sudan in Chapter 6 ('Women's rights and the women's movement in Sudan (1952–2014)'). They argue that:

> Women's movements in the Middle East and Northern Africa are influenced by both an international human rights agenda and the expansion of Islamic and Salafist influences, which are doctrines that place women's rights within an Islamic frame. These conflicting trends have led to polarisation between secular and Islamic approaches to law reform, particularly within the area of family law. The women's movement has thus remained divided in many locations in the Middle East and Northern Africa.

Fatima Sadiqi in Chapter 5 ('The Moroccan feminist movement (1946–2014)') discusses the challenges facing secular feminists to advance their demands for gender equality based on a discourse that emphasises equal rights based on similarity in humanity, unlike the Islamic feminists who challenge them with a discourse based on complementarity. The Islamic discourse highlights a religious and cultural identity that needs to be protected against a Westernised secularist discourse. Sadiqi shows in her chapter how Islamic feminists highlight cultural identity as an unambiguous Islamic identity, whereas secular feminists generally consider religious identity as part of women's multiple identities and highlight religious identity as reductive and crippling, because it complicates the treatment of gender inequality and injustice. This religion-based identity is also often seen as highlighting the male establishment as the supreme authority. For Sadiqi: 'The focus on religious identity by Islamic feminists makes the discussion of women's issues outside religion almost impossible. This is generally seen by secular feminists as a way of reducing a woman's multiple identities to her religion.'

Building alliances

The key challenge for women's rights activists is how to build alliances across ideological and political divisions. Changes in the priorities of women activists have created a challenge for solidarity of action among diverse feminist and activist groups. Some believe that it is crucial to concentrate only on social and economic development issues as priorities without challenging cultural values. Others consider that no substantial change in women's positioning and development can be achieved without addressing the structural root causes of women's subordination and the violence against them. Nana Pratt indicates in Chapter 2 ('The evolution of the women's movement in Sierra Leone') that some women are hesitant to hold the government accountable on certain issues because they are more loyal to the political party in power than to women's concerns and interests. Women from various political parties may not reach a consensus on the actions that would benefit the majority of women because of their party loyalties. Women's movements are not only divided ideologically and politically, but also based on urban versus rural interests, elite versus grassroots differences, as well as class and generational divides.

The aforementioned arguments have also been elaborated on by Al Nagar and Tønnessen in the case of Sudan. They suggest that a generational gap emerged, particularly in opposition to the conservative leadership of the Women's Union, which continued to conform to harmful traditions and customs despite women's entry on a large scale into universities and the workforce. The Union did not take up issues relating to marriage, sexuality and virginity, which were of great importance for young Sudanese women. As one of their interviewees, Nour Muhammed Uthman, explained, the Union 'grew out of touch with the international developments. They still maintained the same programme despite vast demographic and social changes. With time, they lost members. The youth did not identify with the movement because of their dinosauric attitudes. They did not manage to bridge generations.'[2]

Sadiqi highlights the urban–rural divide in the Moroccan context when explaining that both secularists and Islamists remain elitists. She points out that:

> It is important to note that neither the secularist nor the Islamic trend addresses the Berber issue per se in spite of the fact that this language is closely related to the third-wave women's

2 Interview with Nour Muhammed Uthman, Omdurman, 13 October 2012.

movement. This is due to the fact that, geographically, secular and Islamic feminist centres that fight violence against women are concentrated in urban areas, especially the cosmopolitan Rabat and Casablanca. In a sense, both secular and Islamic feminist trends generally represent rural women as 'passive beneficiaries', or 'reasons' for securing national and international funding.

Sheila Meintjes (Chapter 9, 'Women organising for liberation in South Africa') views the diversity within coalitions as ultimately a challenge for the formation of a broader women's movement, leaving individual organisations to work separately while joining forces only on pressing national issues. She also argues that: 'The NGOisation of civil society meant that women's engagement became depoliticised and the women's movement demobilised. The consequences have been that a political and professional elite now dominates the policy terrain to the exclusion and the frustration of community-based activism.'

The lack of democracy

Activists have also confronted non-democratic political contexts that have constrained their mobilisation. The plight of the one-party, non-democratic political system that lasted in most African countries from the 1960s until the 1990s – and in some cases longer – restricted freedoms of organising and expression. To maintain their one-party hegemony over government, leaders established women's organisations as an umbrella for all women, tied to the patronage politics of the single party. They also restricted women's actions to the social welfare context.

Aili Tripp (Chapter 7) describes how the Women's Union under one-party rule in Tanzania was able to make some legislative gains for women, but the autonomy of the organisation was curtailed as the ruling party controlled its agenda, the selection of its leaders and its financial resources.

The women's organisations formed by the government were regarded by many activists as politicised organisations merely used to bring women into political structures and acting as part of the mechanism for ensuring support for the party or government or for preventing opposition from the masses. They were monitored and directed to ensure that they would support various party and government initiatives. Thus, as we explained in Chapter 1

> women's organisations tended to be focused on welfare and domestic concerns and espoused a discourse of 'developmentalism'. At the grassroots level, women's associations were mostly producing handicrafts, promoting literacy, farming, participating in income-generating projects, fighting AIDS, subscribing to faith-based organisations, engaging in cultural expression and other such activities.

Long periods of military rule, which banned the activities of women's movements, radically limited their room for manoeuvre. These military regimes created their own top-down state machineries, without much genuine inclusion of women's groups or oppositional political parties. Because of the strong link between women's groups and ruling political parties, the political engagement of women has suffered from polarisation. The lack of democracy challenged activists with coercion or the threat of it. Such non-friendly contexts threatened both the possibility of solidarity and continuous sustained activism for the achievement of demands. Labidi elaborated on this coercion in discussing the challenges activists faced during dictatorial regimes. Women such as Tunisian Sihem Ben Sedrine, who defended human rights and press freedom, became targets of harassment by the intelligence services and state-owned press under Ben Ali's regime. The press, according to Labidi, called her a 'prostitute, hysterical and delirious' and 'claimed she had sold out to Zionists and Freemasons, and circulated pornographic images on which her face was pasted, in an effort to break her psychologically'.

The harassment of women activists as individuals made many not even report the violence they experienced during the dictatorship. The closures of NGOs and confiscation of their assets were actions that challenged African women's activism. Labidi describes the challenge of facing dictatorship regimes, stating:

> Several women in prison were victims of violence for having challenged the dictatorships of the Habib Bourguiba and Zine el-Abidine Ben Ali regimes, or for having supported a spouse, a

brother, a father or a friend who made such a challenge. Several
organisations produced reports on violence against political
prisoners committed during these periods.

The postcolonial and military resistance period

Nationalist leaders who claim that they are supporters of women's
issues during periods of resistance, whether against the colonialists or
national dictators, sometimes challenge African women's activism.
During post-struggle transitional periods, they change their position
to argue that any consideration of women's issues will detract from
achieving the national agenda of nationalisation or development. They
claim that the women's agendas are alien, Western or individualistic
in orientation. This is highlighted by Sadiqi in the case of Morocco:
'In matters of politics and activism, the second wave feminists
quickly realised that their issues and demands had never constituted
a priority in Moroccan national history, nor in the ideologies of the
country's formal post-independence political parties.' The feminists
of the time were torn between their feminist commitments and their
political allegiances.

This is also emphasised in the Sudanese experience of the general
strike of 1985 against the government of Jafaar Nimeiri, bringing the
country to a halt. Demonstrators opposed rising food, petrol and
transportation prices and many women took part in demonstrations
as part of professional unions. According to Al Bakri: 'It was
important to note that housewives led some demonstrations, held
secret meetings in their homes, and helped to protect the people
attending the meetings. However, gender issues were not raised
during the strike, being considered of secondary importance in
relation to political issues' (Al Bakri 1995).

From theory to praxis

Moving from a legal framework to the implementation of laws
is yet another challenge that African feminists face, in spite of
political gains. Even when constitutions are reformed and women
are guaranteed seats in legislatures and other governmental bodies
through a quota system, the state and the legislature are still controlled
by patriarchy, defeating the spirit of equality and administering
injustice and discrimination. This has been highlighted by several
authors. Mwatha argues in the Kenyan case (Chapter 8, 'The

women's movement in Kenya') for the need for activists to create a critical mass, because the fact that there have been so few women in political institutions has limited their ability to have a significant impact on transforming the male-dominated culture of politics and create more equitable resource allocation.

A further challenge to African women is that women tend to be marginalised in both formal political and economic institutions such as organised labour and political office (Britwum 2012). At the same time, they form the bulk of the African informal economy workforce, as is evident from Chapter 3 on 'Market women's associations in Ghana' by Akua Opokua Britwum and Angela Dziedzom Akorsu.

Brown and Lyons (2010) recognise the challenges informal economy workers face in voicing their concerns and influencing national policies. Collective action, however, provides these workers with opportunities to overcome such limitations, provided that they are strong and can identify with institutions to access these benefits.

In other contexts, the challenges of achieving activists' goals are related to the inability to implement policies, as is evident in the case of South Africa. Meintjes points out that NGOs have engaged the state in ways that have created new, professionalised actors within the policymaking framework, but this has not allowed for the advancement of a feminist agenda within the state. The issue-based focus of the policy process has made it difficult to link up with broader civil society mobilisation.

Logistical challenges

There are several other challenges of a practical nature that can be related to funding, access to the media, inadequate publication and dissemination, and limited professional human resource capacity. The lack of proper mechanisms for information sharing poses challenges for the promotion of the women's movement. Labidi highlights the issue of publishing when she states:

> [I]t is important to note that the French-language writing by women in Tunisia, although significant in volume and often winning awards, has no real presence in France. Also, women novelists cannot survive on the income from their writings and in only a very few cases do publishing houses, local or foreign,

finance their publication. Only within the past few years have a number of French language departments in Tunisian universities shown an interest in the writings of Tunisian women. And university departments of Arabic literature show lower rates of women in the faculty than other departments. Also, censorship has affected publications in Arabic more significantly than those in French.

Labidi also highlighted the lack of integration of women's writing in the secondary curriculum. This observation could be found in other countries as well, where activists are seeking to bring their voices to bear in mainstream curricula and media that would then influence new generations about women's identity, representation, demands and achievements. This type of visibility would allow for these perspectives to be introduced as part of the nation's history and literature. In addition, we see that women writers are more frequently publishing their autobiographies and letters, as well as documents and biographies of women who became active in public space; these are elaborately discussed as success stories in Tunisia, but other countries face challenges that need to be met and women's writing needs to be documented and disseminated.

The other challenge facing activists is the lack of funds, qualified staff and space for women's machinery of government and women's organisations to function effectively. This is clearly indicated by Pratt in the case of Sierra Leone. She argues that the lack of an adequate funding base complicated efforts for sustainable interventions throughout the country. Donors have often dictated organisations' activities. Funding is usually tied to project activities aligned to donor priorities and cease with changes in these priorities. Organisations face challenges in implementing activities that relate to their core issues. Additionally, many donors are reluctant to provide institutional support to organisations, which hinders the effective functioning of their offices. Most of the time, the organisations do not have adequate funds for hiring full-time, appropriately qualified personnel and have to rely on volunteers, who may not be fully committed or even possess the technical and managerial skills necessary to run their offices.

The government-sponsored women's ministries or departments were established as an outcome of African women activists' demands, but they too are challenged by a lack of qualified staff and inadequate budgets and resources, sometimes struggling to even obtain office space. Indeed, some women activists see them as little more than a token gesture towards the consideration of women within political and institutional structures.

Conclusion

The future for African women activists seems brighter due to the use of social media by the younger generation. Women activists have sought to recognise and accept their differences and to combine their action when faced with strong challenges that would undermine their fundamental gains. The main new challenge for African activism is to demonstrate regional and global solidarity against the fundamentalist terrorism of Islamic State and its variants within West, Central and North African countries. The global feminist agenda against terrorism needs to be developed as a roadmap for African women's activism against this latest challenge.

References

Al Bakri, Z. B. (1995) 'The Crisis in the Sudanese Women's Movement' in Wieringa, S. (ed.) *Subversive Women*. London: Zed Books.

Britwum, A. O. (2012) 'Female Union Leadership, Power, Dynamism and Organised Labour in Ghana' in Ledwith, S. and Hansen, L. L. (eds) *Gendering and Diversifying Trade Union Leadership*. London: Routledge.

Brown, A. and Lyons, M. (2010) 'Seen but not Heard: Urban Voice and Citizenship for Street Traders' in Lindell, I. (ed.) *Africa's Informal Workers: Collective Agency, Alliances and Trans-national Organizing in Urban Africa*. London: Zed Books.

Dudman, J. (2015) 'The UK Has a Lot to Learn about Gender Equality from Countries like Rwanda'. *The Guardian*, 24 March.

Logan, C. (2009) 'Selected Chiefs, Elected Councillors and Hybrid Democrats: Popular Perspectives on the Co-existence of Democracy and Traditional Authority'. *Journal of Modern African Studies*, 47(1), 101–28.

Quartey, P., Owusu, G. and Bawakyillenuo, S. (2014) 'Are Ghana's Women More Entrepreneurial than its Men?' *Brookings* [online], 19 August. Available at http://www.brookings.edu/blogs/africa-in-focus/posts/2014/08/19-ghanaian-women-entrepreneurs-owusu-quartey-bawakyillenuo.

Social Institutions and Gender Index (2016) *Sub-Saharan Africa SIGI Regional Report*. Paris: Organisation for Economic Co-operation and Development (OECD).

Tønnessen, L. and Al Nagar, S. (2016) *Criminalizing Female Genital Mutilation in Sudan: A Never Ending Story?* CMI Insight. Bergen: Chr. Michelsen Institute.

Tripp, A. M. (2015) *Women and Power in Post-conflict Africa*. New York: Cambridge University Press.

ABOUT THE EDITORS AND CONTRIBUTORS

Balghis Badri is a professor of social anthropology and director of the Regional Institute for Gender, Diversity, Peace and Rights at Ahfad University for Women, Sudan. She has previously taught at the universities of Khartoum and Riyadh, and was head of research at the Arab Centre for Training and Research in Tunis. In addition to her academic research, she is active in struggles for women's legal rights and empowerment, has headed several NGOs, and has worked as a consultant on gender issues to several UN agencies and government ministries.

Aili Mari Tripp is professor of political science and Evjue Bascom professor of gender and women's studies at the University of Wisconsin-Madison in the United States. She has published extensively on gender and politics and on women's movements in Africa and globally. She is author of several award-winning books such as *Women and Power in Postconflict Africa* (2015) and co-author of *African Women's Movements: Transforming Political Landscapes* (2009).

Angela Dziedzom Akorsu is associate professor and director, Centre for Gender Research, Advocacy and Documentation, University of Cape Coast, Ghana. She has specialised in the areas of employment and labour issues in development studies for the past ten years, authoring publications on gender and employment, informality, labour relations, human resource planning, employee training, trade unionism and labour standards.

Akua Opokua Britwum is a senior research fellow at the Centre for Development Studies at the University of Cape Coast, Ghana. Her teaching and research interests cover gender-based violence, gender and economic policy as well as trade union democracy and informal sector labour force organisation.

Lilia Labidi is an anthropologist and psychologist, co-founder of the Association of Tunisian Women for Research and Development (AFTURD) and the Tunisian Association for Health Psychology. She is the author of publications on the feminist movement, the construction of identity, and the aftermath of the Arab Spring. She served as minister for women's affairs in the provisional Tunisian government and has held fellowships and visiting professorships at numerous international institutes and universities, including the Woodrow Wilson International Center for Scholars (Washington, DC), the American University in Cairo (Egypt) and the National University of Singapore.

Sheila Meintjes has been professor of political studies at the University of the Witwatersrand since 1989. She teaches African politics, political theory and feminist theory and politics. She was a full-time commissioner in the Commission on Gender Equality between May 2001 and March 2004 and is the chair of Tshwaranang Legal Advocacy Centre against Violence. She has published widely on the politics of gender and on gender violence, including three co-edited books.

Regina G. Mwatha is a sociologist specialising in gender equality and women's rights. She chaired the National Gender and Development Commission between 2008 and 2011. She was instrumental in introducing gender-responsive budgeting to the government, developing Kenya's National Action Plan of the United Nations Security Council Resolution 1325 and maintaining the principles of gender equality in the new Kenyan constitution. She then joined the Commission on Administrative Justice (Office of the Ombudsman) in November 2011, pursuing the gender agenda. In recognition of her achievements in the area of gender and women's rights, she was awarded the Moran of the Burning Spear (MBS) by His Excellency the President of Kenya in 2010.

Samia Al Nagar is an independent researcher, currently working on several research projects with Dr Liv Tønnessen on women's rights, quotas and violence against women. She previously worked as a researcher at the National Research Centre in Sudan, with the United Nations Population Fund and United Nations Development Programme in Khartoum, and as a part-time lecturer and researcher with the Regional Institute of Gender, Diversity, Peace and Rights, Ahfad

University, Sudan. She has published on women's rights and gender issues, and is a member of the Advisory Board of the Babiker Badri Scientific Association, as well as of the Asma'a Association.

Nana Claris Efua Pratt is a leader of the women's movement in Sierra Leone, having served as coordinator of the National Organisation for Women-Sierra Leone. She was secretary-general of Global Network of Women Peacebuilders and was appointed to the African Union Women's Committee, which is the highest advisory body in Africa to the Women's Commission. As a leader of the Mano River Women's Peace Network (MAWOPNET), she has been at the forefront of the mediation processes that brought about peace in Sierra Leone and Liberia. A chemist by training, Pratt has been a lecturer at Fourah Bay College at the University of Sierra Leone.

Fatima Sadiqi is professor of linguistics and gender studies at the University of Fez, Morocco. Her work focuses on women's issues in modern North Africa, the Middle East and the Mediterranean. She is author and editor of numerous volumes and journal issues, including *Women, Gender and Language* (2013), *Women and Knowledge in the Mediterranean* (2013), *Moroccan Feminist Discourses* (2014) and *Women's Movements in Post-'Arab Spring' North Africa* (2016). Sadiqi is a public speaker in several languages and a member of many scholarly and policy-making boards. Professor Sadiqi was a Fellow at the Woodrow Wilson Center (2015–2016) and her forthcoming book will focus on Jihadism and the escalation of violence against women in the Middle East and North Africa.

Liv Tønnessen is a senior researcher at the Chr. Michelsen Institute in Bergen, Norway. She is the coordinator of a research cluster on gender politics and is leading several research projects, including one with Dr Samia Al Nagar at Ahfad University for Women in Sudan. Tønnessen has published extensively on women's rights and Islamic law, Islamic movements and gender politics. She has a track record in the Middle East and Northern Africa, with long-term stays in Sudan, Lebanon and Syria. Tønnessen is a board member of the Nordic Society for Middle Eastern and Islamic Studies.

INDEX